IMAGES
of America

GRANVILLE COUNTY
Revisited

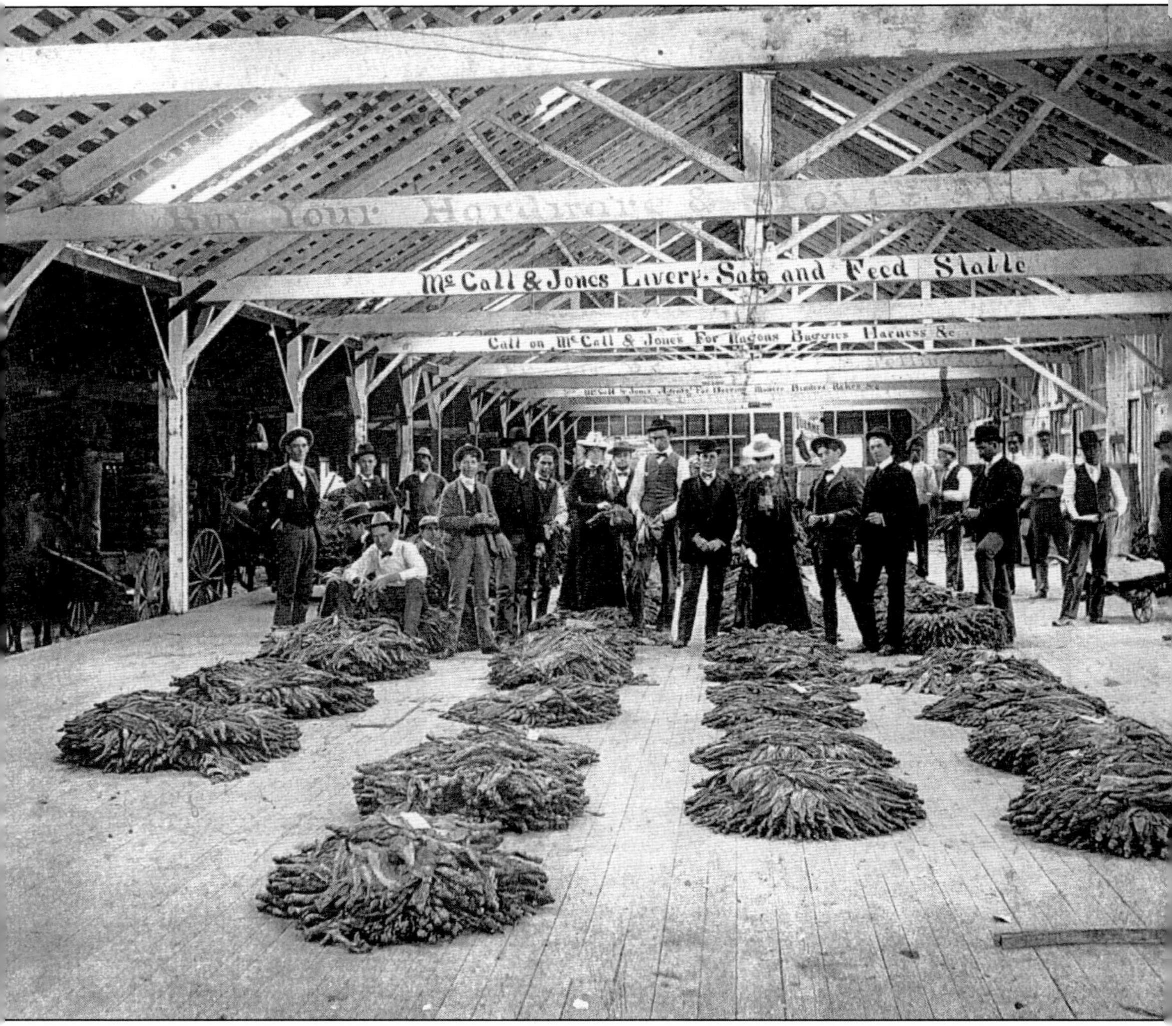

Piles of tobacco wait to be sold at a tobacco auction in Oxford in 1900. The two interior signs say, "McColl and Jones Livery and Feed Stable," and "Call on McColl and Jones for Wagons, Buggies, Harness." (Courtesy of Herbert Gregory Jr.)

IMAGES
of America

GRANVILLE COUNTY
Revisited

Lewis Bowling

ARCADIA
PUBLISHING

ISBN 978-0-7385-1585-4

Published by Arcadia Publishing
Charleston, South Carolina

Printed in the United States of America

Library of Congress Catalog Card Number: 2003111066

For all general information contact Arcadia Publishing at:
Telephone 843-853-2070
Fax 843-853-0044
E-mail sales@arcadiapublishing.com
For customer service and orders:
Toll-Free 1-888-313-2665

Visit us on the Internet at www.arcadiapublishing.com

This book is dedicated to my siblings. Lee is, and always will be, my big brother, whom I look up to very much. My sisters Martha, Dale, Bonnie, Phyllis, and Deborah have all looked after me, "the baby of the family." I love you all.

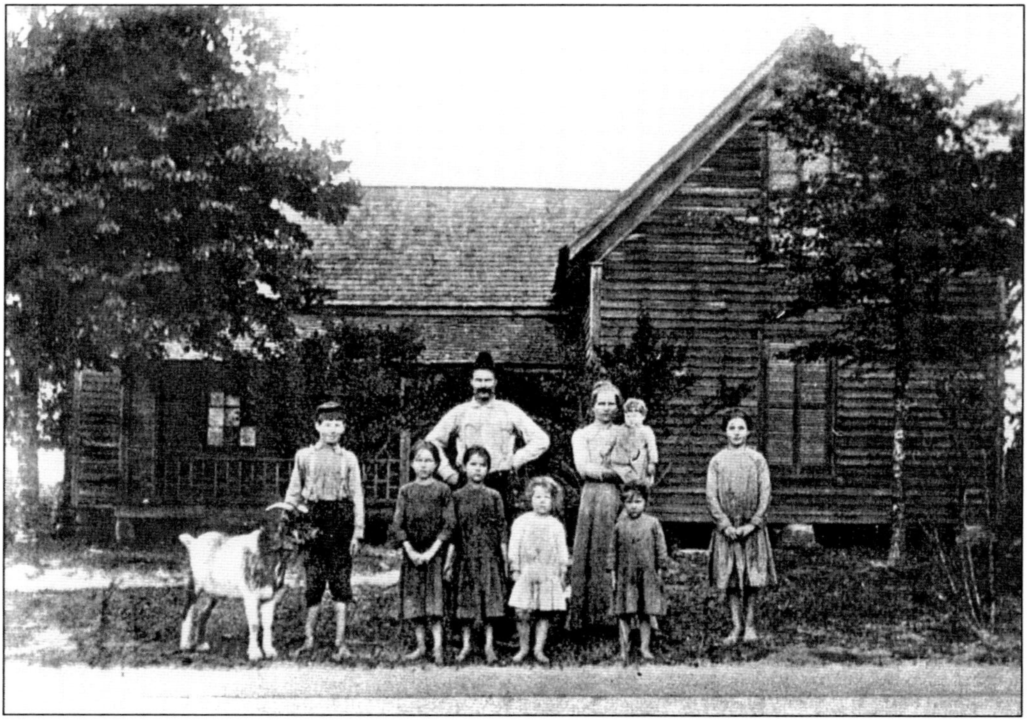

The Kearney family and their goat pose for the camera in 1915. This home was located in the Wilton area. (Courtesy of Barbara Wilkerson.)

Contents

ACKNOWLEDGMENTS

Words cannot give justice to the people who have helped in writing this book. Individuals and families have been very helpful in loaning me pictures and other memorabilia. While gathering material for this book, I was given tours of homes and farms, was fed, and was treated warmly wherever I went. I would like for all of you to know how much I appreciate your help.

Just as with my first book, *Granville County*, this second one is available now largely due to Beth Harward. Beth traveled with me on some of my picture-hunting trips, so quite a few of you have met her. She typed this book and helped me in selecting appropriate pictures. If you have met her, you can not help but to love her. She, more than I, should get credit for being the author of this book.

My mother, Mary Bowling, through her store in Oxford, has been an intermediary for me in collecting pictures. Some of you know her better than you know me and dropped the pictures off to her. I dedicated my first book to my mother, but for all she has done for me, I can never repay her.

Others to thank are Nellye Tunstall; Bobby and Nancy Blackwell; Catherine Noblin; Shirley Currin; Rowena Wheeler; Liz Falkner, for your gigantic scrapbook of memories; Glen Green; Nettie Dickerson, who is a joy to sit and talk with; Rachel Thomas, who I am proud to call a friend; Becky Jennings; Josh Mangum, a young man who is quite the historian himself; Nellie Brame; William Adcock of Adcock Realty; Mary Harris; Mary Watkins Eason, your brother Billy will never be forgotten in this county; Patsy Wells; Carol Sharron; Nellie McFarland; Peter Tocci, thanks for the use of your great postcard collection; Julia Gooch Vaughn; Betty Chappell; Pat Colenda, your poetry is beautiful; Hiram Webb; Margaret Moss Cooper, you really had some great pictures; Opal White, a tiny, sweet lady of Oxford; Jean Gill, for helping me with both books; William and Lisa Burwell; June Cross; Betty Roberts Moody; Taylor and Martha Jackson; Ramona Byrd; Barbara Wilkerson; Anita Adcock; Ada Lee Cozart; Marguerite Stem; Virginia Clay; Joe Haskins; James and Dorothy Harward; Barbara Davis; Emmy Lou Day; Harvey Ellinton Jr.; Ronald Ragland; Al Woodlief; and Fann Montague of the Richard Thornton Library in Oxford, who has been very helpful in the production of both of my Granville books.

Thanks also to Bob and Judy Hunt, for the pictures, farm tour, and the great meal. Thank you, Herbert Gregory Jr., for driving me around the Gregory farm and for the pictures. I must admit this now to Lillian Gill: I purposely kept borrowing pictures from you so that I would have an excuse to come back to your house, hoping you would give me another loaf of your homemade bread. You are a great cook and such a kind woman.

I owe a big thank you to Harry Coleman of the *Butner-Creedmoor News*, who helped me advertise for pictures through his newspaper. Harry also let me rummage through his boxes of pictures and has been very supportive of my efforts. David Rogers of the *Butner-Creedmoor News* collected pictures for me through his contacts and deserves much credit for the Creedmoor chapter. David and I both are night owls, so we called each other at times when most decent people were sleeping.

Ronnie Critcher of the *Oxford Public Ledger* was very helpful in letting people know that I was preparing this new volume. I hope to lend more details to my first two books through my "Looking Back" column in the *Oxford Public Ledger*.

Thanks also go to David and Sharon Morgan of PIP in Durham for copying so many pictures for me.

Granville County Timeline

1700	Indians live in Granville County, including the Sopona, Tuscarora, and Occanechi.
1701	John Lawson travels through what is now Granville County, calling the land the "Flower of Carolina," for the fertility of the land.
1728	William Byrd surveys the area now known as Granville County and notes the abundance of game, including deer, bears, and buffalo.
1746	Granville County is established; its name is derived from Lord John Carteret, Earl of Granville.
1749	The population of the county is 2000.
1759	Granville land riots result from questions of the Earl of Granville's legal rights to land in the area.
1774	Granville citizens express their intent in the "General Meeting of Freeholders" to revolt against English rule.
1776	Thomas Person of Granville is on the committee to draft North Carolina's Constitution. John Penn of Stovall signs the *Declaration of Independence*.
1779	Granville Hall Academy is chartered, becoming one of the first classical schools in the state.
1788	Nutbush Seminary, later named Williamsboro Seminary, is founded.
1802–1805	James Turner of Granville serves as governor of North Carolina.
1805	Bost Gooch invents the crossweave tobacco basket upon which tobacco was stacked on the warehouse floor. Gooch also invents the first iron plow used in America, called Gooch's Twist.
1811	Oxford Male Academy and Oxford Female Academy are chartered.
1811–1814	William Hawkins of Granville serves as governor of North Carolina.
1816	Oxford is incorporated.
1840	Tobacco is established as the staple crop of Granville, which produced 3,912,822 pounds—more than any other county in the state.
1840	The Raleigh and Gaston railroad, which runs through Granville County, is completed. This helps farmers market their product outside of the county and state.
1840	The Oxford Courthouse is completed.
1842	Robert Potter, a former resident of Granville County, dies. A Texas county is named for Potter, who served Texas as secretary of the navy.
1850	Oxford Female College is formed.
1851	Horner Military Academy is formed.
1857	St. John's College is chartered.
1861–1865	Over 1,500 men serve our nation in the War between the States, including the Granville Grays.
1866	The first warehouse in Granville County is built by Leonidas Taylor.
1873	Oxford Orphanage opens.
1881	Oxford's first railroad is completed.
1883	Stovall is incorporated.
1887	Central Children's Home opens.
1889–1893	Henry Cheatham serves in the United States Congress; he later serves as superintendent of the Central Children's Home.

1890	Mary Potter School opens.
1904	Buckhorn Mineral Springs is discovered.
Early 1900s	The Gregory brothers, William and Francis, introduce flue-cured tobacco to Canada.
1905	Creedmoor is incorporated.
1911	C.G. Credle School opens.
1911	Oxford Tobacco Research Station opens and becomes the largest tobacco research facility in the world.
1911	Stem is incorporated.
1916	The streets of Oxford are paved.
1917–1918	Many Granville County people participate in World War I.
1932	Hoover Cart Rodeo is held in Oxford during the Depression, attracting 15,000 spectators.
1941–1945	World War II involves many Granville County citizens.
1942	Camp Butner opens.
1946	The bicentennial of Granville County is celebrated.
1969	Man lands on the moon. James Webb, from Oxford, serves as administrator of National Aeronautics and Space Administration from 1961 to 1968. Webb is major force behind the moon landing.
1971	Oxford-Henderson Airport is built.
1972	Interstate 85 passes through Granville County.
1974	Thad Stem receives the North Carolina Literature Award.
1976	Vance Granville Community College opens.
1980s	Major manufacturing companies move to Granville County.
2003	Granville County continues to be a great place to call home.

One

Oxford

OUR TOWN

Beautiful old homes overlooking shady streets,
Where the branches of old trees rustle as they meet.
There's a feeling of forever as if time will not let go,
An intertwining past and present that ever will be so.

Buildings that through the years have stood the test of time,
Churches with steeples soaring and ivy creeps and climbs.
Schools ever-feeding the minds of our town's youth,
Growing minds seeking for wisdom and truth.

In the glory of color the fall season is here,
In our little town a special time of year.
The mist in the morning and chill in the night,
Beautiful days all golden and bright.

In the cold of the winter — the beauty of snow,
The season of moisture to make things grow.
The coming alive in the spring of our town,
When flowers and Dogwood bloom all around.

The planting and growing and tilling the sod,
The music and laughter and worship of God.
The joy of just being a part of a place
Filled with such beauty, warmth, charm and grace.

Pat Colenda, archivist at the Masonic Home for Children, writes inspiring poetry. Mrs. Colenda wrote this poem about Oxford. To borrow the last two lines, we should all feel lucky to experience "the joy of just being a part of a place/ Filled with such beauty, warmth, charm, and grace." (Courtesy of Pat Colenda.)

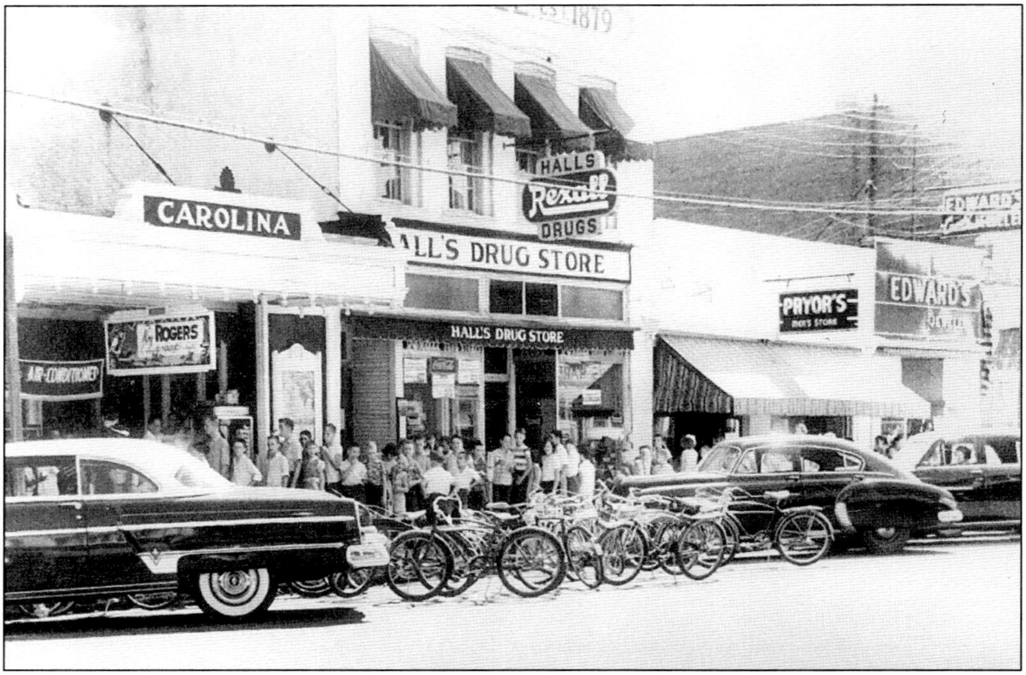

A Roy Rogers movie has kids lined up along Main Street to get into the Carolina Theater in the 1950s. Hall's Drug Store, Pryor's Store, and Edwards Jewelers can also be seen. Many of the kids have their bicycles parked outside.

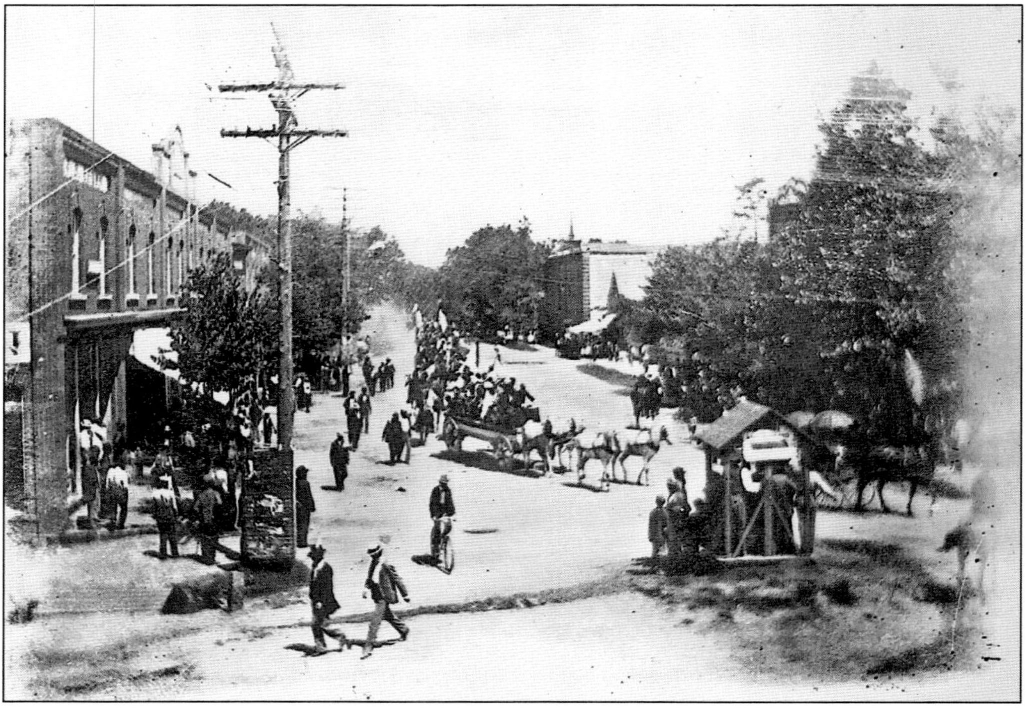

College Street in Oxford was quite a busy place in the early 1900s. People can be seen traveling by foot, bicycle, and horse as they tend to their business. Oxford, in 2003, remains one of the prettiest, most historic towns in North Carolina. (Courtesy of Liz Falkner.)

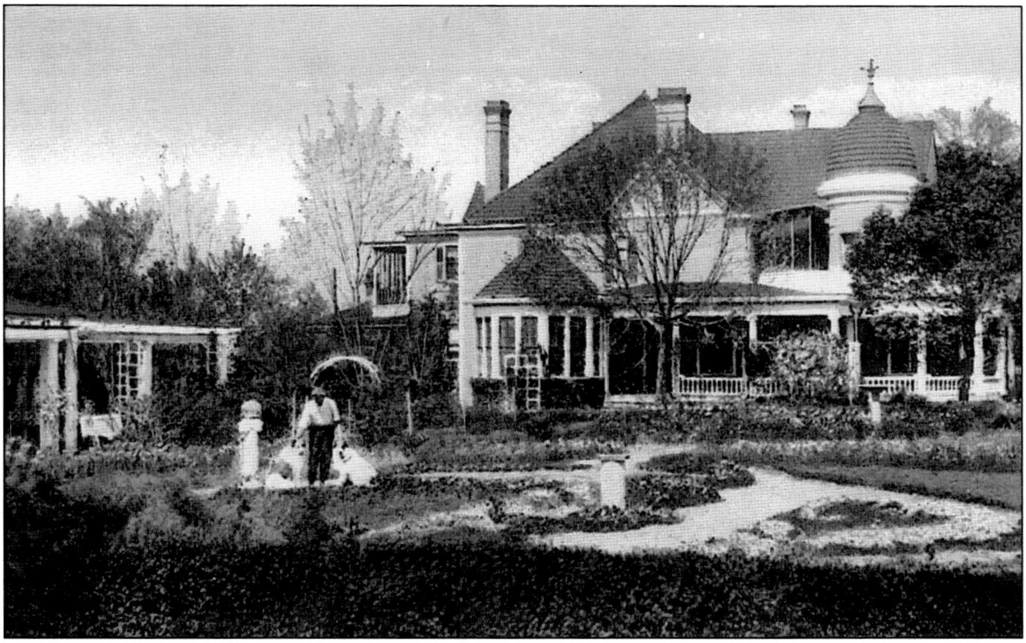

This beautiful garden belonged to R.G. Lassiter of Oxford. Mr. Lassiter built what is known as the Lassiter House, located in front of the garden but not seen in this picture. Peter Tocci and Ricky Dixon now live in this home. The Powell House, which was built in 1886, can be seen in this photograph. (Courtesy of Peter Tocci.)

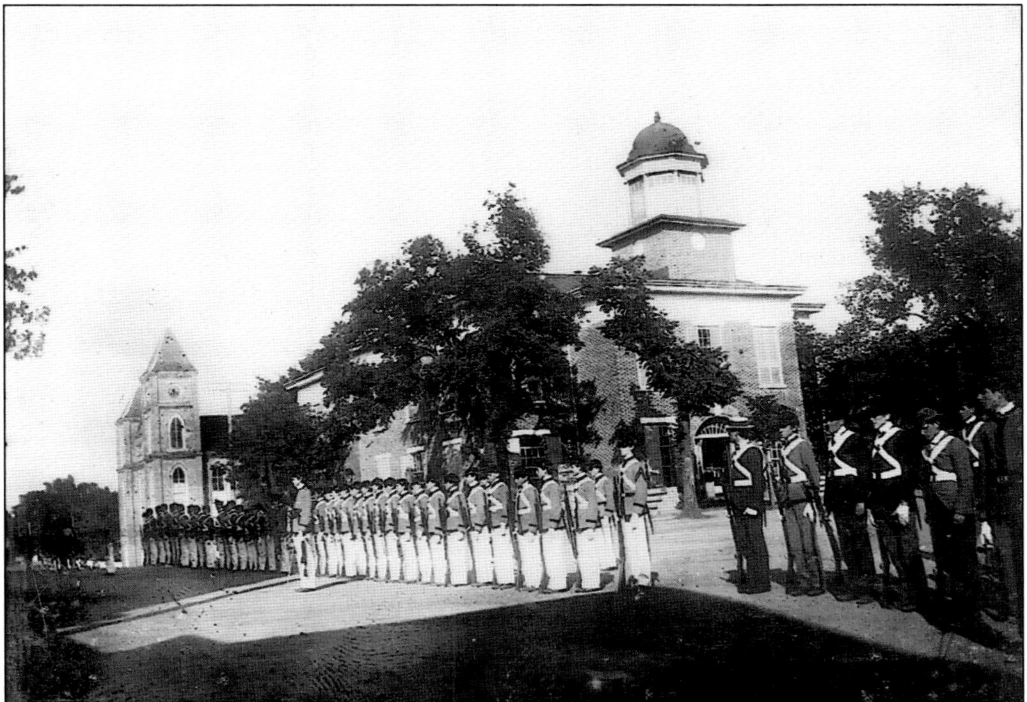

Horner Military School Cadets stand at attention in Oxford in 1905. The ornate Opera House can be seen on the left and the Granville County Courthouse is on the right.

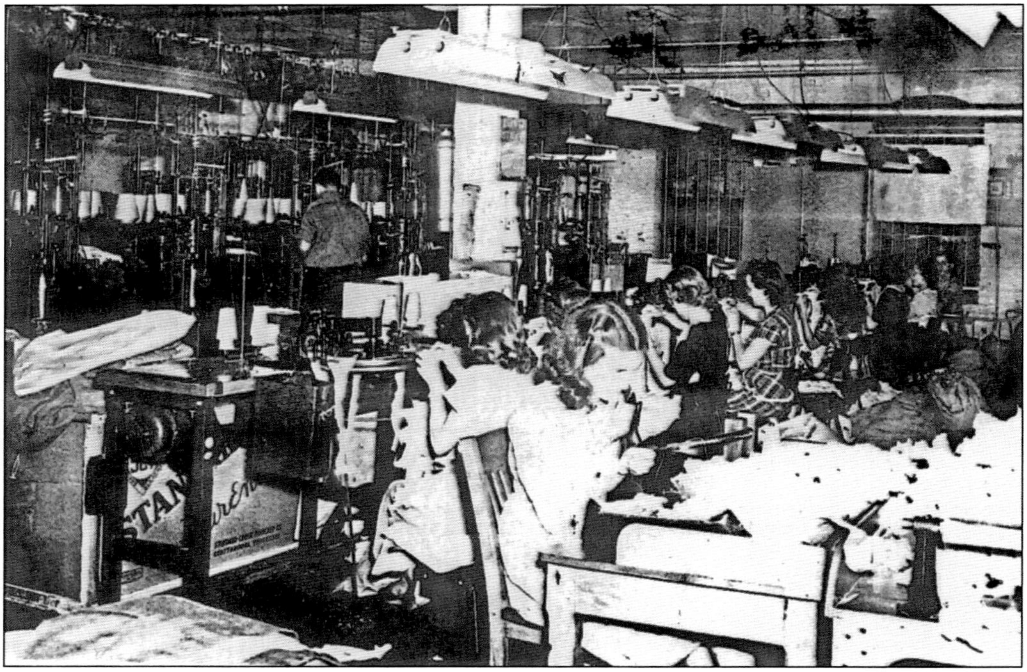

Employees of the Vogue Hosiery Mills in Oxford are busy at their jobs. This factory was owned by Henry Jennings Jr. (Courtesy of Becky Jennings.)

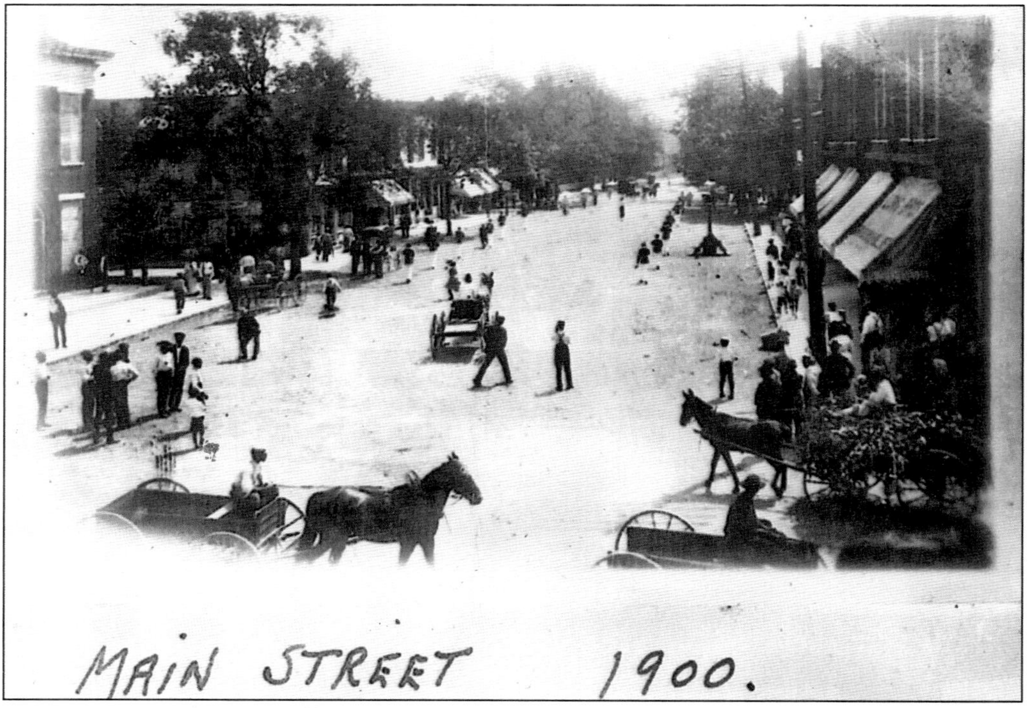

You are passing the Granville County Courthouse on your left as your horse pulls you down Oxford's Main Street in 1900. Traveling is slow and dusty, but your family is in short supply of flour, tobacco, and fabric for sewing. With a few cents left over, you plan to stop by Hall's Drug Store for a piece of chocolate or a soda fountain drink for the kids. (Courtesy of Liz Falkner.)

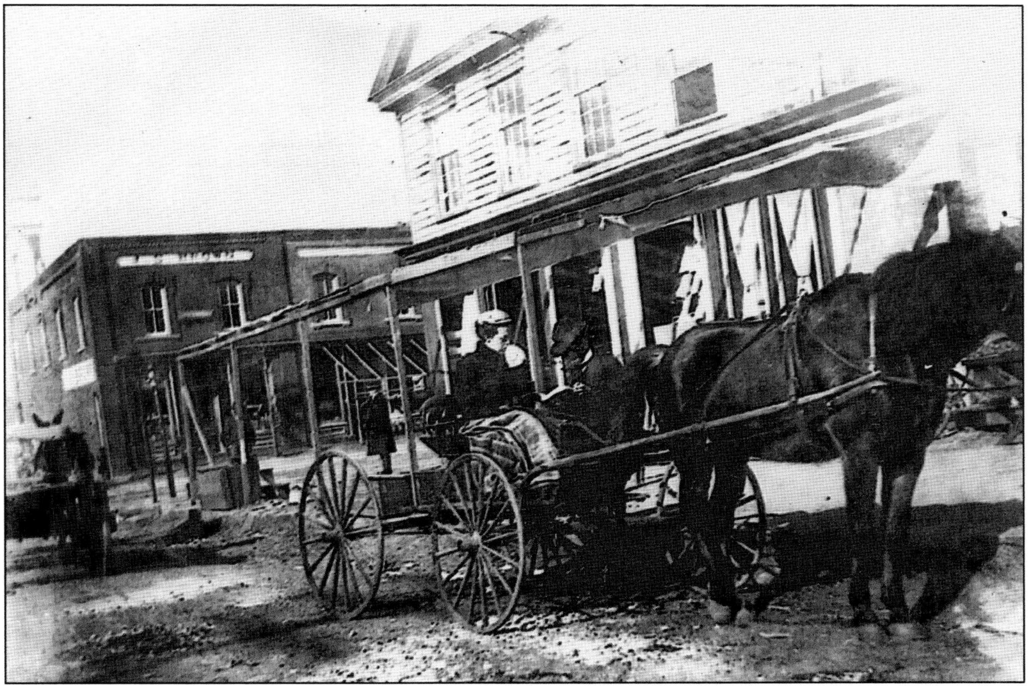

In the very late 1800s, Anne Delacroix pauses to speak to a gentleman in front of Mary Belles Millinery Shop in Oxford. (Courtesy of Liz Falkner.)

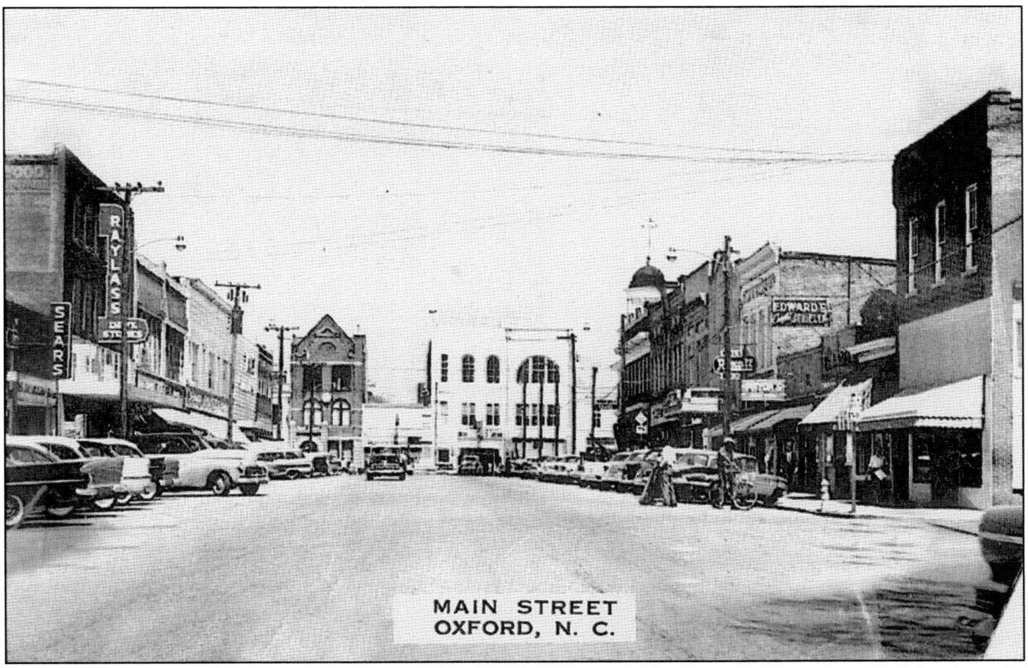

Sears and Raylass Department Stores are seen on the left of Oxford's Main Street and Edward's Jewelers is on the right. Notice the Confederate Monument standing in its original location. This picture is from the 1950s.

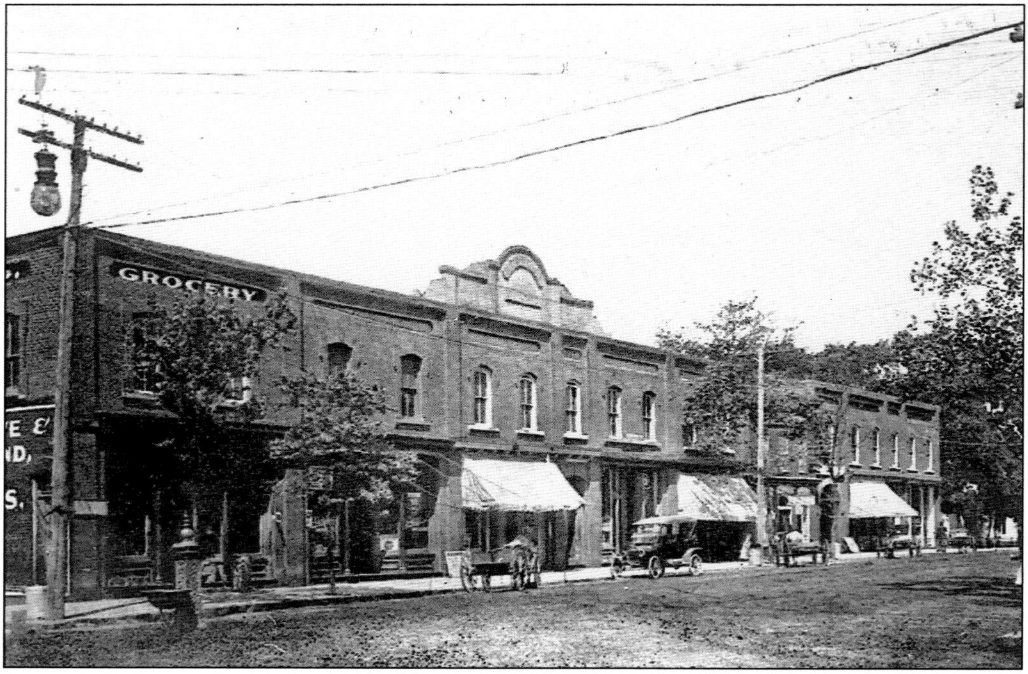

An early 1900s car faces a horse and buggy on Cottage Street in Oxford. No problem: the wide streets would accommodate both as America and Granville County continue to change.

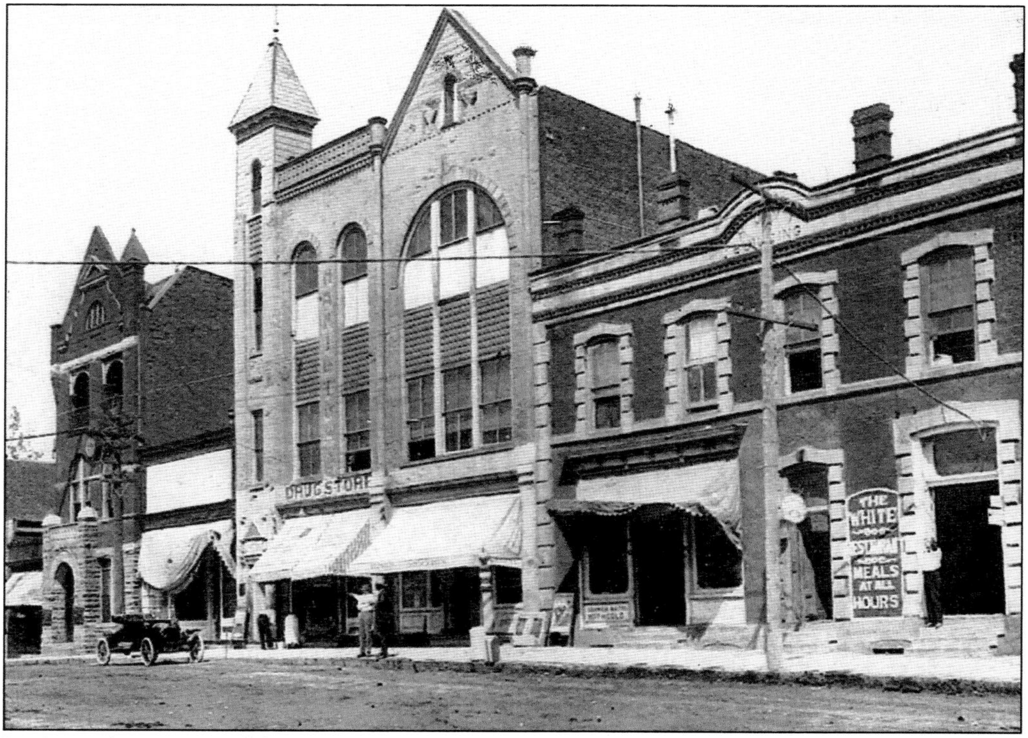

In the early 1900s, Hillsboro Street offered Oxford a variety of shopping options. The building on the right was the White Restaurant, advertising "Meals At All Hours" and "Baths Hot and Cold." Notice the "horseless carriage" on the left.

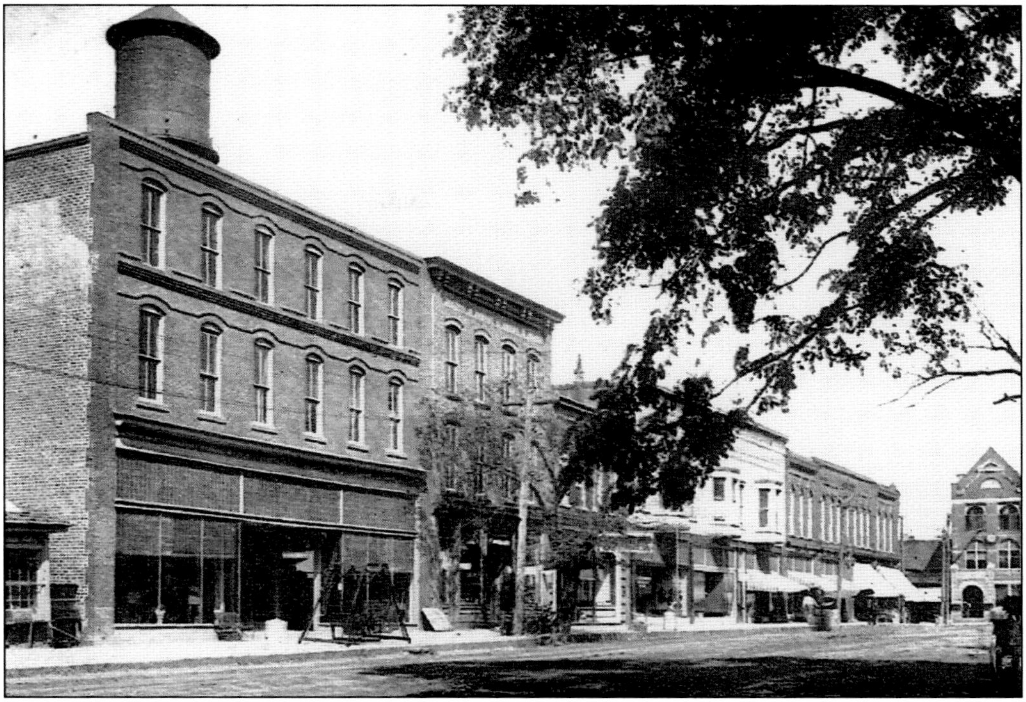

Under the overhanging shade tree looks like a nice place to stop with your horse and buggy. This is Oxford's Main Street in the early 1900s.

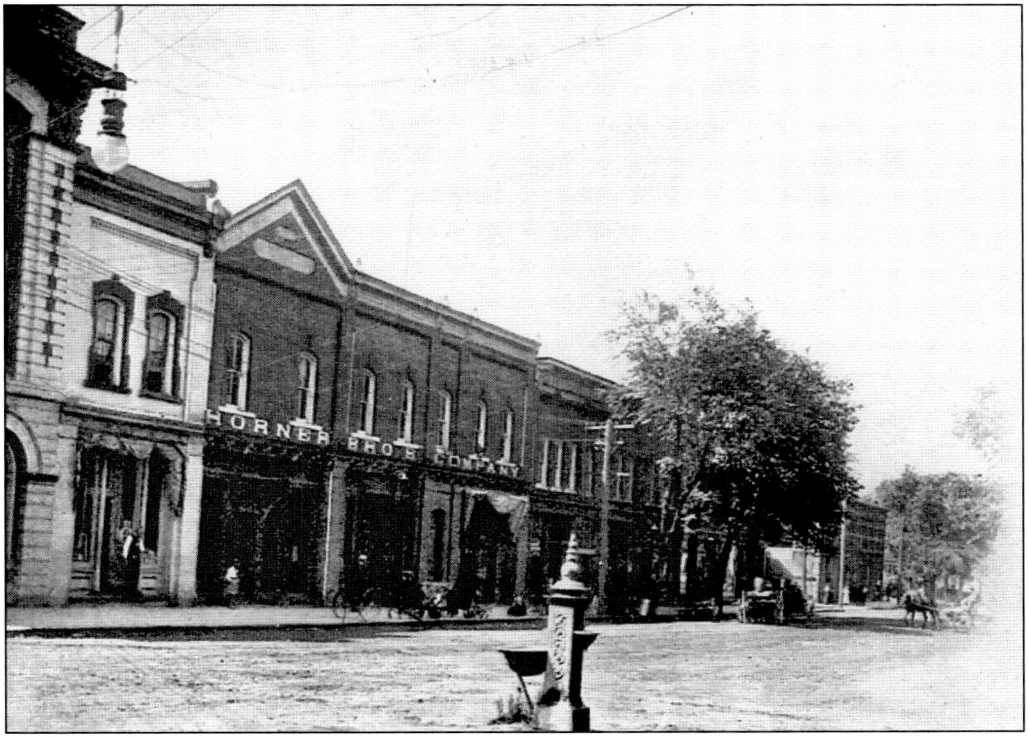

The Horner Brothers Company can be seen in Oxford around the turn of the century. Notice the water trough on the unpaved street and the old light in the upper left corner.

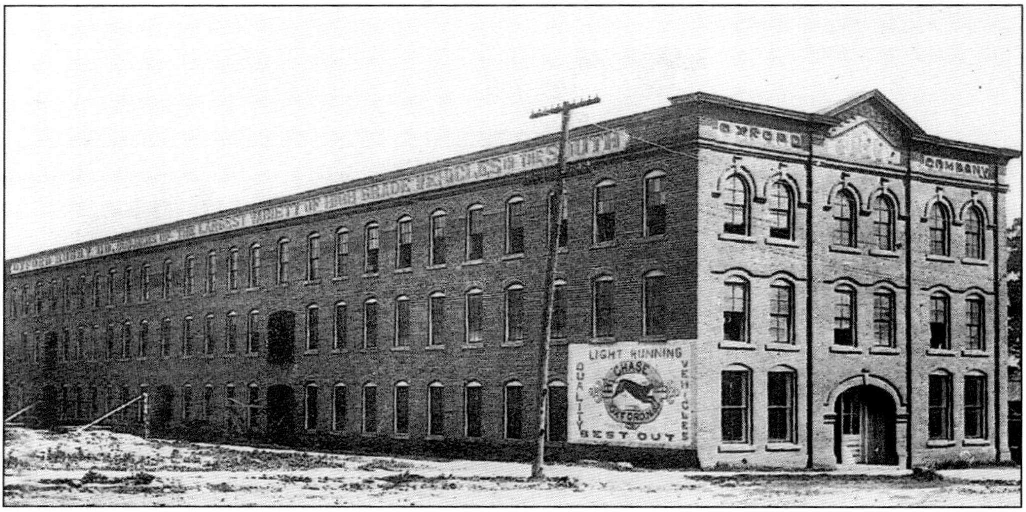

The Oxford Buggy Company is depicted in the early 1900s. The sign on the side of the building says, "Oxford Buggy Co., Builders Of The Largest Variety Of High Grade Vehicles In the South."

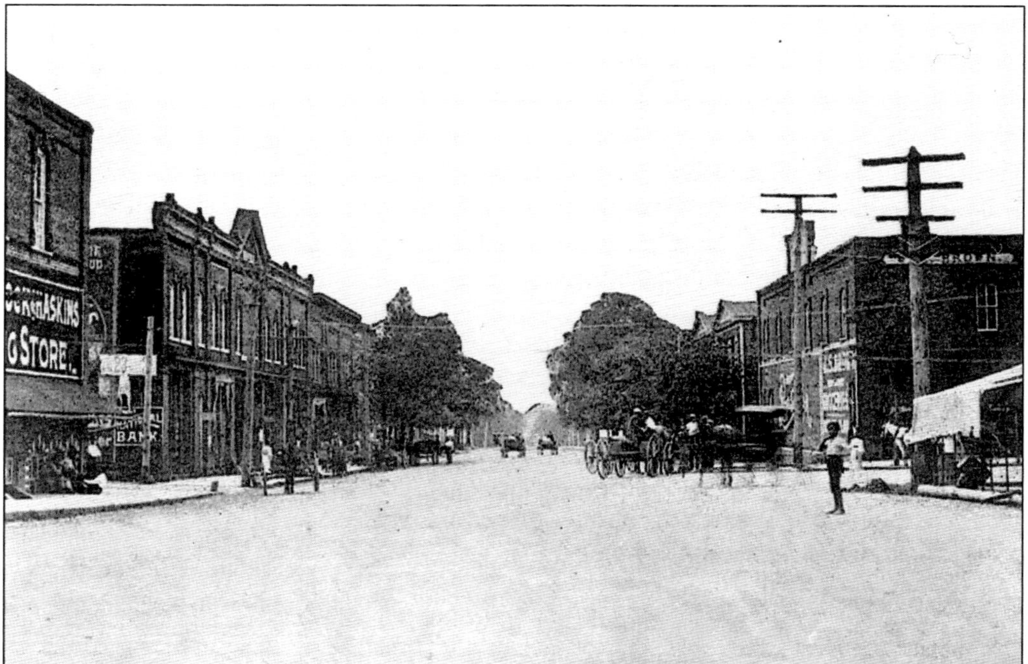

Notice Oxford's wide streets in this very early 1900s picture.

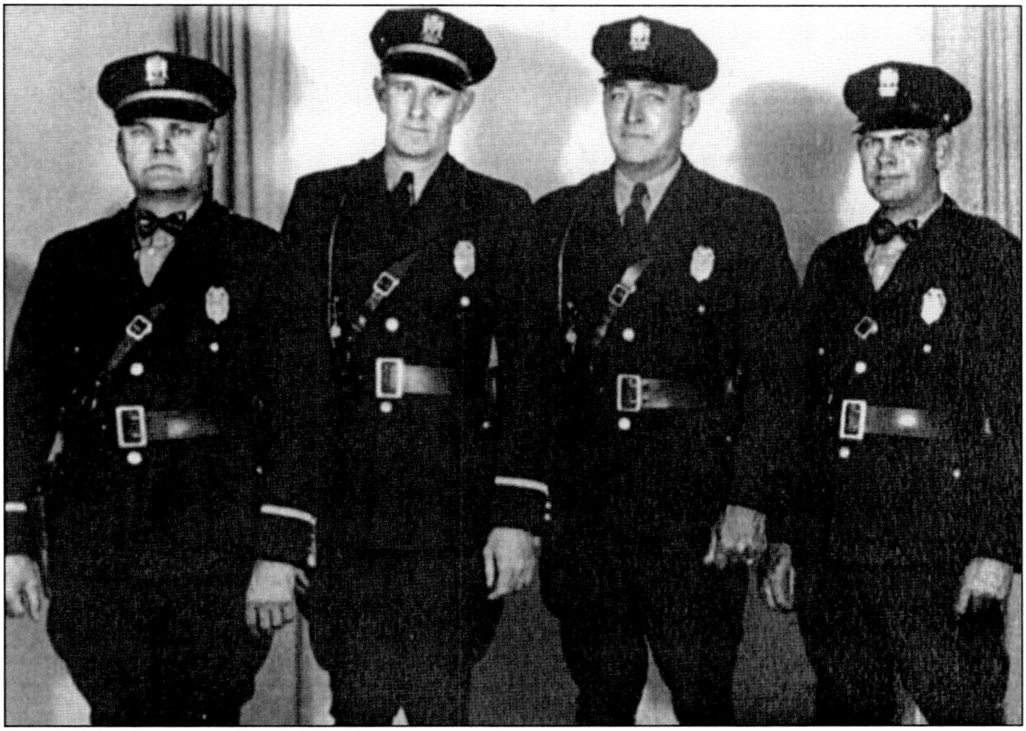

The entire police force of Oxford is assembled in this 1940s photograph. Chief H.J. Jackson is on the left, followed by J.L. Cash, Will Strickland, and Hugh Wheeler. Chief Jackson became the street superintendent of Oxford after retiring as police chief. During the 1940s, these four men worked 12 hours on duty and 12 hours off duty, sometimes for 7 days a week. (Courtesy of Taylor Jackson.)

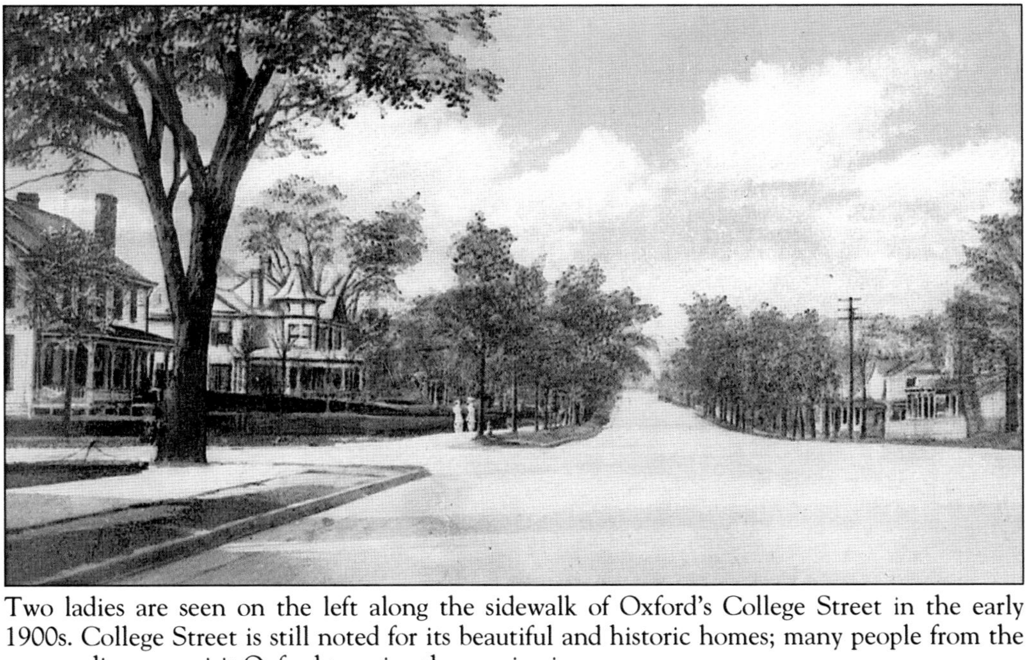

Two ladies are seen on the left along the sidewalk of Oxford's College Street in the early 1900s. College Street is still noted for its beautiful and historic homes; many people from the surrounding area visit Oxford to enjoy the scenic views.

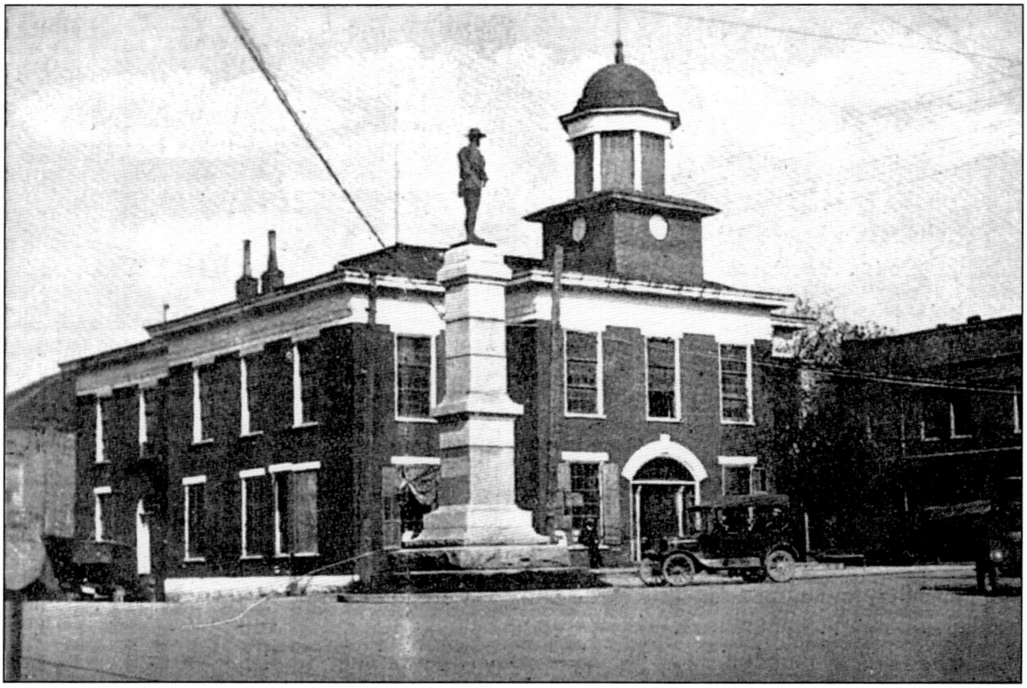

Completed in 1840, the Granville County Courthouse was 163 years old in 2003. The Confederate Monument was erected in 1909 and this picture was taken in the 1910s. This Courthouse Square has been the site for parades, speeches, and many other significant events in our county's history.

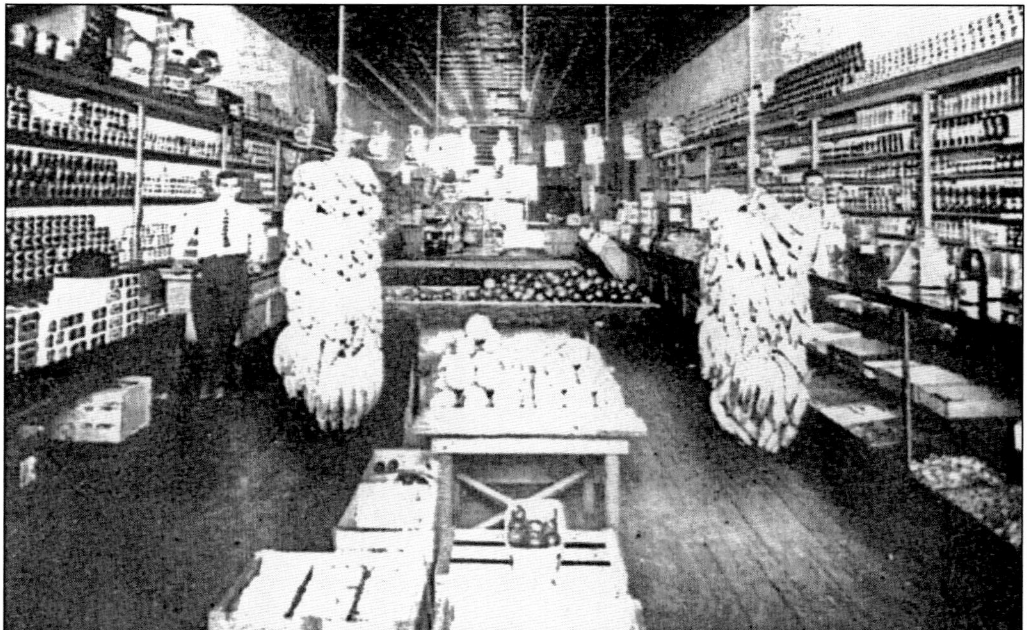

This early 1900s picture of Oxford's Taylor Brothers, the Sanitary Grocers proves at least one thing—shoppers in need of bananas would find them at Taylor's. Other types of fruit, candy, and canned goods are also neatly stacked and ready for sale.

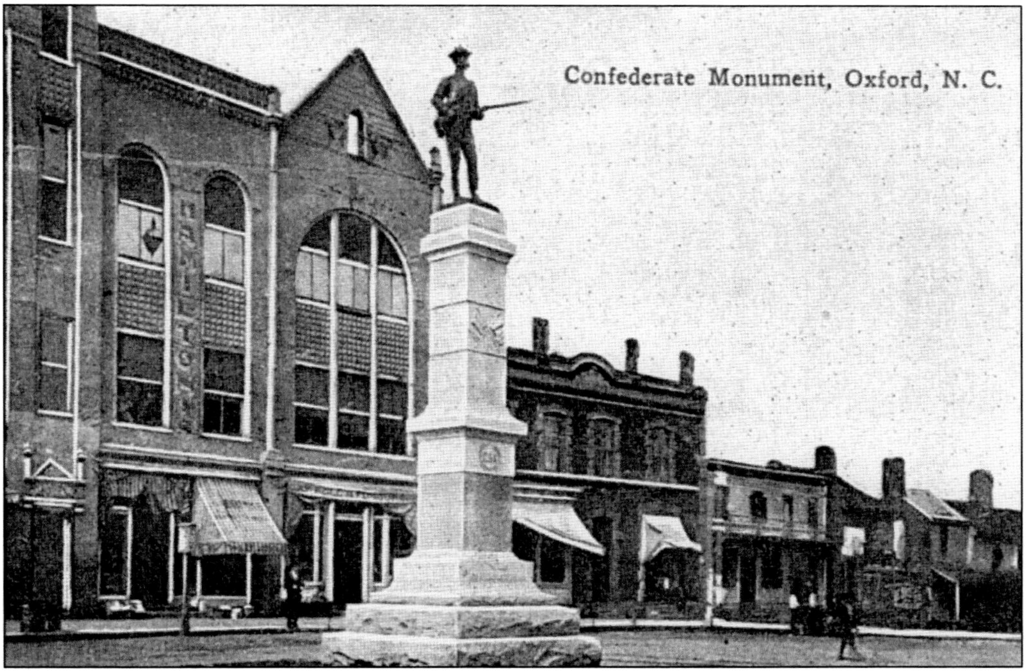

The Confederate Monument is shown a couple of years after its completion in 1909.

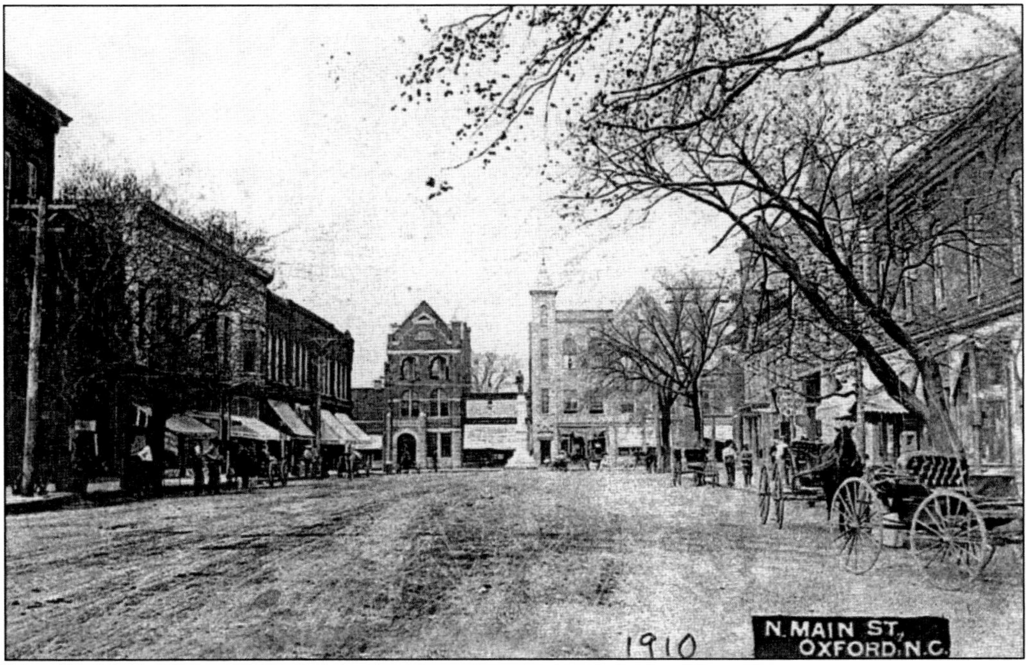

Ride with me down Oxford's Main Street in 1910 and let us experience the stores, businesses, traffic, people, smells, and sounds of a town proud of its past, yet looking eagerly to the future.

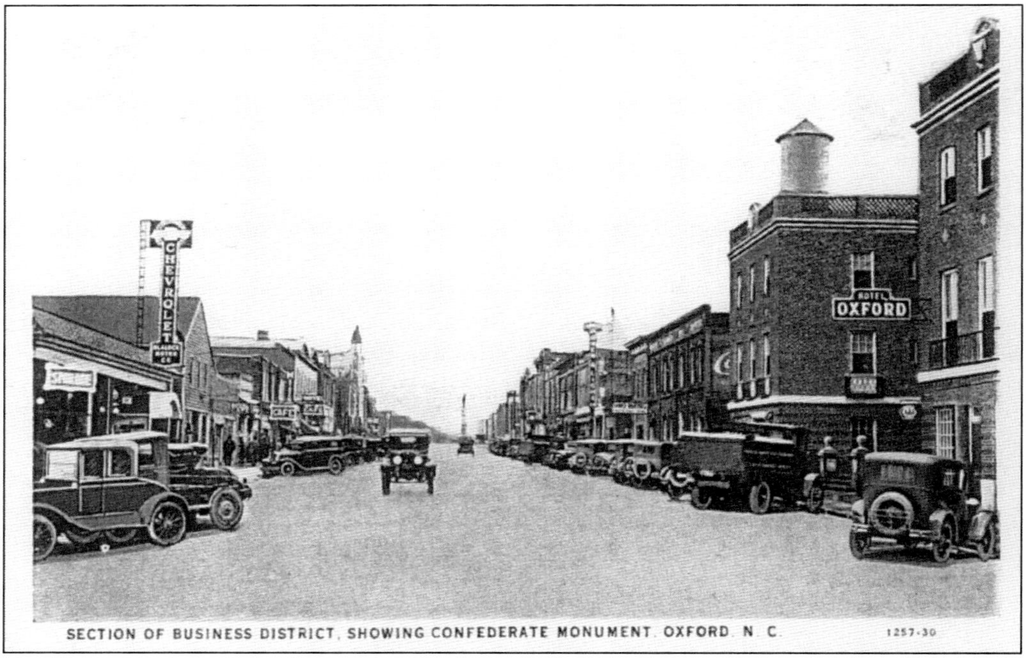

SECTION OF BUSINESS DISTRICT, SHOWING CONFEDERATE MONUMENT. OXFORD. N. C. 1257-30

Let us ride down Hillsboro Street in Oxford. Blalock Motor Company is on the left. We may just stay the night at the Hotel Oxford, located on the right.

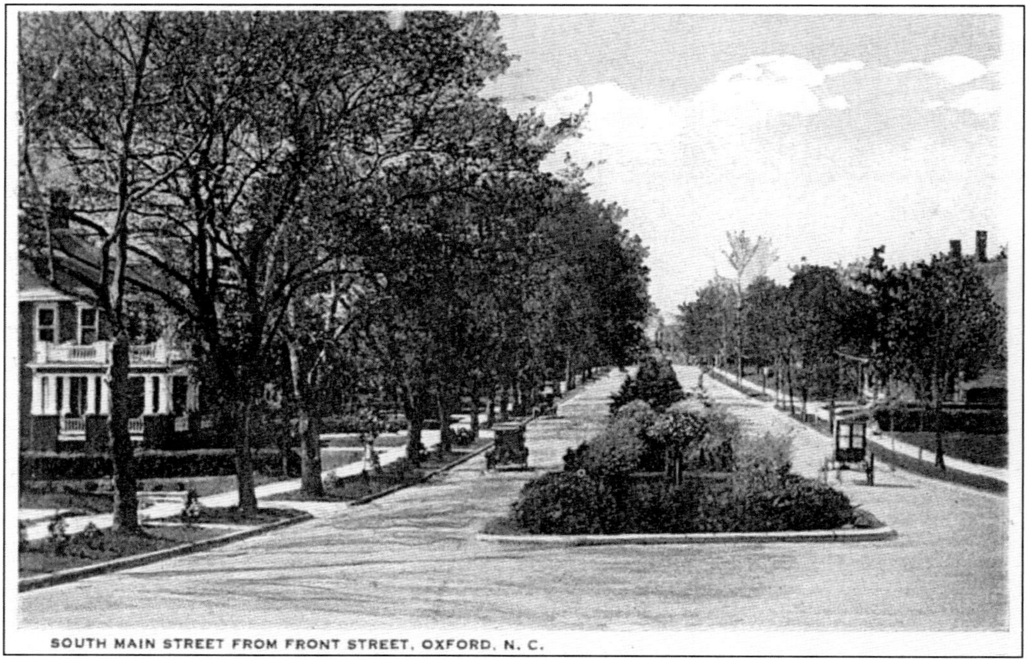

SOUTH MAIN STREET FROM FRONT STREET, OXFORD, N. C.

Continuing on our riding tour of Oxford, we turn off Front Street onto South Main Street and travel into the business district. As we drive in, we see another one of those mysterious "horseless carriages," kicking up dust and coughing out noise. Now let us enjoy the pretty tree-lined streets and gaze at the nice homes.

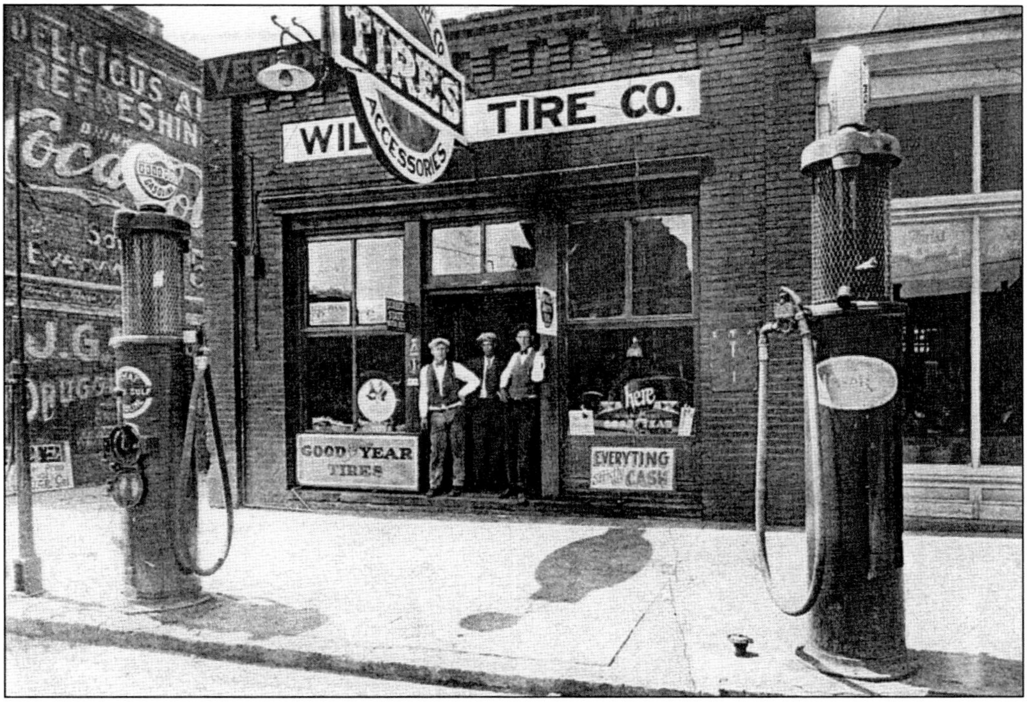

We should stop at Wilson Tire Company and grab a Coca-Cola. There is no credit here though; the sign says, "Everything Strictly Cash." Oh well, I'll loan you the nickel needed for the purchase. L.L. Wilson, the owner, is on the left, and J.B. Yeargin is on the right. It looks as if they are glad to see us. (Courtesy of Jean Gill.)

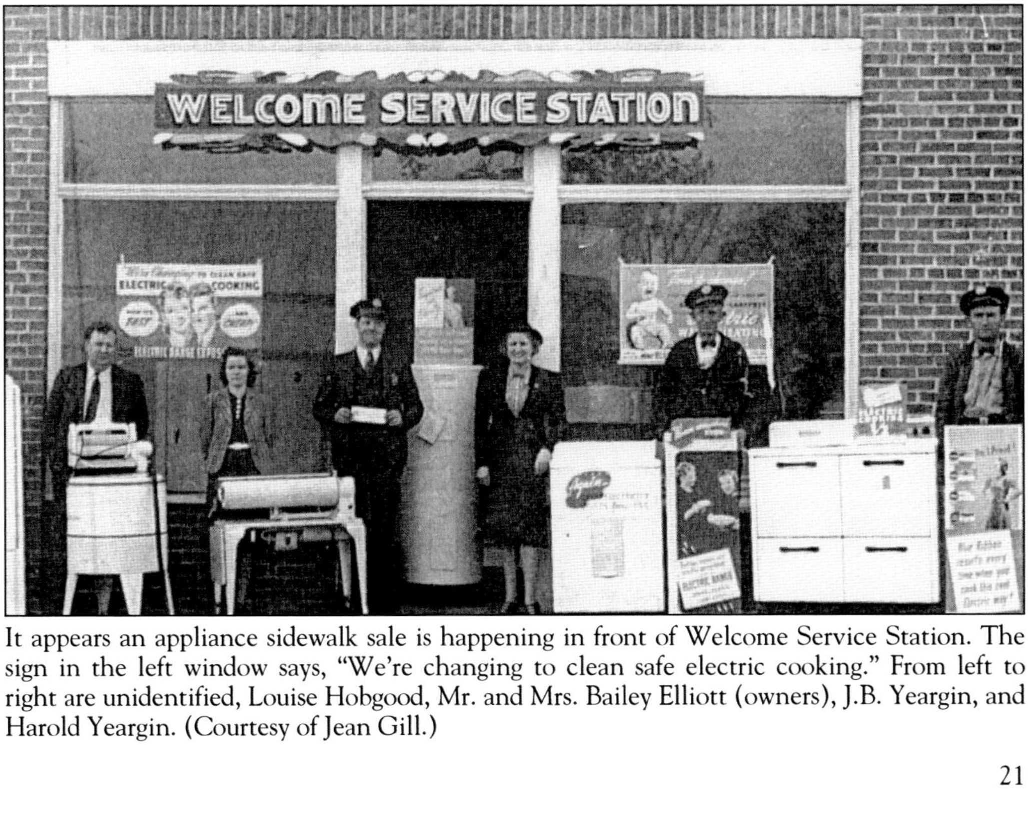

It appears an appliance sidewalk sale is happening in front of Welcome Service Station. The sign in the left window says, "We're changing to clean safe electric cooking." From left to right are unidentified, Louise Hobgood, Mr. and Mrs. Bailey Elliott (owners), J.B. Yeargin, and Harold Yeargin. (Courtesy of Jean Gill.)

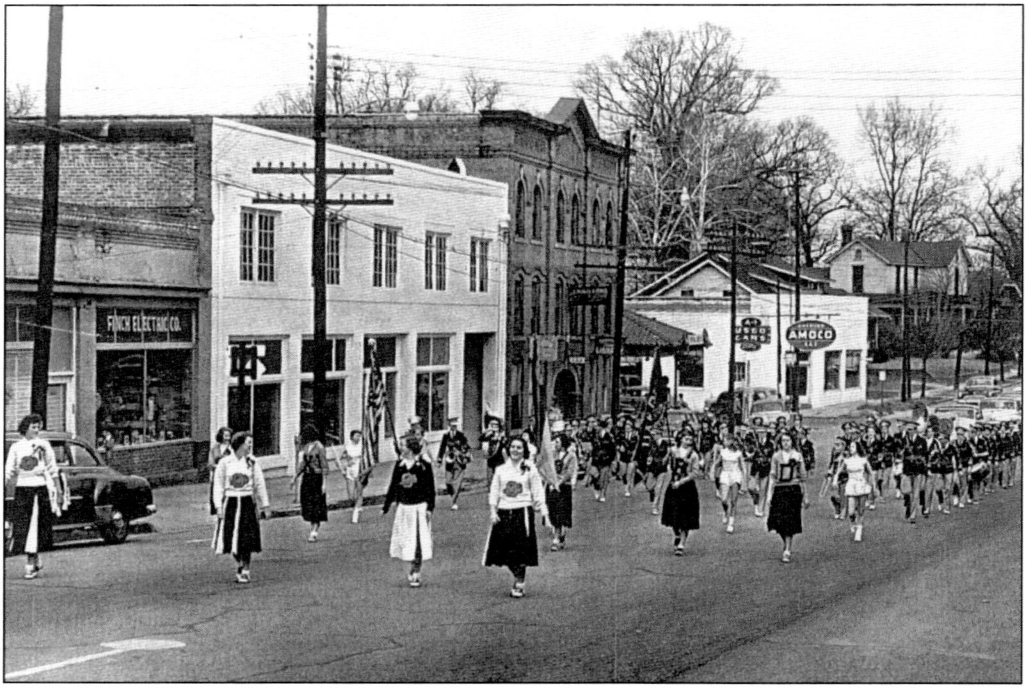

An Oxford High School pep rally takes place in the 1950s. High school football was a big event in Oxford at one time, generating lots of excitement.

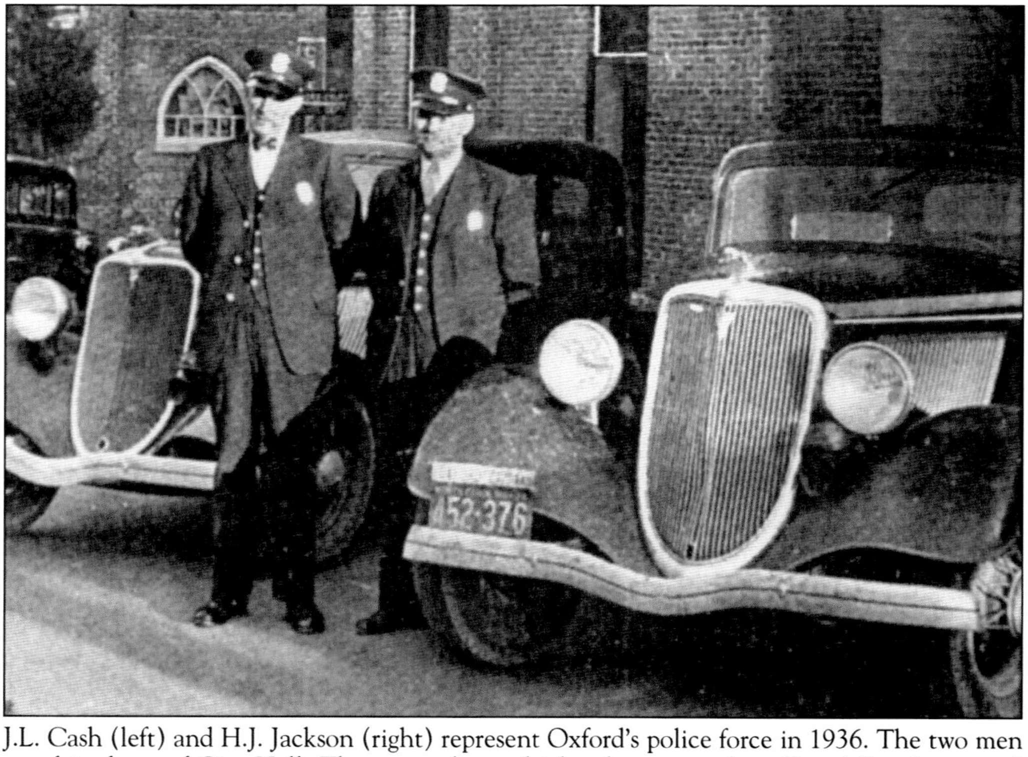

J.L. Cash (left) and H.J. Jackson (right) represent Oxford's police force in 1936. The two men stand in front of City Hall. The two police vehicles shown are the officers' "headquarters." (Courtesy of Taylor Jackson.)

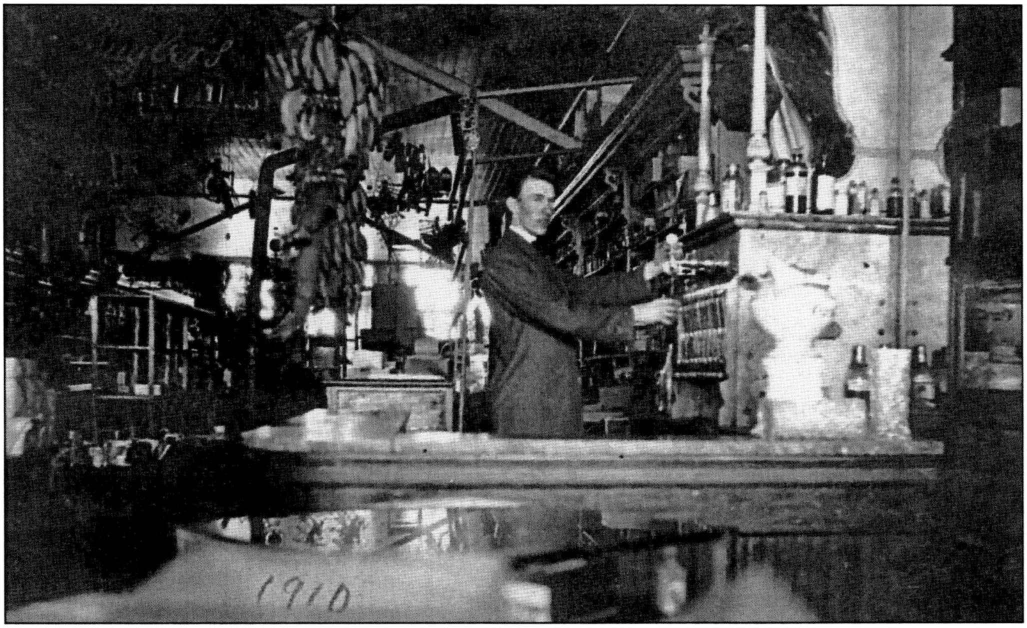

A cold drink is being prepared inside Hall's Drug Store in 1910. (Courtesy of Virginia Clay.)

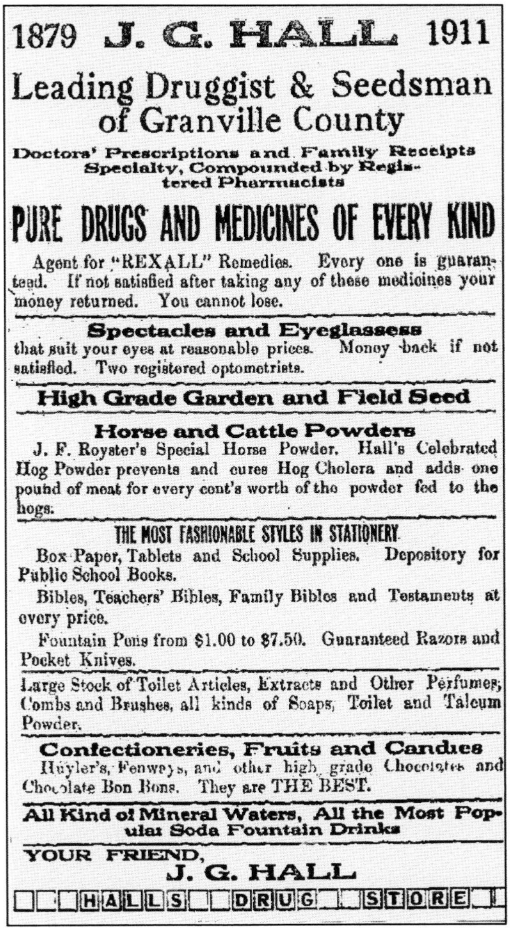

1879 **J. G. HALL** 1911

Leading Druggist & Seedsman of Granville County

Doctors' Prescriptions and Family Receipts Specialty, Compounded by Registered Pharmacists

PURE DRUGS AND MEDICINES OF EVERY KIND

Agent for "REXALL" Remedies. Every one is guaranteed. If not satisfied after taking any of these medicines your money returned. You cannot lose.

Spectacles and Eyeglassess
that suit your eyes at reasonable prices. Money back if not satisfied. Two registered optometrists.

High Grade Garden and Field Seed

Horse and Cattle Powders
J. F. Royster's Special Horse Powder. Hall's Celebrated Hog Powder prevents and cures Hog Cholera and adds one pound of meat for every cent's worth of the powder fed to the hogs.

THE MOST FASHIONABLE STYLES IN STATIONERY

Box Paper, Tablets and School Supplies. Depository for Public School Books.

Bibles, Teachers' Bibles, Family Bibles and Testaments at every price.

Fountain Pens from $1.00 to $7.50. Guaranteed Razors and Pocket Knives.

Large Stock of Toilet Articles, Extracts and Other Perfumes, Combs and Brushes, all kinds of Soaps, Toilet and Talcum Powder.

Confectioneries, Fruits and Candies
Huyler's, Fenways, and other high grade Chocolates and Chocolate Bon Bons. They are THE BEST.

All Kind of Mineral Waters, All the Most Popular Soda Fountain Drinks

YOUR FRIEND,
J. G. HALL

HALLS DRUG STORE

In 1911, Hall's Drug Store carried a wide assortment of products. (Courtesy of Oxford Banner.)

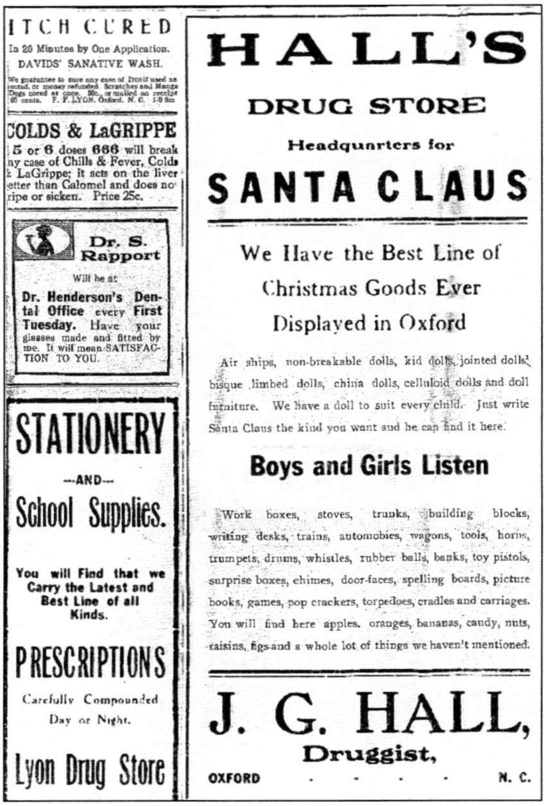

ITCH CURED

In 20 Minutes by One Application.

DAVIDS' SANATIVE WASH.

We guarantee to cure any case of Itch if used as [di]rected, or money refunded. Scratches and Mange [on] Dogs cured at once. 50c., or mailed on receipt 65 cents. F. F. LYON, Oxford, N. C. 1-9 9m

COLDS & LaGRIPPE

5 or 6 doses 666 will break [a]ny case of Chills & Fever, Colds [&] LaGrippe; it acts on the liver [b]etter than Calomel and does no[t] [g]ripe or sicken. Price 25c.

Dr. S. Rapport

Will be at

Dr. Henderson's Dental Office every First Tuesday. Have your glasses made and fitted by me. It will mean SATISFACTION TO YOU.

STATIONERY

—AND—

School Supplies.

You will Find that we Carry the Latest and Best Line of all Kinds.

PRESCRIPTIONS

Carefully Compounded Day or Night.

Lyon Drug Store

HALL'S

DRUG STORE

Headquarters for

SANTA CLAUS

We Have the Best Line of Christmas Goods Ever Displayed in Oxford

Air ships, non-breakable dolls, kid dolls, jointed dolls, bisque limbed dolls, china dolls, celluloid dolls and doll furniture. We have a doll to suit every child. Just write Santa Claus the kind you want and he can find it here.

Boys and Girls Listen

Work boxes, stoves, trunks, building blocks, writing desks, trains, automobies, wagons, tools, horns, trumpets, drums, whistles, rubber balls, banks, toy pistols, surprise boxes, chimes, door-faces, spelling boards, picture books, games, pop crackers, torpedoes, cradles and carriages. You will find here apples, oranges, bananas, candy, nuts, raisins, figs and a whole lot of things we haven't mentioned.

J. G. HALL,

Druggist,

OXFORD . . . . N. C.

As a child in the Oxford area in 1913, your eyes would probably open wide as you walked past Hall's Drug Store and saw the selection of Christmas goods for sale. No computers or video games were available, so children of today may not be very impressed.

Many young school girls entered through this main entrance to Oxford College and, upon graduation, emerged a young educated woman of culture. The college advertised thusly: "At one end goes in a school girl, rough and rude and void of culture; from the other comes a lady, a wise and well accomplished woman."

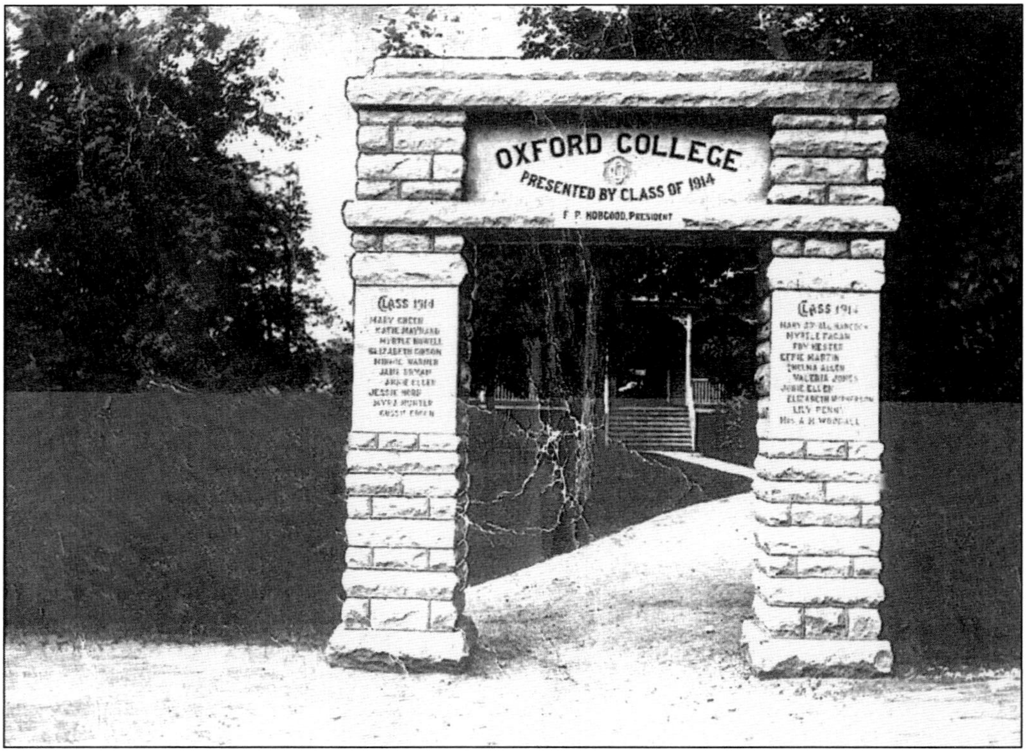

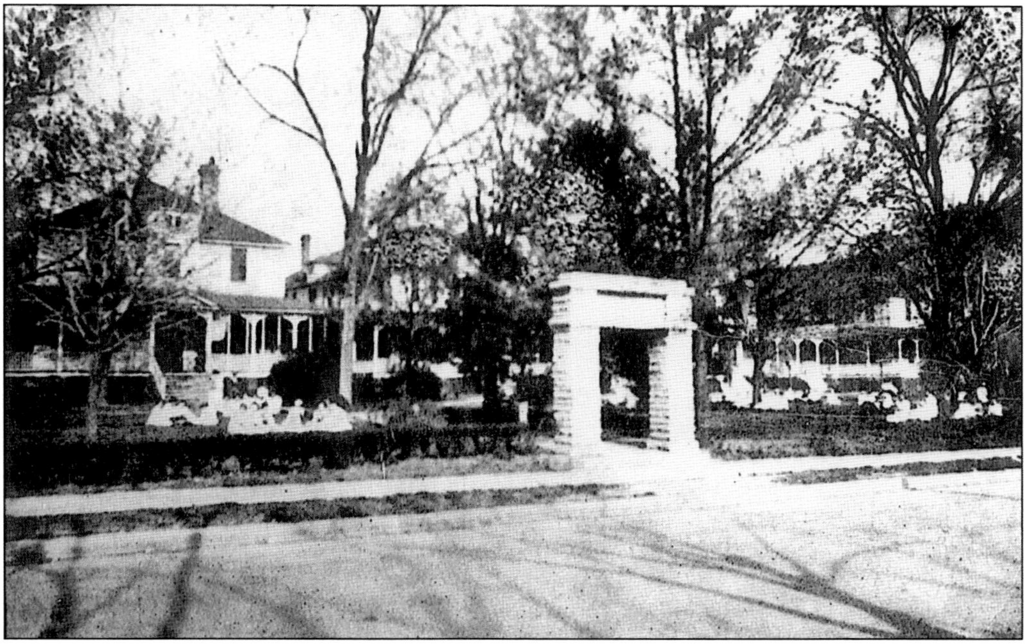

Young ladies spread out on the lawn of Oxford College in the early 1900s. Many women came from North Carolina and Virginia, as well as from other states around the country, to be educated in such subjects as ethics, metaphysics, literature, Latin, vocal music, embroidery, and physical culture.

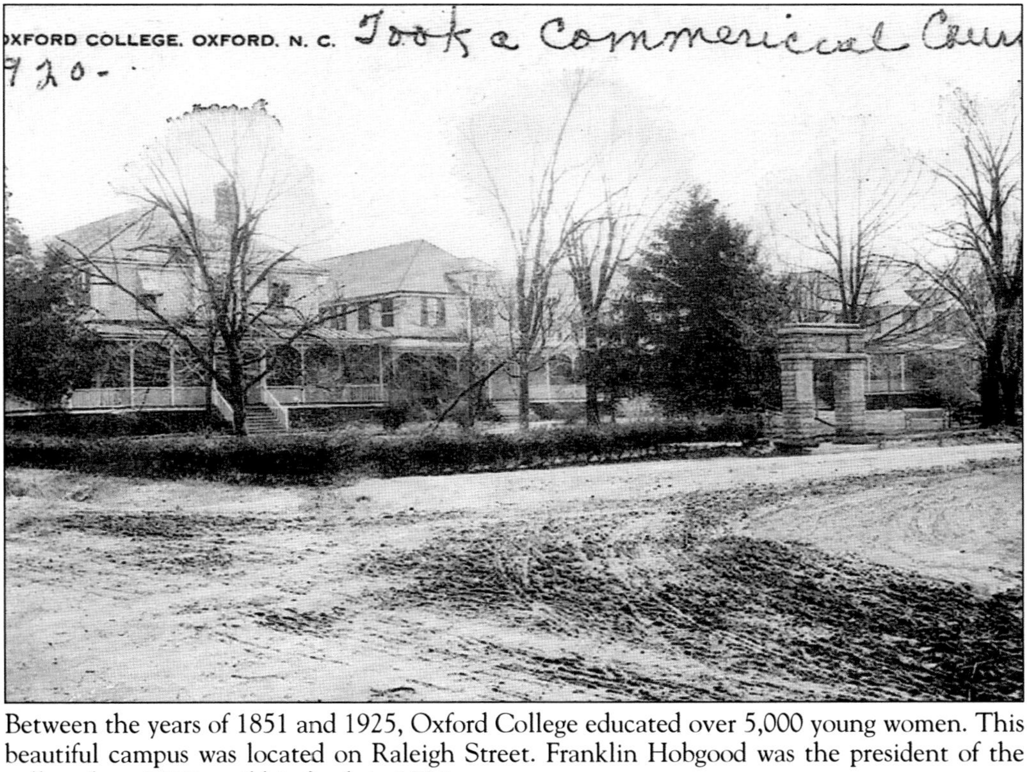

Between the years of 1851 and 1925, Oxford College educated over 5,000 young women. This beautiful campus was located on Raleigh Street. Franklin Hobgood was the president of the college from 1880 until his death in 1924.

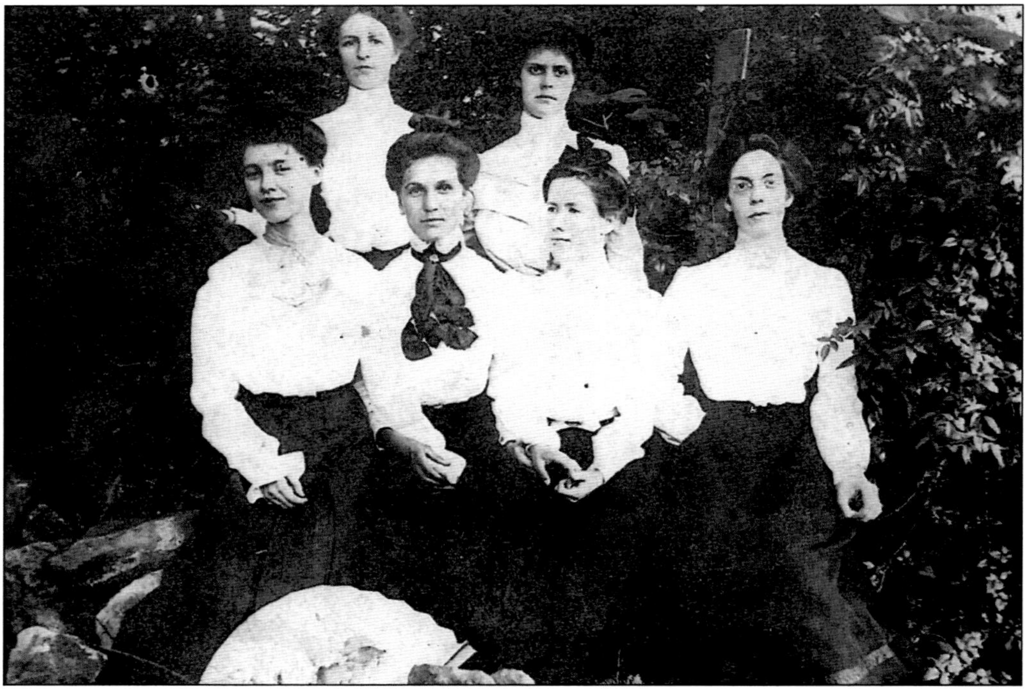

Oxford College students take a break from their studies to pose for this picture in the early 1900s. On the first row, from left to right, are Belle Norwood, Thula Norwood, Ophal Jones, and Minnie Elliott. The two on the back row are unidentified. (Courtesy of Mary Watkins Eason.)

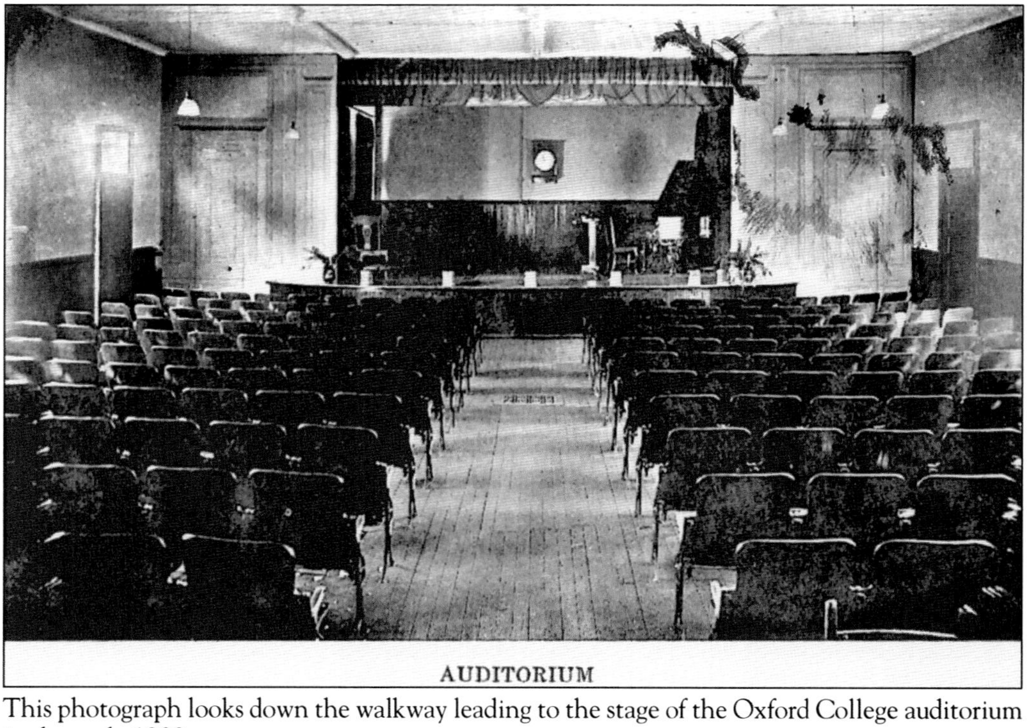

This photograph looks down the walkway leading to the stage of the Oxford College auditorium in the early 1900s.

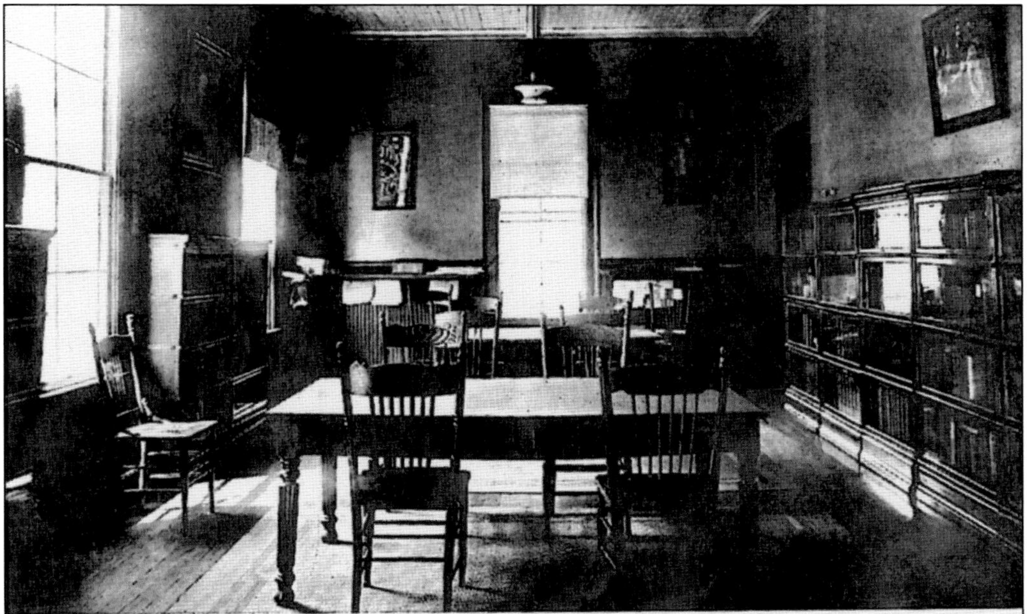

SECTION OF LIBRARY

Oxford College had a reputation of vigorous academic requirements; therefore, one doubts that this library was empty very often. Notice the bookcases on the right in this picture from the early 1900s.

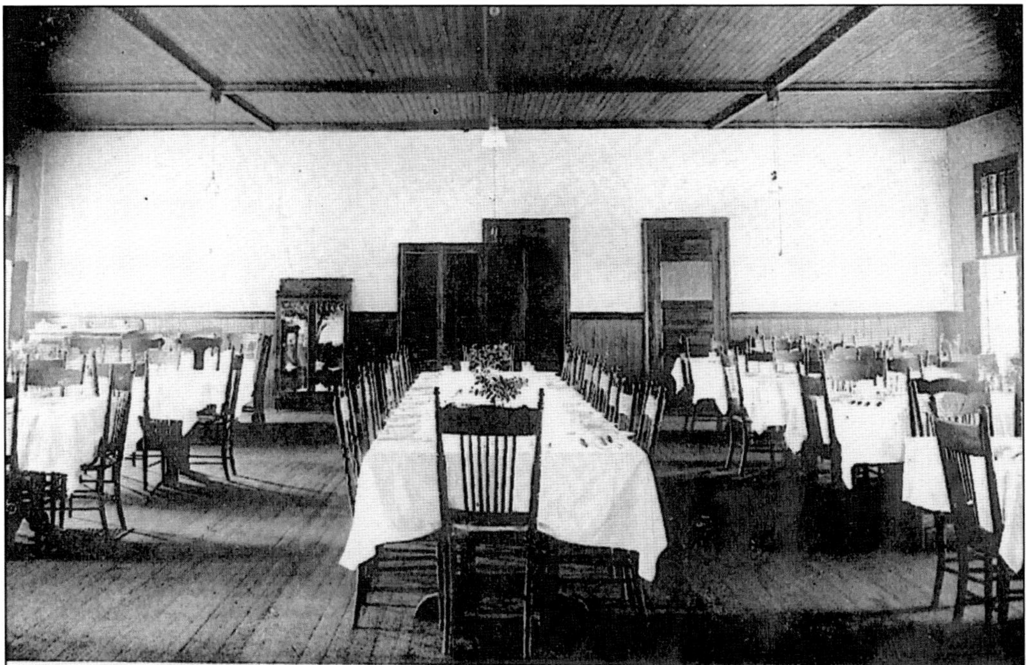

SECTION OF DINING ROOM

The Oxford College dining room looks very inviting in this 1920s photograph.

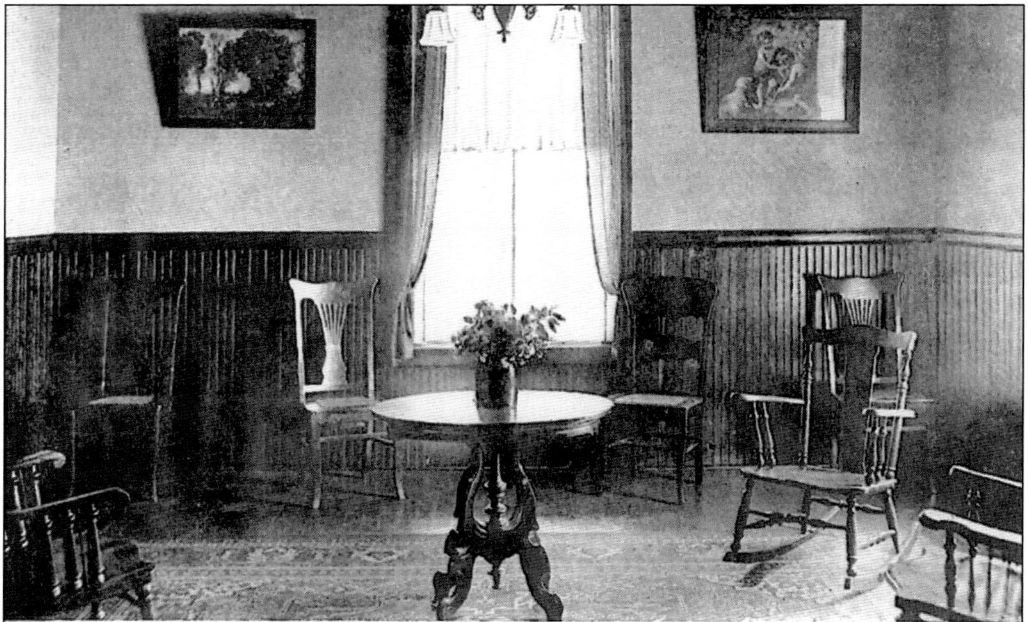

ONE OF PARLORS

This parlor offered a cozy place for good conversation and visiting with others. Despite its strict academic rules, Oxford College offered ample opportunity for rest and recreation. The young ladies were encouraged to get plenty of rest and to engage in walks around the campus or play such sports as tennis and basketball.

OXFORD

FEMALE ACADEMY.

This Institution, located in the healthful town of Oxford, in an elevated region of Middle Carolina, has been in successful operation for sixty years, having been founded in the year 1817. During that period it has been sustained by patronage from nearly all the Eastern and Middle counties of the State, and has contributed in a great measure to the high reputation which the town of Oxford has so long enjoyed as a centre of education and refinement.

It is the aim of the undersigned, as joint principals, assisted by competent instructors, to maintain for this Institution the character it has hitherto sustained as a finishing school of high grade.

The prices of board and tuition have been placed as low as the proper care of the pupils and their thorough instruction in the course of study will warrant, and in the boarding department everything required for the comfort of the pupil is furnished without extra charge.

The government of the School is intended at all times to inculcate elevated views of propriety and deportment. The prescribed rules of discipline are therefore few, but a strict observance of these will be required, and no pupil will be retained in the School who persists in a course of disobedience to them.

The control of day scholars, or those boarding in private families, *whilst away from School*, is not assumed by the Principals, except that such pupils upon leaving the School premises will be required to go immediately to their homes, and in no case will they be allowed to take part in public entertainments or exhibitions out of the School, during the session.

Occasional social receptions will be given in the School on Friday evenings, to which the pupils will be allowed to invite their friends.

The School is unsectarian. Especial care is devoted to biblical and religious instruction, and pupils boarding in the School will be required to attend divine service in one of the four churches in the place, Methodist, Episcopal, Presbyterian, or Baptist, every Sabbath—unless for good excuse—and always in company with one of the teachers; but no merely doctrinal bias is inculcated, and no sectarian disputation allowed.

The course of instruction is intended to be thorough, rather than hurried and superficial, and no pupil will be advanced in studies beyond her attainments, *except upon the special request of the parent.* About seven hours each day are devoted to school exercises, four in the forenoon and three in the afternoon, with suitable intermissions for recreation, according to the age of the pupil.

Quarterly reports of the progress of pupils in their respective studies will be made to parents and guardians.

Terms per Session of Twenty Weeks:

Board, including washing, fuel, lights, &c.,	$75 00
Tuition in English branches, $10 to	15 00
Music on Piano or Organ, with use of instrument,	20 00
Music on Guitar, with use of instrument,	15 00
Latin,	10 00
French,	5 00
Drawing,	10 00
Painting in Oil,	20 00
Wax Work,	5 00

Price of Board and tuition due at beginning of session.

MRS. SALLIE DUTY HAYS,
MISS HATTIE N. COUSINS.

Oxford Female Academy, as seen in this 1877 advertisement, referred to itself as a finishing school of high grade. The purpose of the school was to "inculcate elevated views of propriety and deportment." The advertisement also states that no "pupil will be retained in the School who persists in a course of disobedience." It continues to establish that "especial care is devoted to biblical and religious instruction," and that "no pupil will be advanced in studies beyond her attainments." These regulations are a contrast to many of our schools today, to say the least. (Courtesy of Bob and Judy Hunt.)

Addie Hester attended Oxford Female Academy in 1877. The courses offered at this time appear to differ from the curriculum of today. (Courtesy of Bob and Judy Hunt.)

OXFORD FEMALE ACADEMY.

QUARTERLY REPORT,

Fall Session, 1877.

Sir: For the quarter ending Septr 28th

Miss Addie Hester has been absent from school 2 times, tardy 1 times, and has received 0 demerits

Her grade of scholarship in her respective studies is as follows, 7 representing the highest and 1 the lowest mark:

Spelling,	6½	Botany,	
Reading,	6	Astronomy,	
Penmanship,	6	Moral Philosophy,	
Composition,	5-½	Mental Philosophy,	
Geography,		Rhetoric,	6
History,		Logic,	
English Grammar,		French,	
Mathematics,	6½	Latin,	5-¼
Natural Philosophy,		Music,	6
Physiology,		Drawing,	
Chemistry,	6¾	Painting,	
Geology,		Wax Work,	

Deportment, 7

We expect to have a better report from Miss Addie [illegible]

OXFORD, N. C.-- DEEP NIGHT, SUMMER

The town's fast asleep as a child
Spent from play. Dim streets are rolled up
Like trundle beds and tucked under
Blue-black hillsides. Slight raindrops
Beat an elfin tattoo on bedded down gutters
And roof-tops, slowly rubbing out
The blackberry jam fingerprints that day left.
And down the deep well of a cool, forgotten street
The milk horse beats his cloppity-clop requiem
For zooming bees and sun-swept lanes.
The echoes go spilling on sleeping gardens
Like a flood of question marks.

Oxford's gone to velvet dreams
Like a child spent from play.
There's hardly a whir among the linden trees
Where the moon goes walking on tip-toe.

Thad Stem was one of North Carolina's greatest writers. Oxford was home to Stem, who wrote books, newspaper columns, and poetry. Enjoy this poem about Oxford by Stem. (Courtesy of Marguerite Stem.)

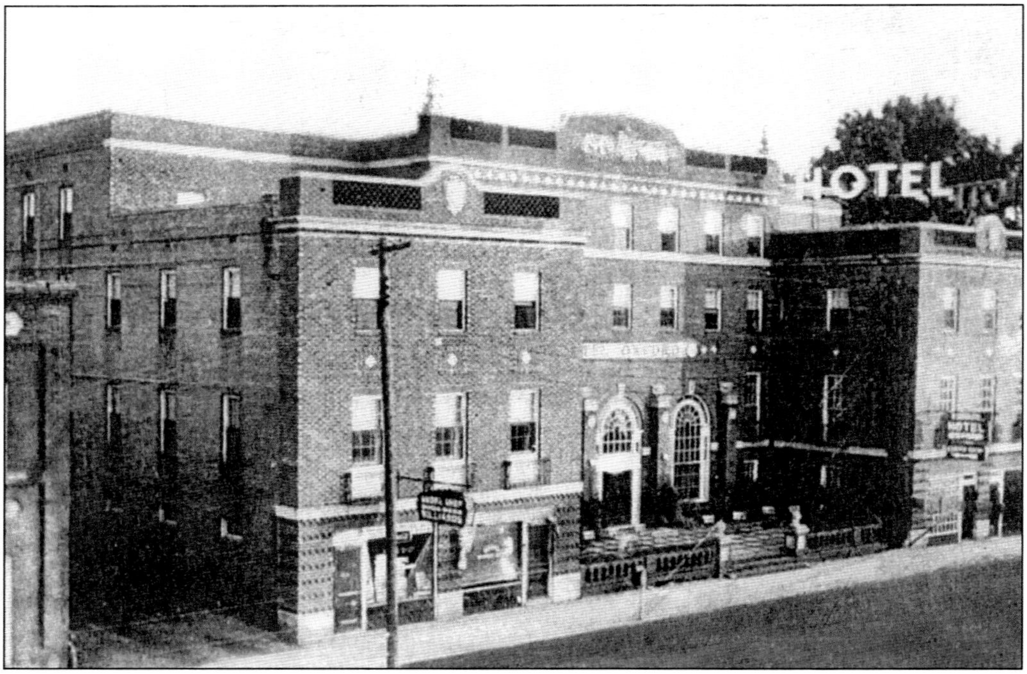

This is the exterior of Hotel Oxford.

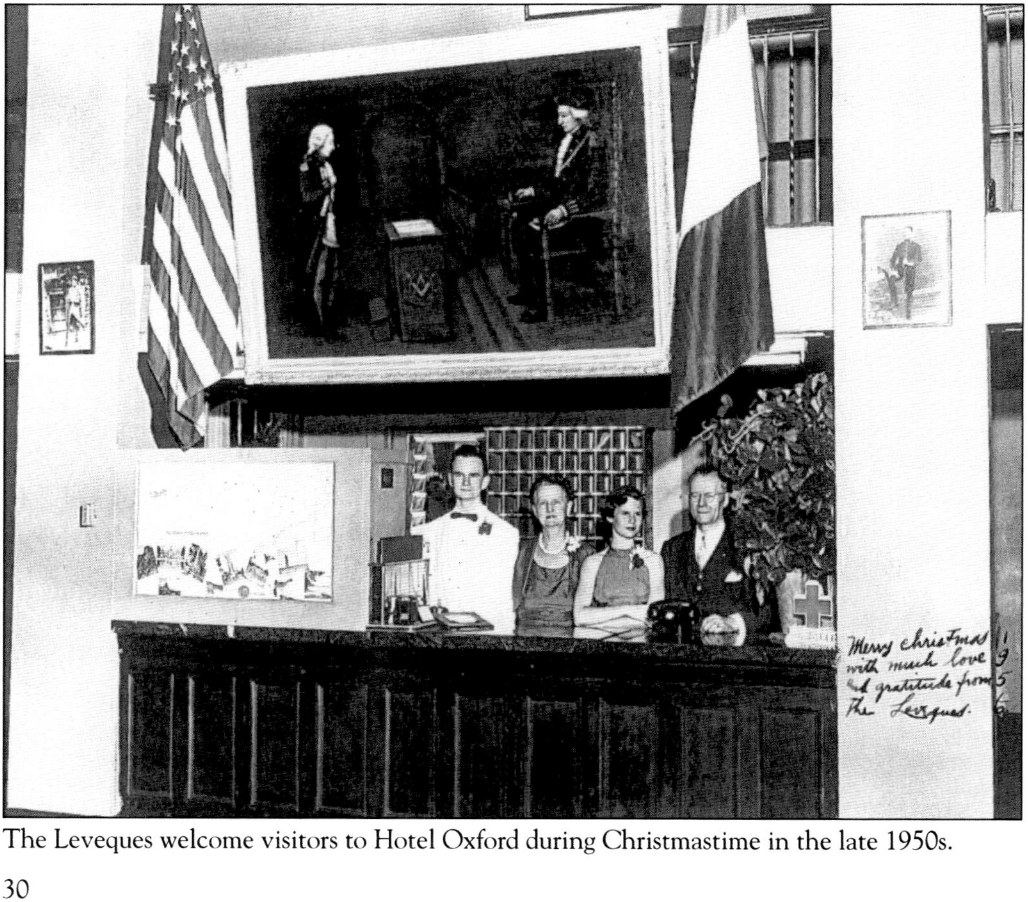

The Leveques welcome visitors to Hotel Oxford during Christmastime in the late 1950s.

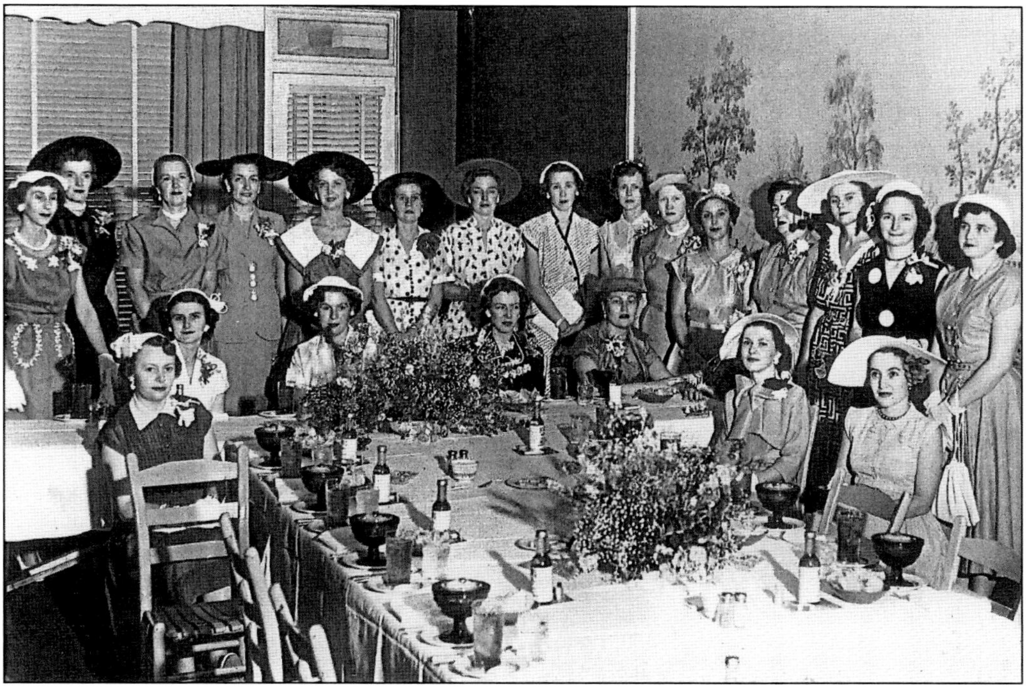

This picture presents the inside of the Hotel Oxford during a Literary Club meeting in 1950. This is quite a gathering of beautiful women. From left to right are the following: (seated at table) Helen White Finch, Hilda Watkins, Maria Kerr Blackwell, Beth Yancey, Helen Rose Duffy, Gwen Pryor, and Audrey Gholson; (standing) Hope Currin, Ruth Yancey, Grace Arthur, Marguerite Stem, Mrs. John Myers, Rachel Thomas, Mary Green Harns, Kay Hancock, Mittie Belle Powell, Becky Jennings, Marjorie Watkins, Elizabeth Sullivan, Virginia Mitchell Watkins, Kathryn Webb, and Caroline Breedlove. (Courtesy of Rachel Thomas.)

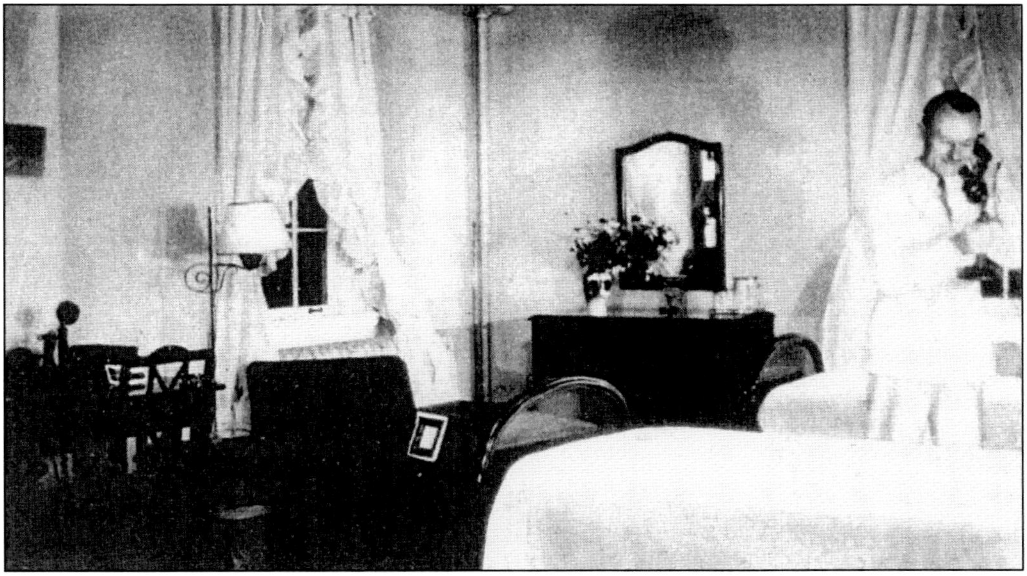

This is one of the rooms at Hotel Oxford with a view of Hillsboro Street. Hotel Oxford was a landmark of the city; with good service and fine accommodations, it hosted meetings and conventions.

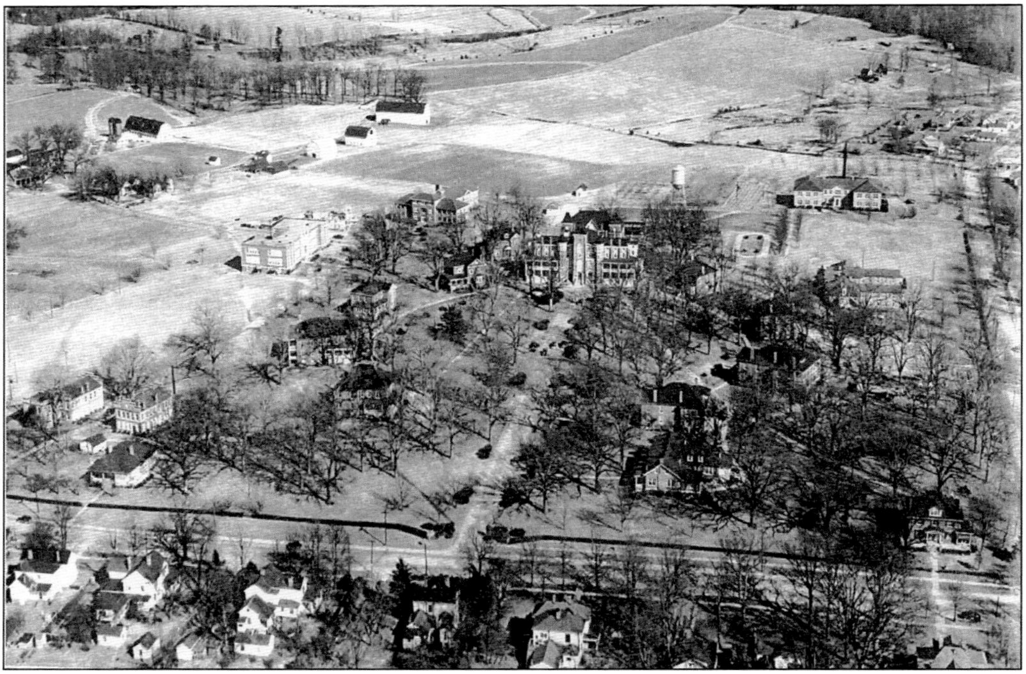

This is a 1951 aerial view of the Masonic Home for Children campus, formerly known as the Oxford Orphanage. Farmland and barns are visible in the background and at the bottom is College Street and some its houses. (Courtesy of Masonic Home for Children Archives.)

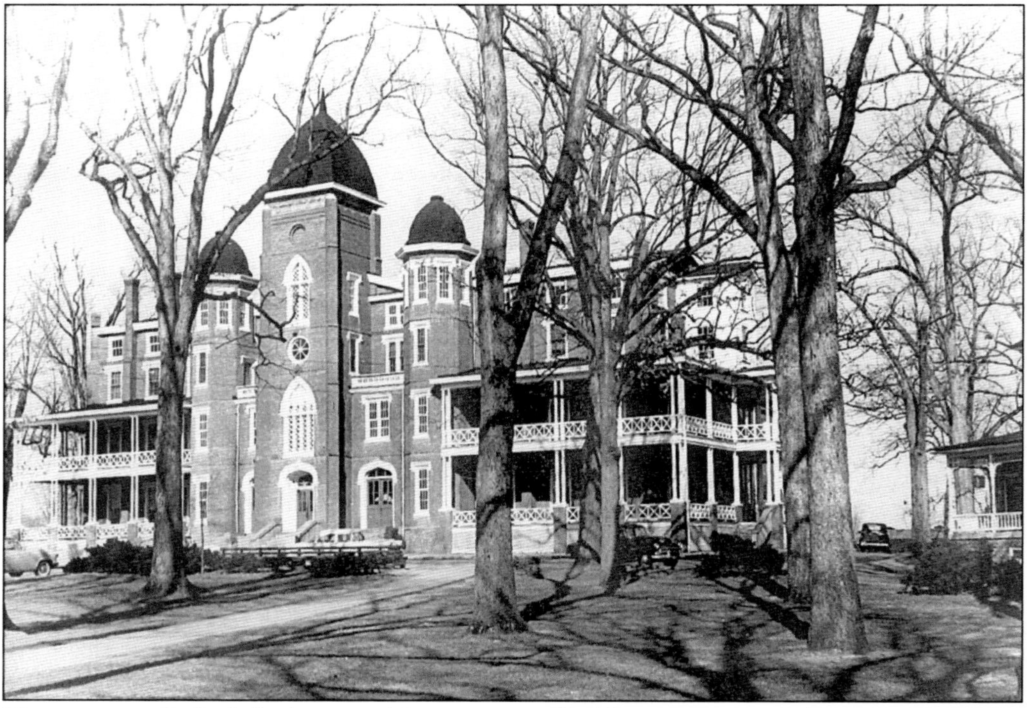

The majestic Oxford Orphanage Administration Building towers over the campus. At one time this structure served as the St. Johns College Building. (Courtesy of Masonic Home for Children Archives.)

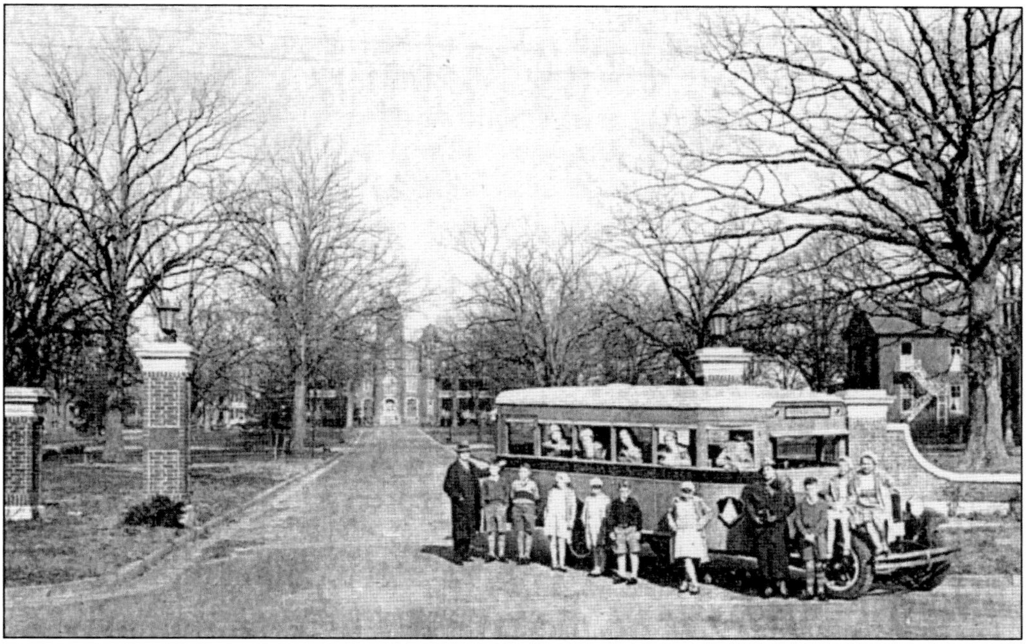

The Oxford Orphanage Singing Class is on their way to perform in the 1930s. The singing classes were a tradition for many years and were enjoyed all over the state.

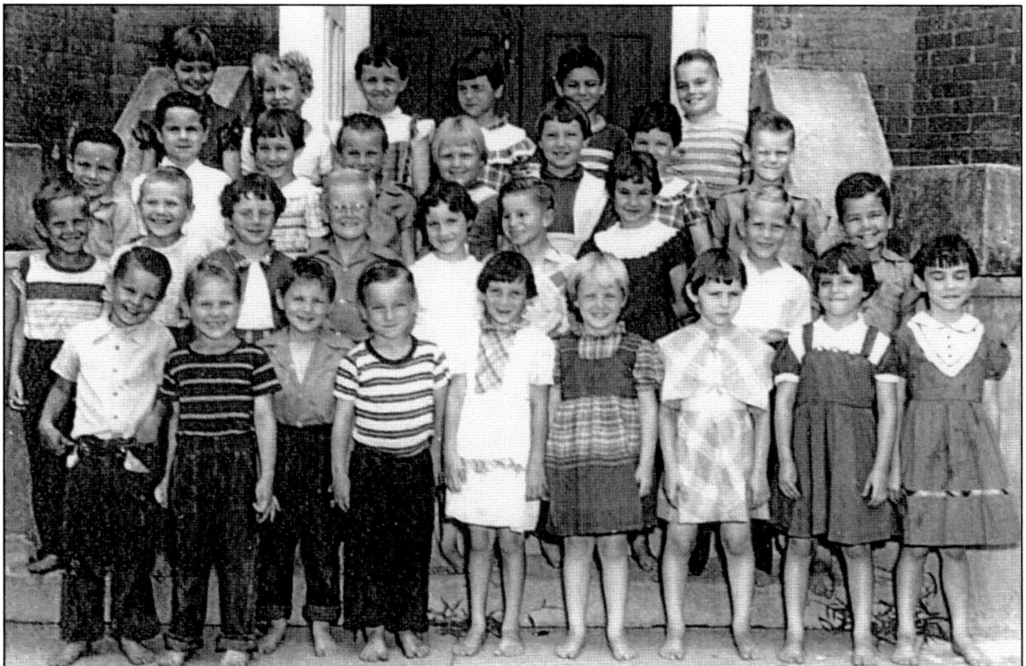

These children are from the "baby cottage" at the Oxford Orphanage in 1955. (Courtesy of Masonic Home for Children Archives.)

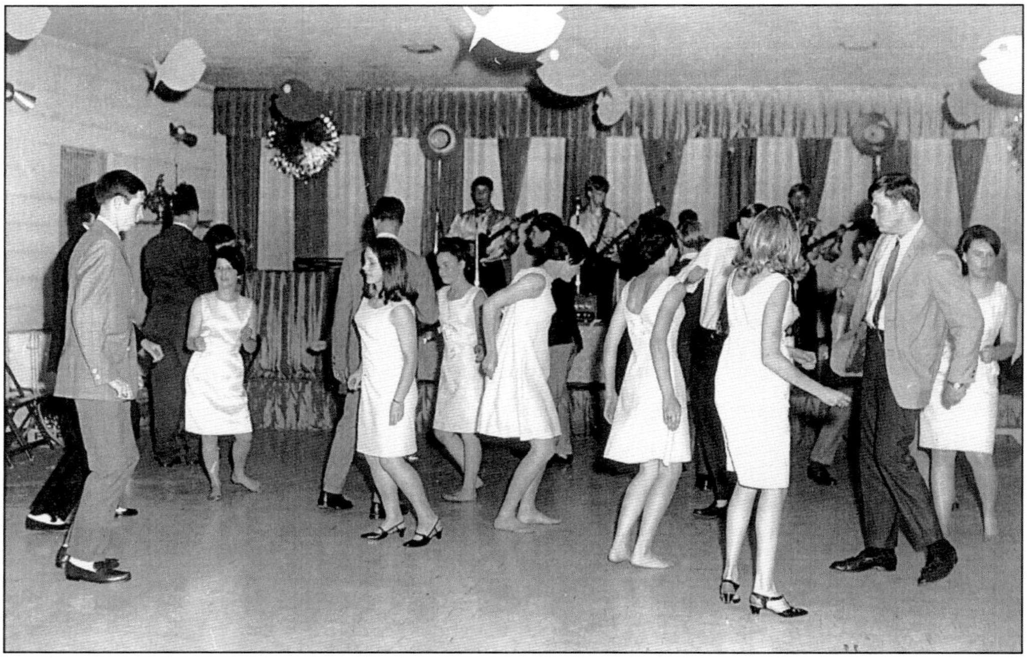

The seniors of the Oxford Orphanage put their best foot forward at a dance in 1967. (Courtesy of Masonic Home for Children Archives.)

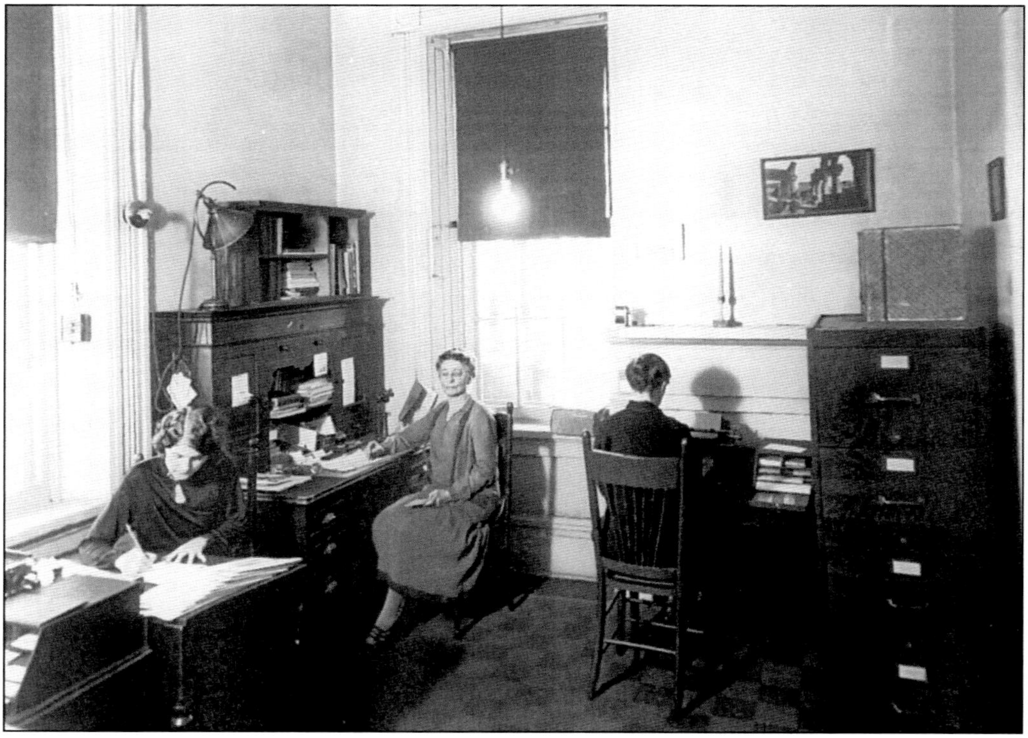

Mrs. Nettie Bemis, lady supervisor at the Oxford Orphanage, works in her office with two assistants. Mrs. Bemis faces the camera. (Courtesy of Masonic Home for Children Archives.)

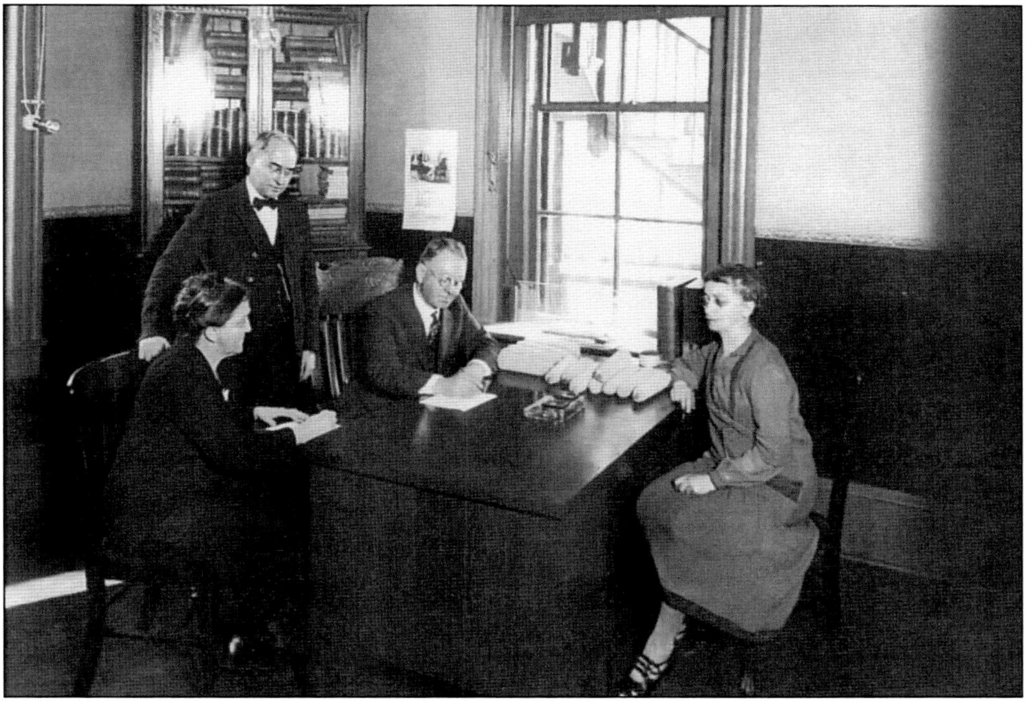

Papers are signed inside the administrative office at the Oxford Orphanage in the early 1900s. Mrs. Nettie Bemis is on the right and Mr. R.L. Brown is standing. (Courtesy of Masonic Home for Children Archives.)

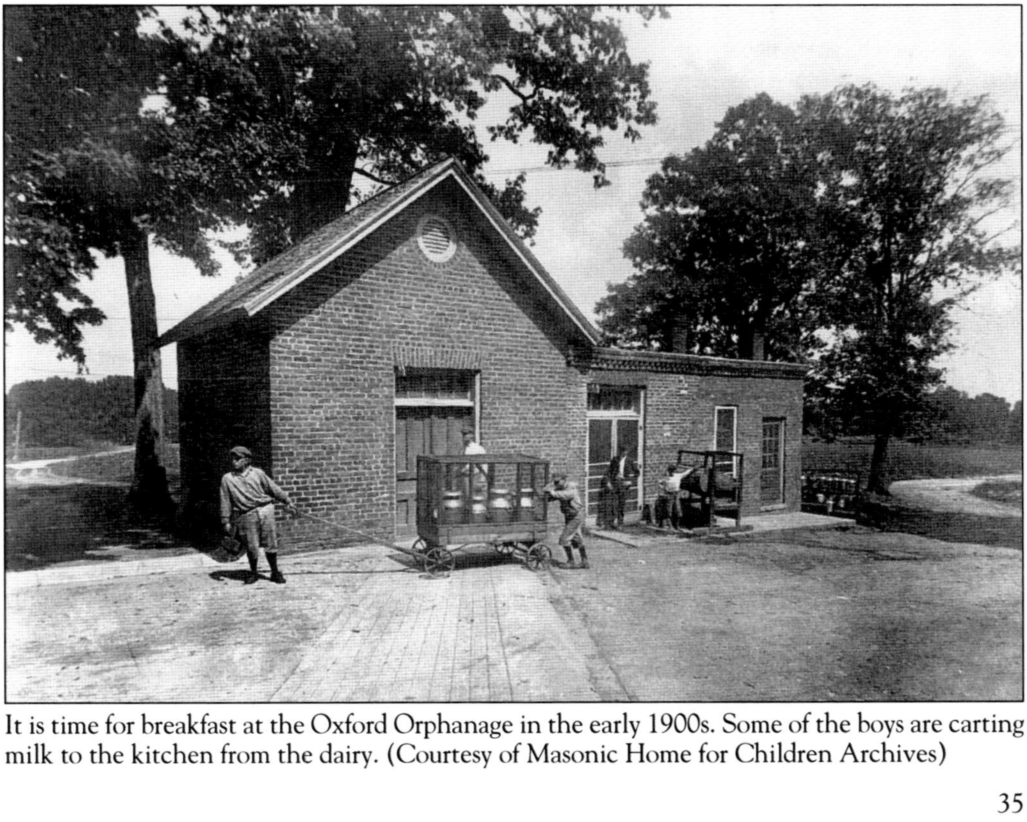

It is time for breakfast at the Oxford Orphanage in the early 1900s. Some of the boys are carting milk to the kitchen from the dairy. (Courtesy of Masonic Home for Children Archives)

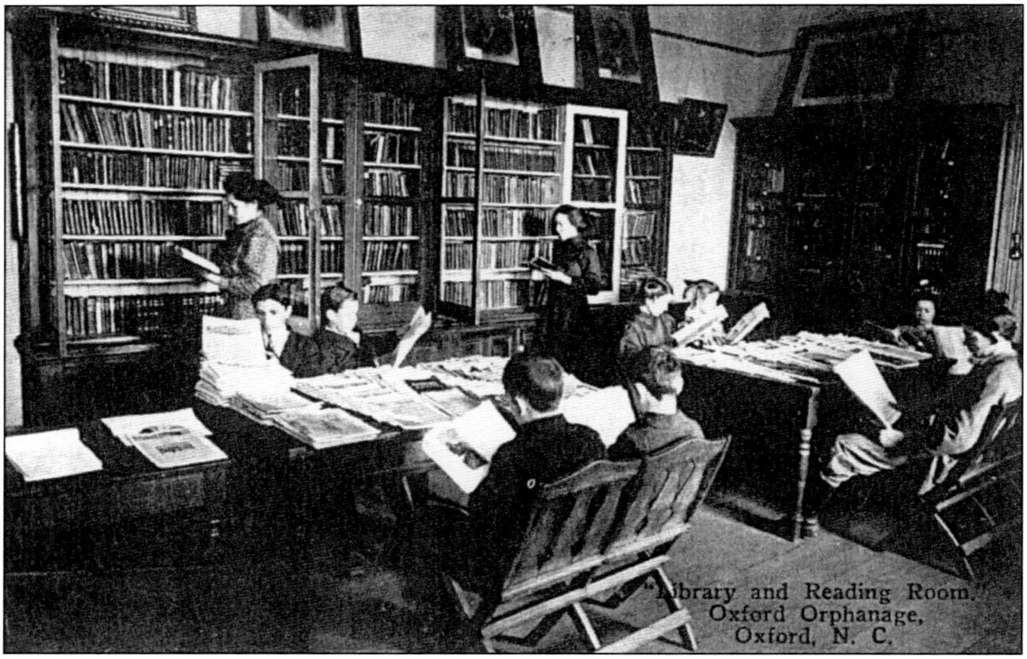

Travel the world, win great battles, fall in love, experience success and failure, learn from masters—all of this a child can do by opening a book and entering the magical world of reading, as shown here at the Oxford Orphanage Library in the early 1900s.

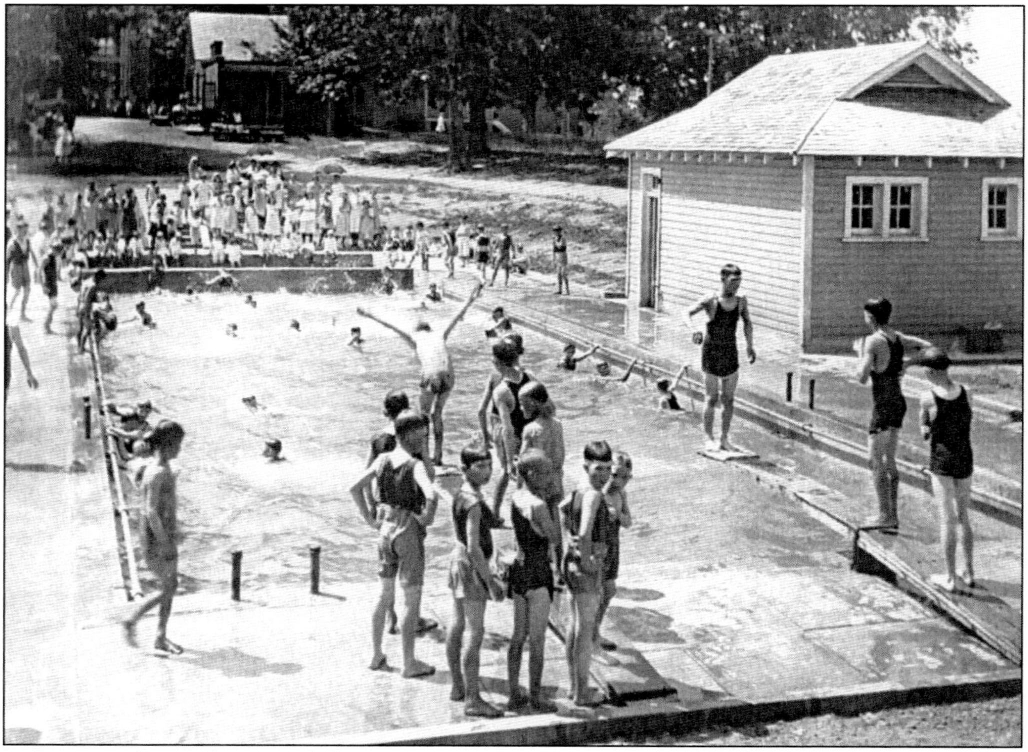

Kids enjoy the cool water of the Oxford Orphanage pool in the 1920s. (Courtesy of Masonic Home for Children Archives.)

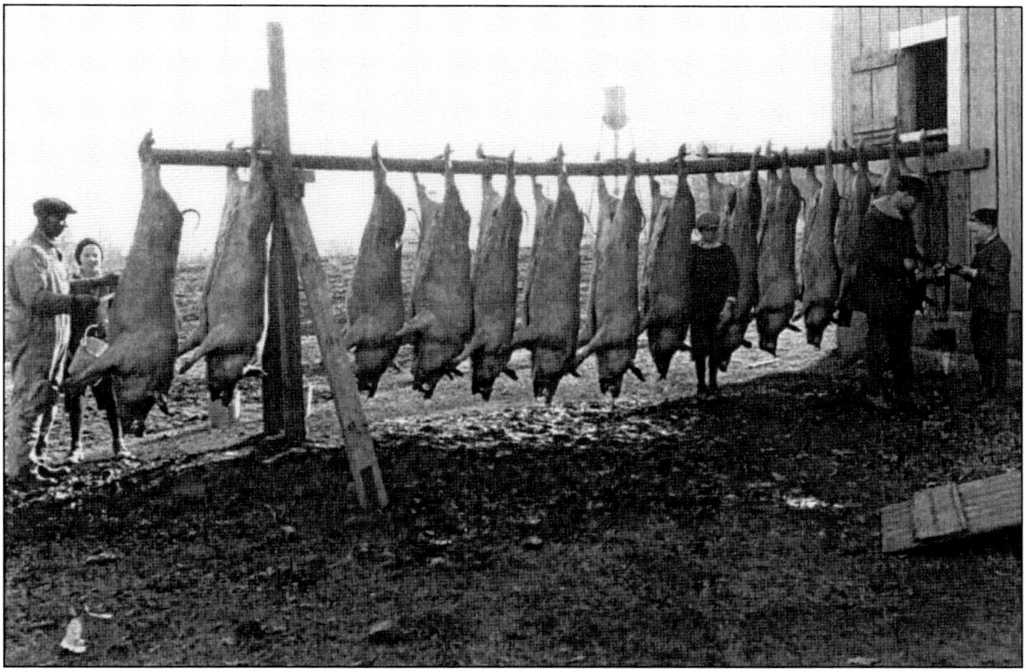

Hog-killing day at the Oxford Orphanage required the skill and hard work of many, including children and staff. For years the orphanage produced much of its own food; a farm was managed by staff and children on the campus. (Courtesy of Masonic Home for Children Archives.)

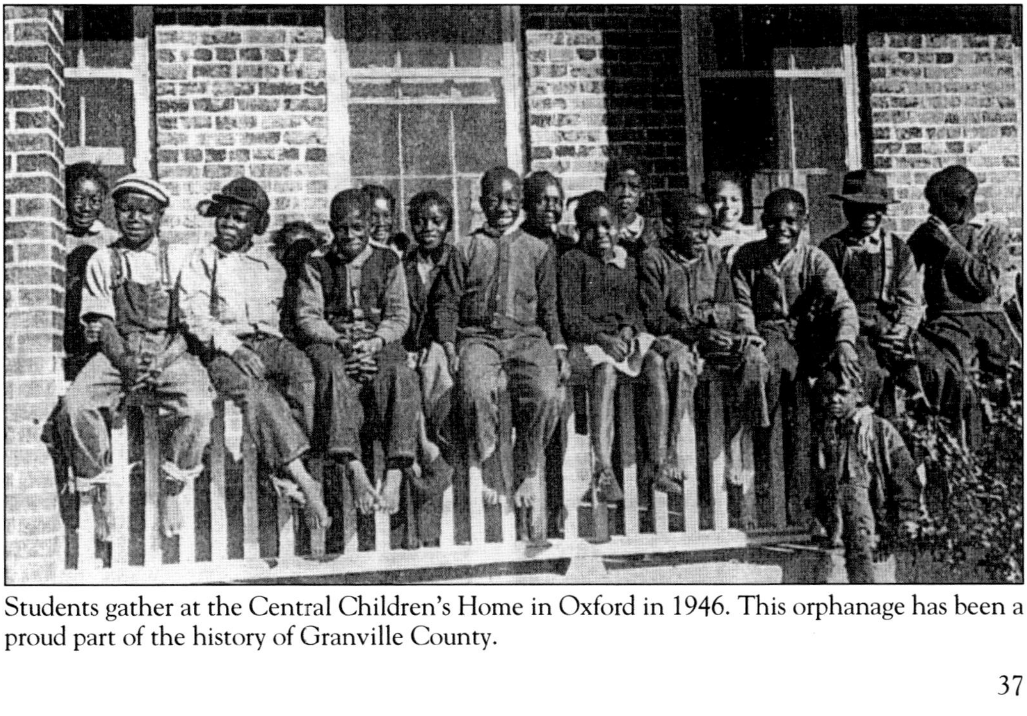

Students gather at the Central Children's Home in Oxford in 1946. This orphanage has been a proud part of the history of Granville County.

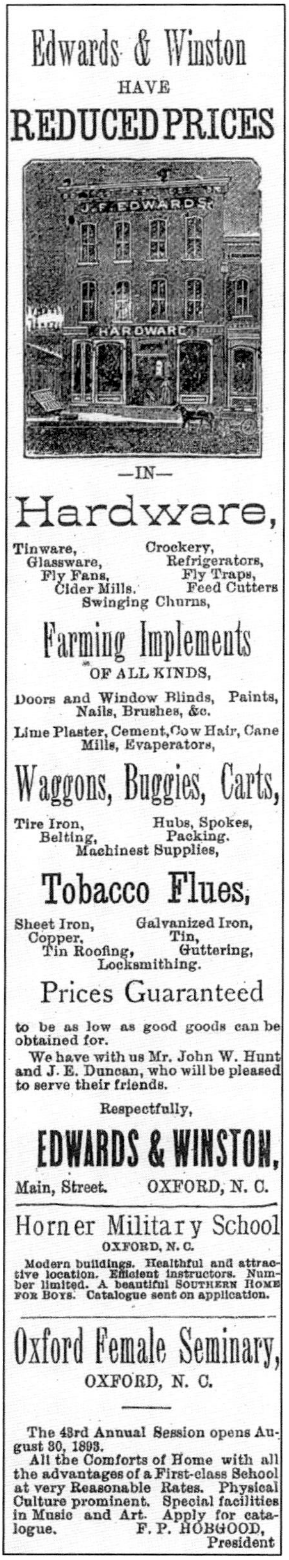

A hardware store, Oxford Female Seminary, and Horner Military School are advertised in the *Orphan's Friend* newspaper in 1893. (Courtesy of *Orphan's Friend*.)

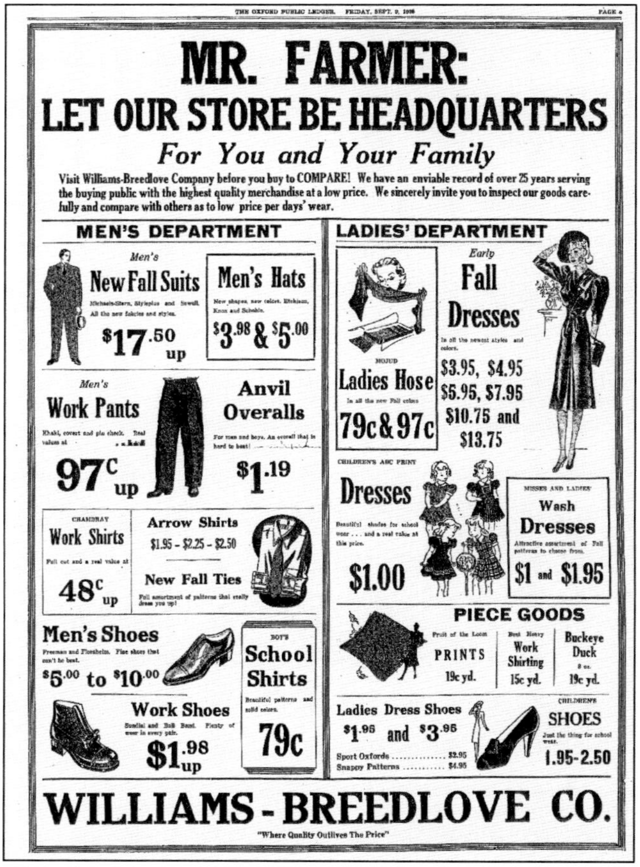

The tobacco industry once employed more than 50 percent of Granville's population in some capacity, and advertisers catered to them. This Williams-Breedlove advertisement appeared in 1938, offering men's suits for $17.50, men's pants for 97¢, dresses for $1, and various other items. (Courtesy of *Oxford Public Ledger*.)

This advertisement appeared in the *Oxford Public Ledger* in the 1930s. It proclaims exactly where to turn in the Bible for problems or situations you may encounter. (Courtesy of *Oxford Public Ledger*.)

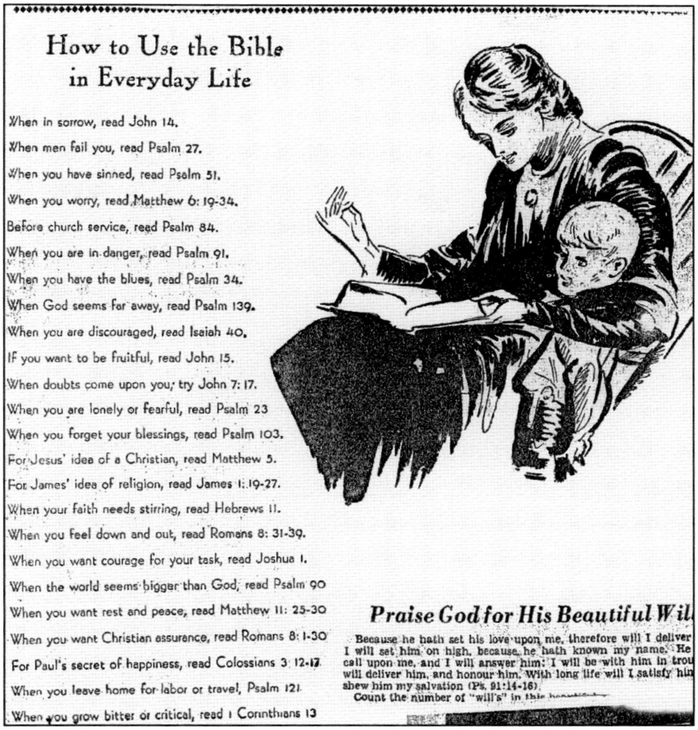

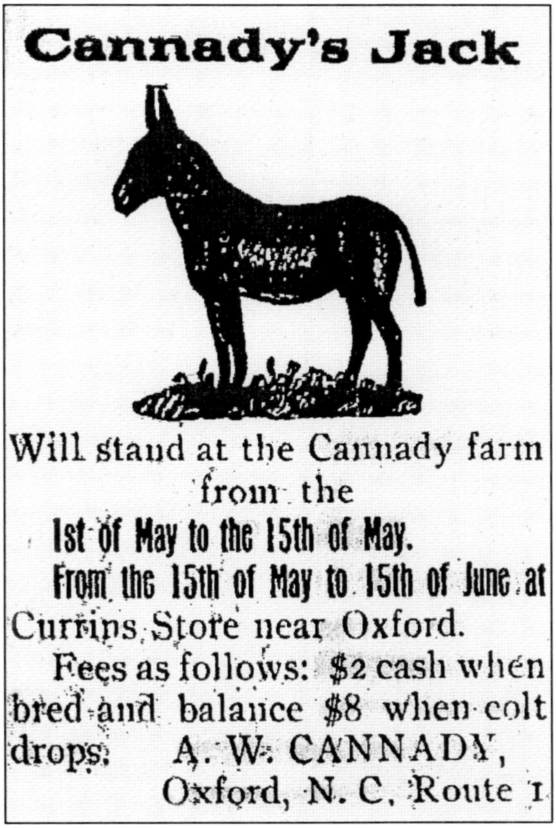

This is an advertisement from the *Oxford Banner* newspaper in 1911. (Courtesy of Oxford Banner.)

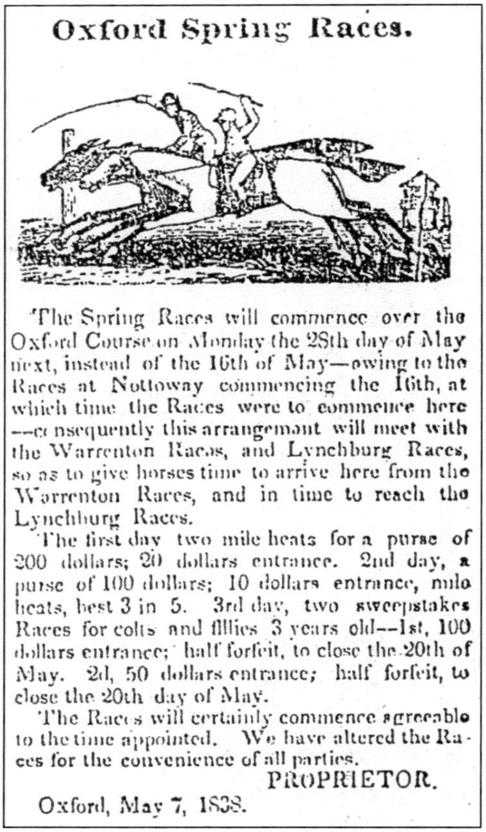

Horse racing was Granville County's favorite sport, especially in the 1800s. This advertisement promoted races at the Oxford Course; it appeared in the *Oxford Examiner* in 1838.

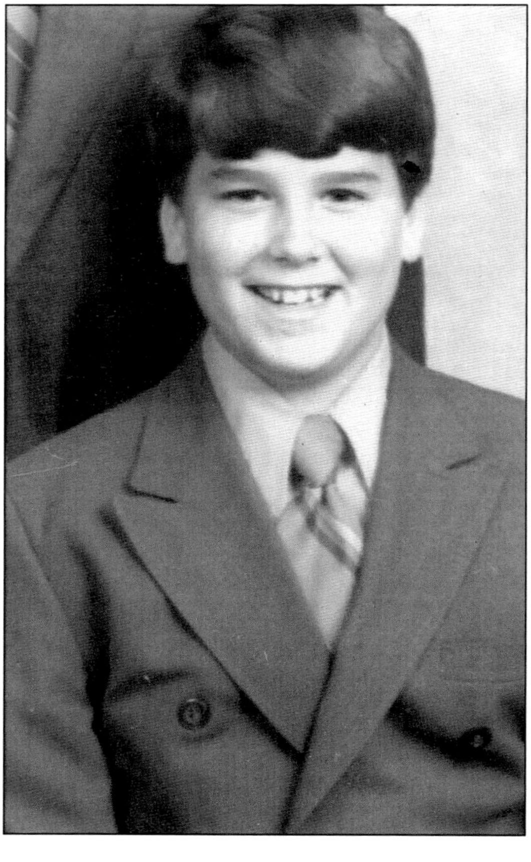

Richard Moore is pictured at the age of 12. He grew up in Oxford and graduated from J.F. Webb High School. Moore is now the treasurer for the state of North Carolina; he previously served as head of the North Carolina Crime Control and Public Safety Department. (Courtesy of G. Tingley Moore.)

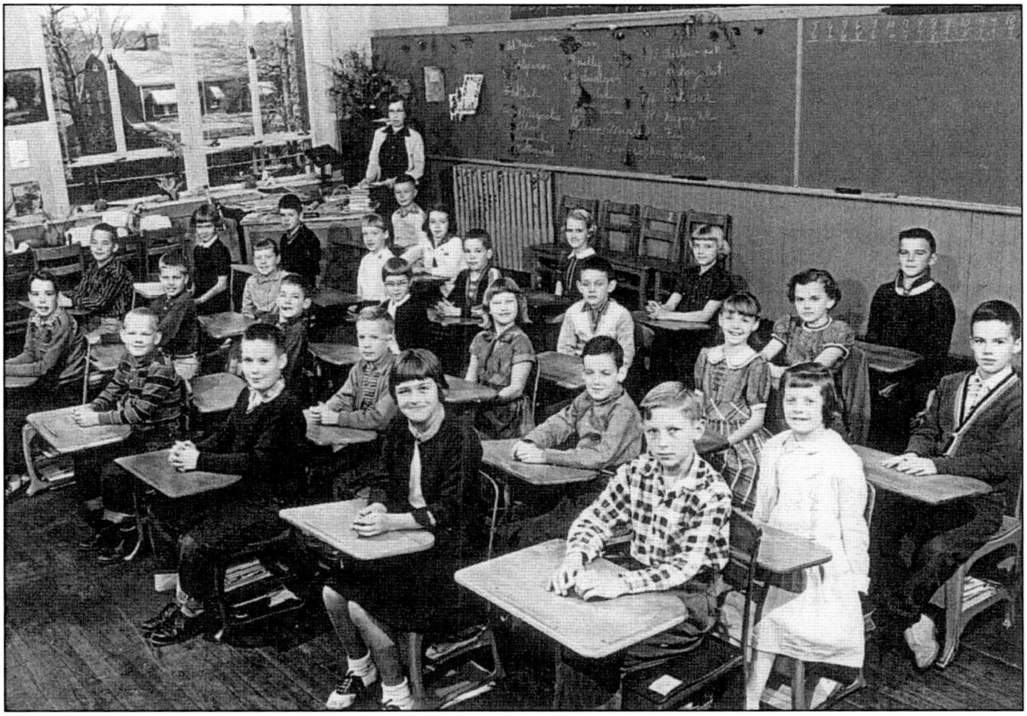

Miss Sue Bryan is shown with her fourth grade class at C.G. Credle School in Oxford in 1959. Miss Bryan taught school for over 40 years and was very instrumental in forming the Granville County History Museum. (Courtesy of William and Lisa Burwell.)

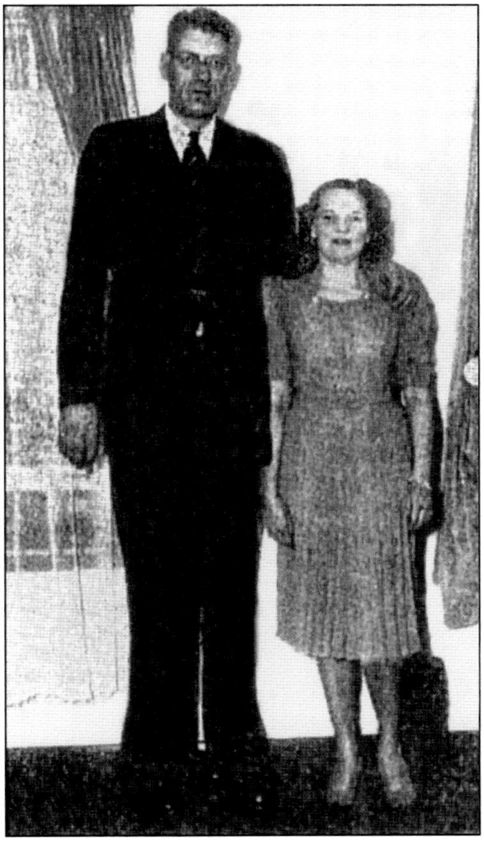

Cliff Thompson, shown here on a visit to Oxford in the 1930s, was at the time the world's tallest human, standing 8 feet, 7 inches tall. Thompson was in town promoting Blatz Brewing Company. He had previously spent many years making circus appearances. Thompson is 36 years old in this picture, weighs 460 pounds, and wears a size 22 shoe. Needless to say, Mr. Thompson probably was not challenged to a wrestling match while visiting Oxford.

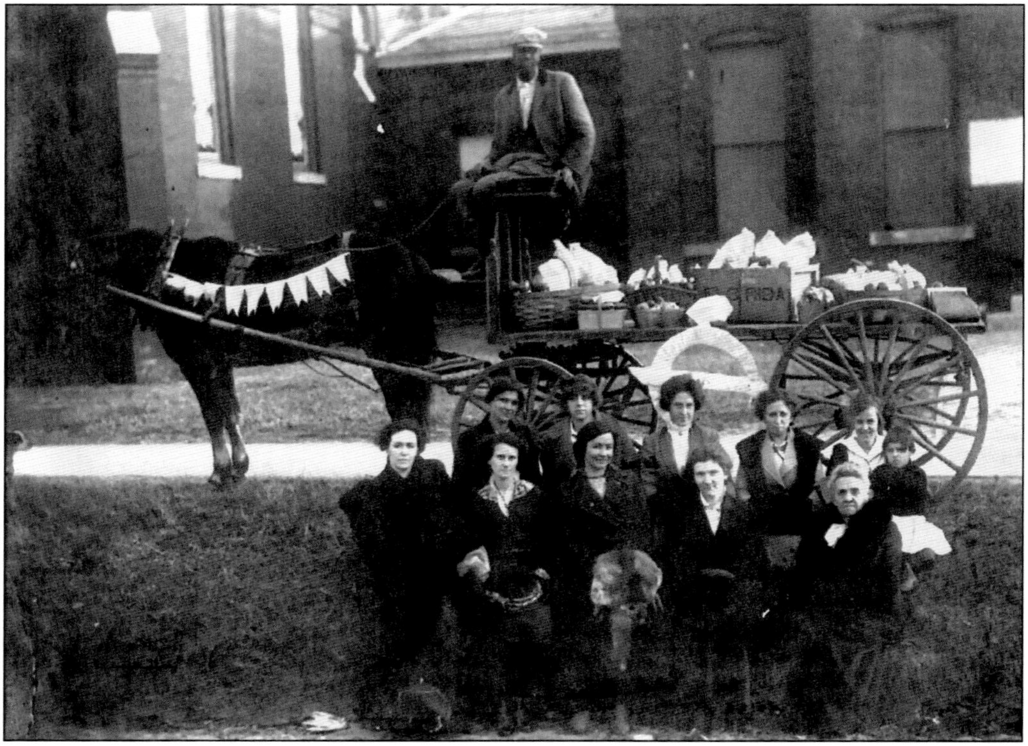

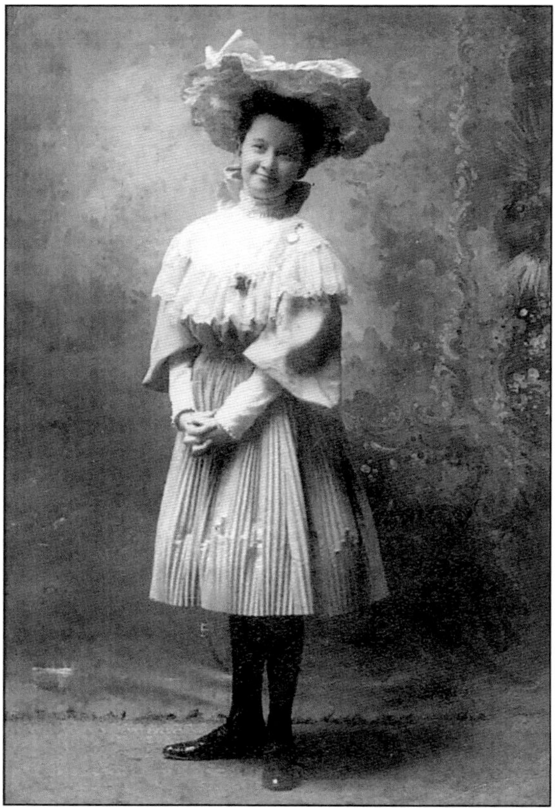

The Philathea Class at Oxford Methodist Church is shown in this 1914 photograph. Prince is the horse and Rob is the driver. Part of th e church can be seen in the background. (Courtesy of Rachel Thomas.)

This is Estelle Bullock at the age of 14 in 1907. Estelle later married Dr. W.N. Thomas of Oxford, a well-known and respected physician and one of the founders of Granville Hospital. Estelle Thomas was an avid historian and kept many scrapbooks of information regarding the history of Granville County. (Courtesy of Rachel Thomas.)

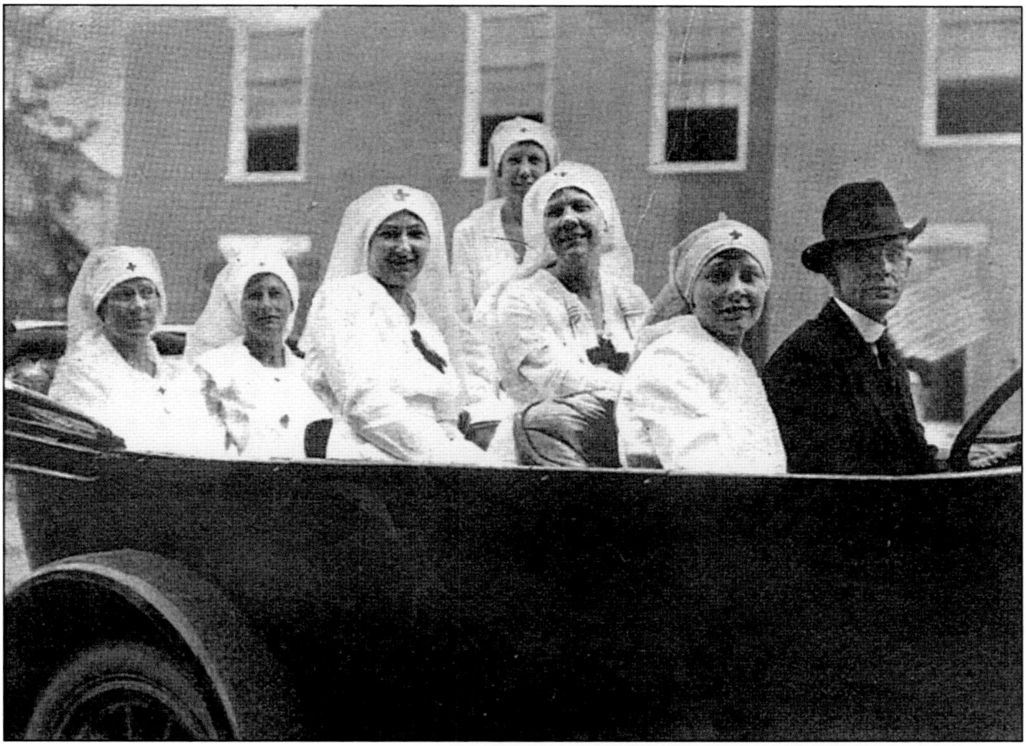

During World War I, many Granville County women helped in the war effort by working for the American Red Cross. Granville County women shown here, from left to right, are Mrs. J.C. Robards, Mrs. S.H. Pritchard, Mrs. A.A. Chapman, Mrs. Graham Roberts, Miss Esther Mitchell, and Miss Mary Webb. The man is unidentified.

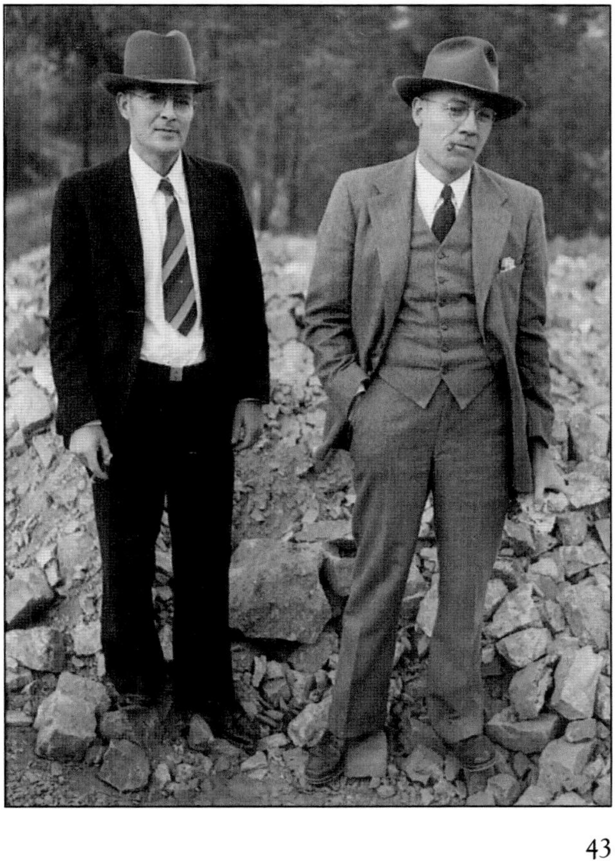

When this picture was taken in 1942, Tungsten Mine was the largest producer of tungsten in North Carolina. This mine was located in Vance County. Richard Hamme (left) and Joseph Hamme (right), both of Granville County, operated the mine. (Courtesy of Catherine Noblin.)

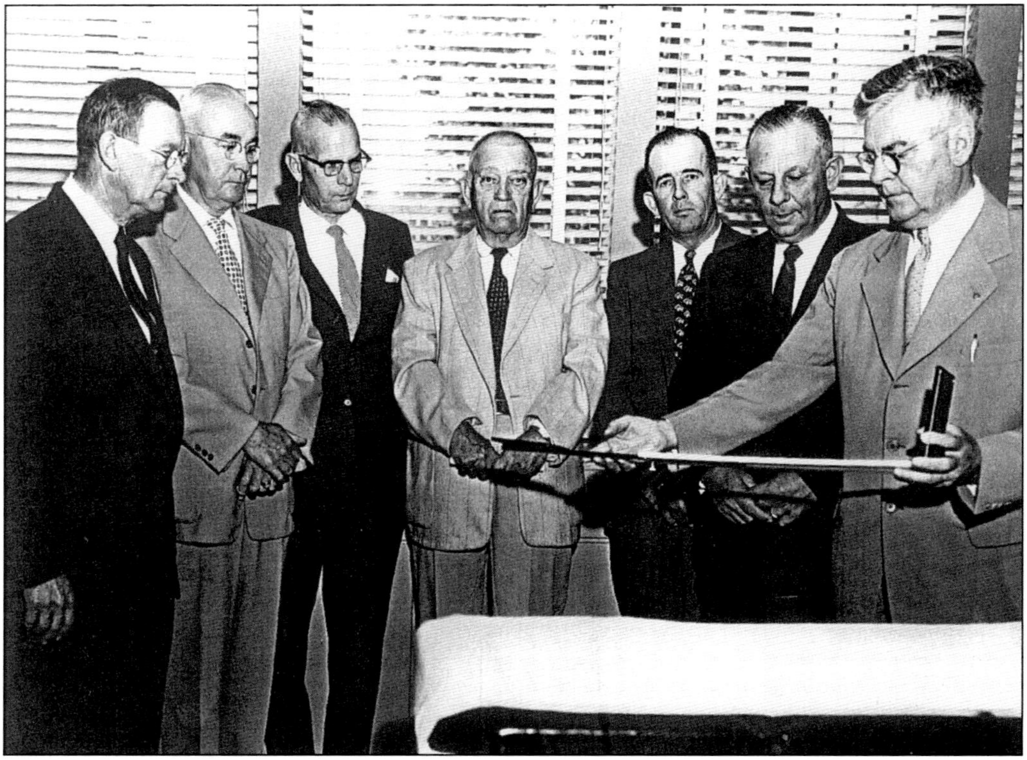

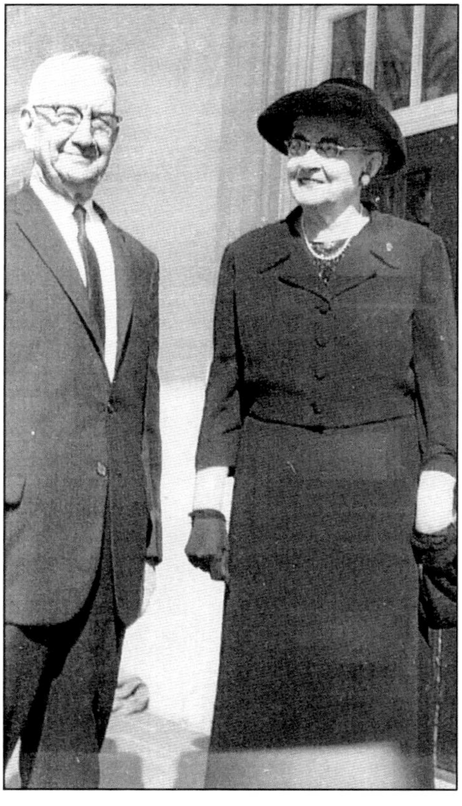

The dedication of the Granville County Health Center took place in 1954. From left to right are R.R.Herring, Dr. Finch, David Hicks, Dr. Joe Thomasson, W.W. Yeargin, Will Mitchel, and Dr. Wampler. (Courtesy of Jean Gill.)

This is Mr. and Mrs. C.G. Credle in Oxford in 1961. C.G. Credle School was named for Mr. Credle, a longtime county educator. (Courtesy of Masonic Home for Children Archives.)

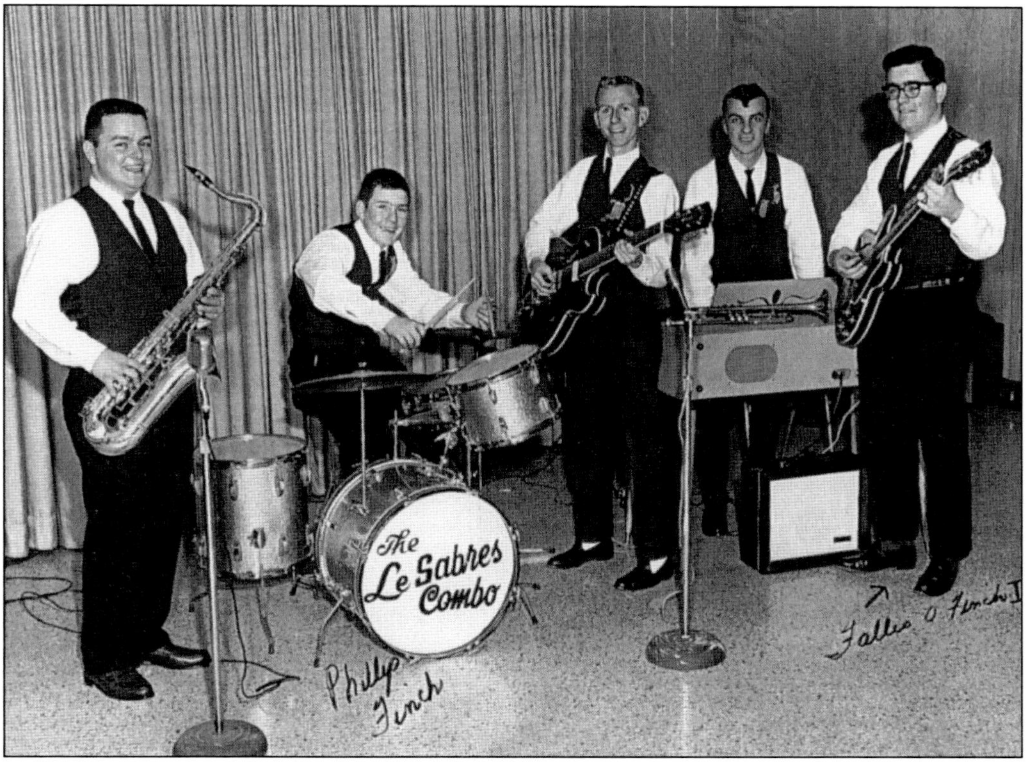

Phillip Finch (second from the left) and F.O. Finch (far right) were members of a band called the LeSabres Combo. (Courtesy of Opal White.)

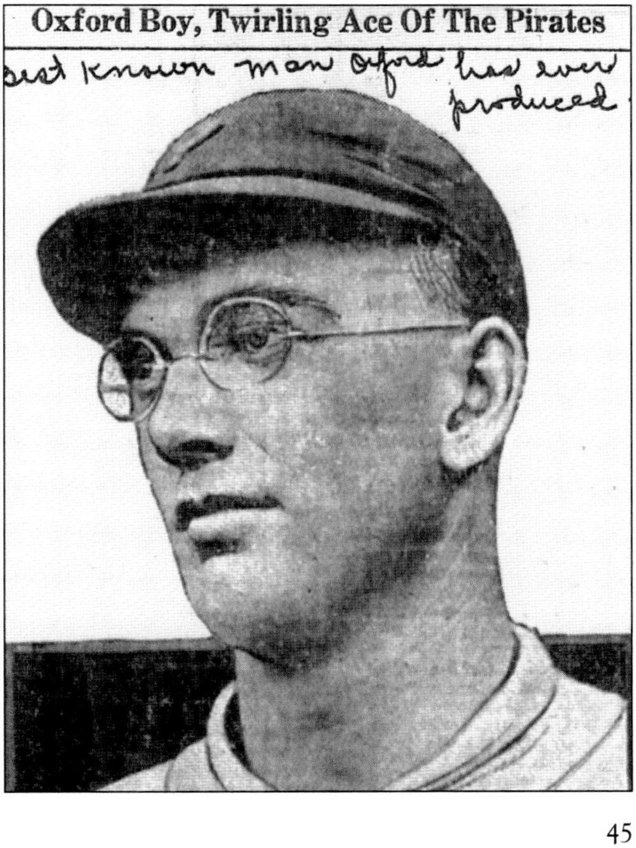

One of the few Oxford men to make it to the major leagues was Lee Meadows, who played for the Pittsburgh Pirates baseball team. Meadows competed in the World Series against the mighty New York Yankees.

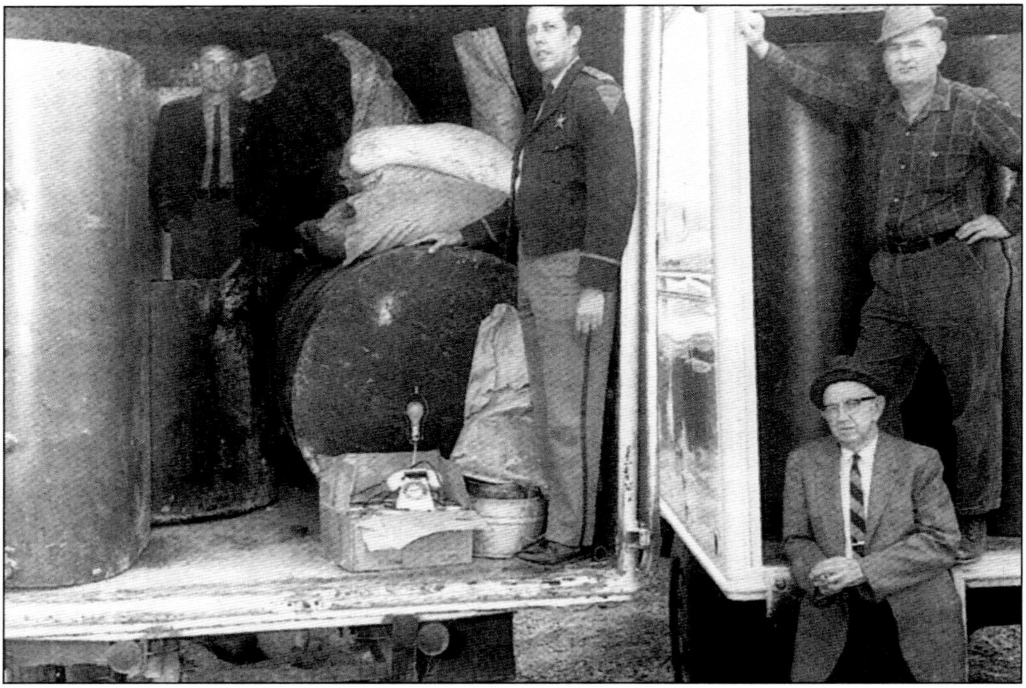

These trucks contain some illegal whiskey-making equipment confiscated in Granville County in the 1960s. Inside is a 500-gallon still, hundreds of pounds of grain, boilers, pipes, and glass containers, among other items. From left to right are H.T. Brame, Bunny Thompson, and Arthur Ray Currin, all of the Granville County Sheriff's Department. The man on the ground is unidentified. (Courtesy of Nellie Brame.)

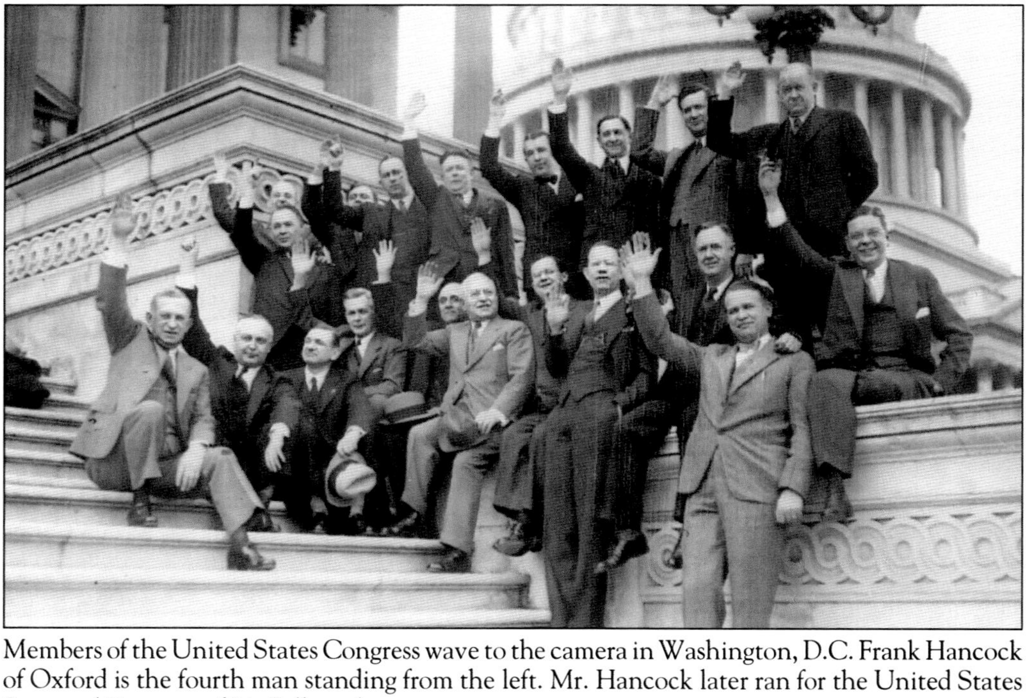

Members of the United States Congress wave to the camera in Washington, D.C. Frank Hancock of Oxford is the fourth man standing from the left. Mr. Hancock later ran for the United States Senate. (Courtesy of Liz Falkner.)

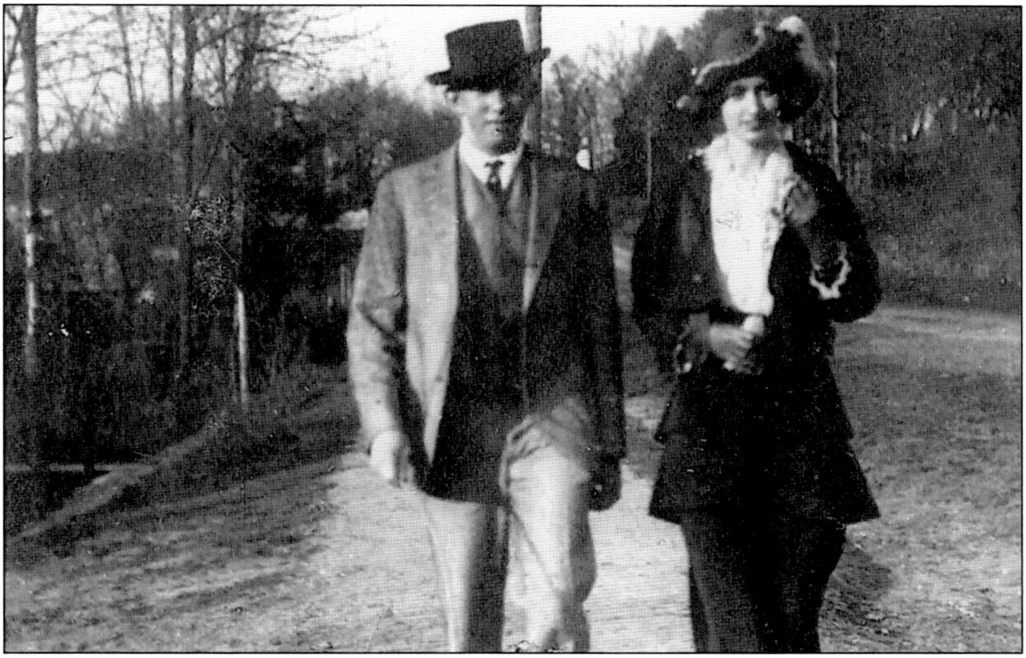

In the early 1900s, a section of Green Acres in Oxford was known as "Lovers Lane." Here Frank Hancock and Lucy Landis, dressed to impress, stroll along and enjoy each other's company. Upon seeing the camera, formality was called for. Frank and Lucy later married. (Courtesy of Liz Falkner.)

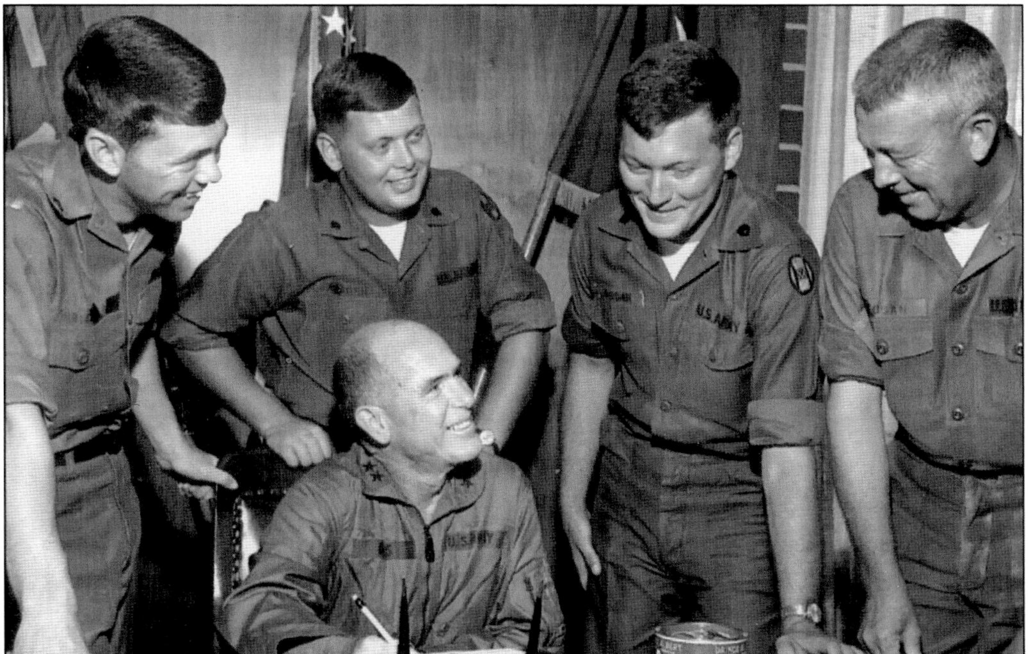

Adj. Gen. Gerald Davis is shown at his desk as the Riggans of Oxford look on. All four Riggan men were members of the National Guard. From left to right, they are Jody, Jay, Wayne, and Johnny. This picture was taken in the 1960s. (Courtesy of Nettie Dickerson.)

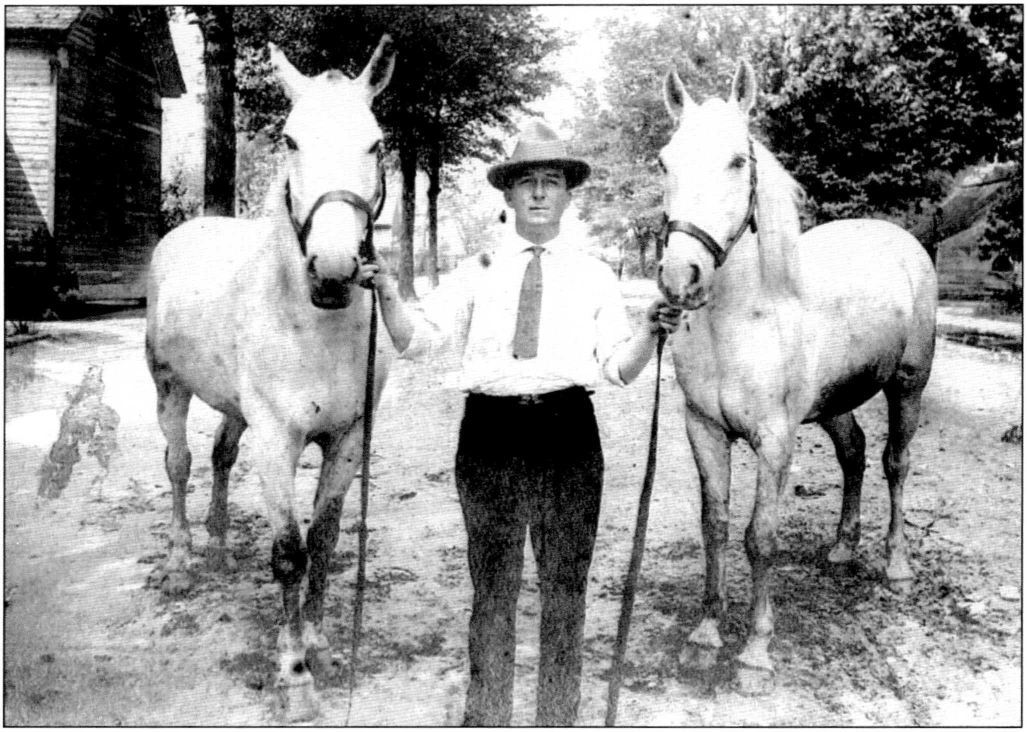

Bob Walker holds two of his horses on McClanahan Street in Oxford in 1905. (Courtesy of Nettie Dickerson.)

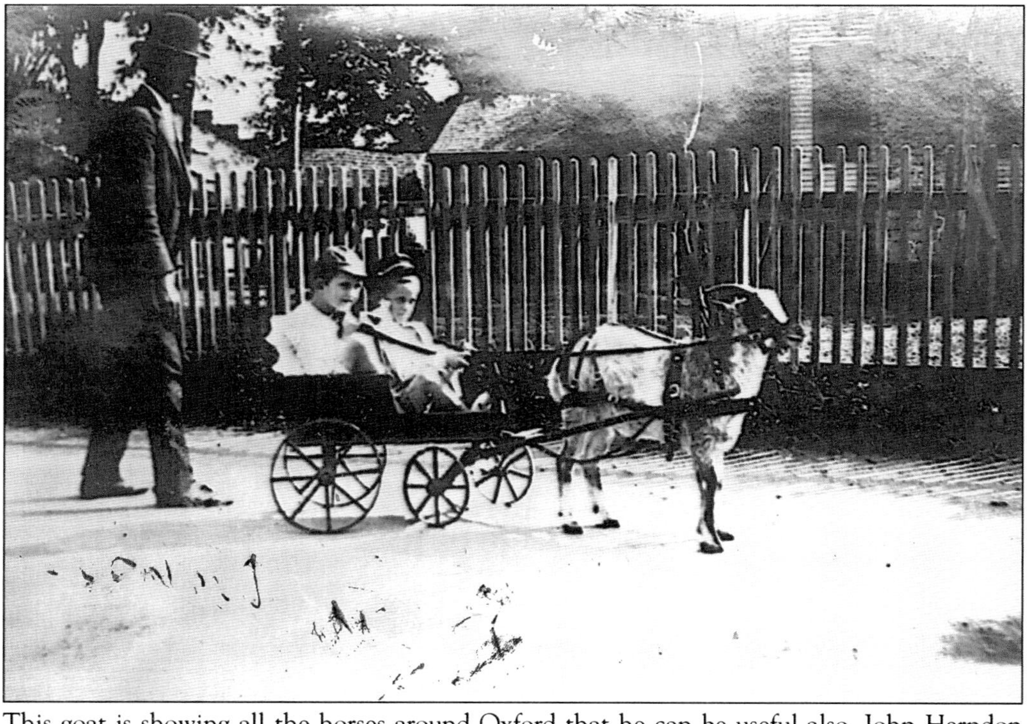

This goat is showing all the horses around Oxford that he can be useful also. John Herndon follows John and Laura Stedman as the proud goat marches on. (Courtesy of Liz Falkner.)

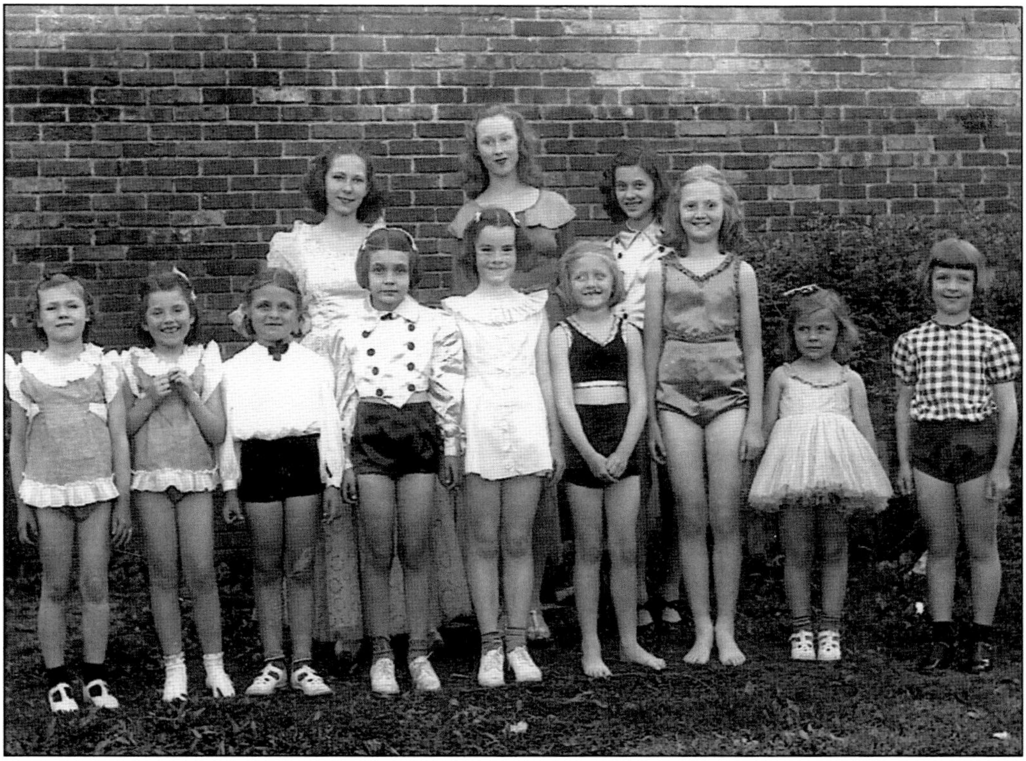

The Julia Jones Dance Class in Oxford was ready to dance in 1939. From left to right are Ann Crymes, Sara Bullock, Dale Bunn, Joyce Grimm, Emma White, Carolyn Crews, Julia Jones, Joan Parker, Gerry Dixon, Julia Noblin, Anna Bunn, and Bobbie Reynolds. (Courtesy of William Adcock.)

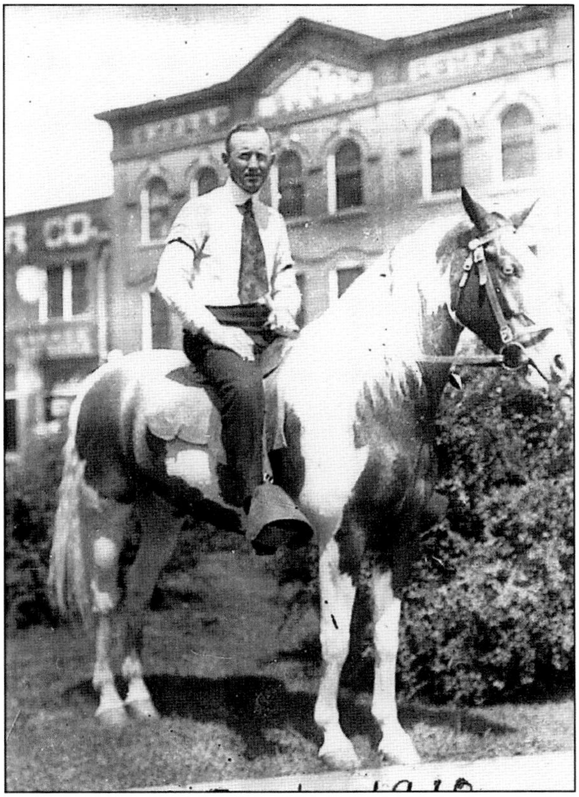

Riding around Oxford on a horse now would be quite a spectacle, but in 1918 Fred Peed probably saw quite a few other riders. Mr. Peed and his beautiful companion stand in front of the Oxford Buggy Company. (Courtesy of William Adcock.)

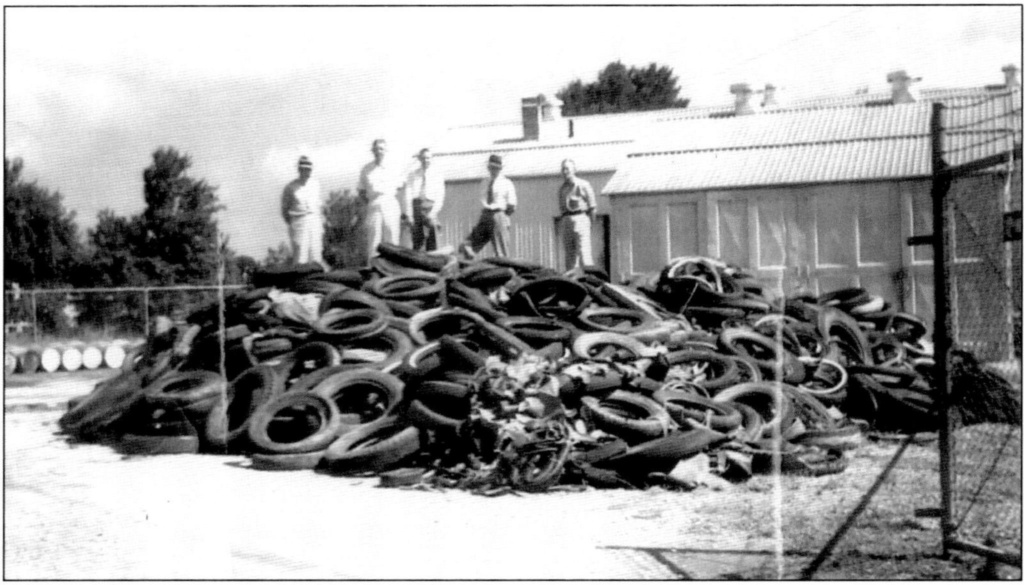

A group of Granville County men collected tires so they could be recycled to help in our nation's participation in World War II. The men, from left to right, are unidentified, O.D. McFarland, Jake Medford, Tom Johnson, and unidentified. This is now Oxford Oil Company. (Courtesy of Nelly McFarland.)

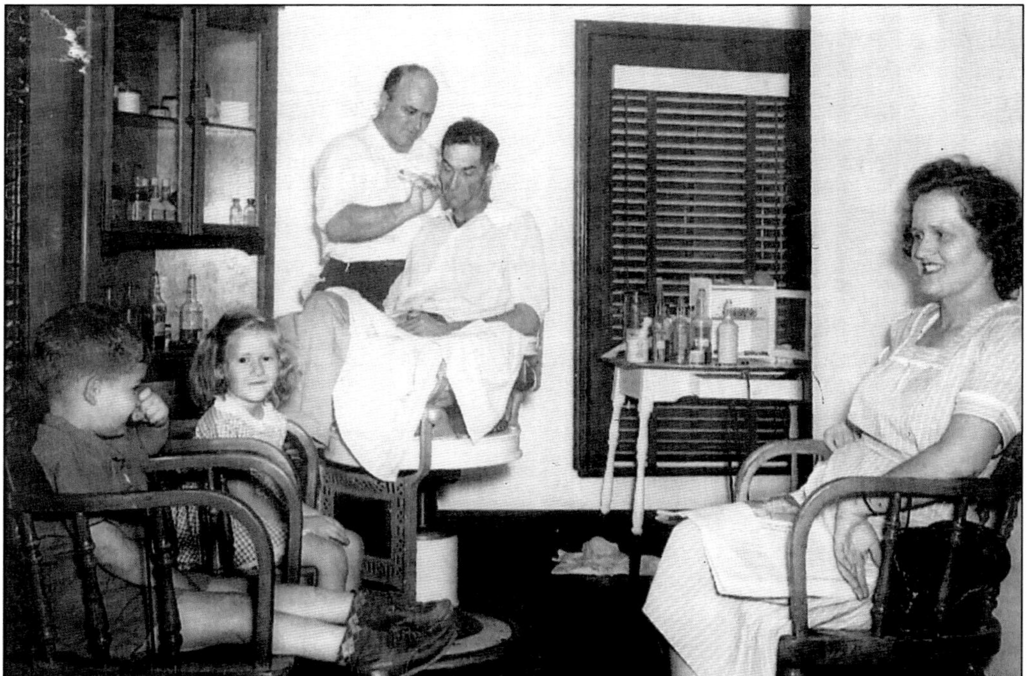

Sam Taylor cuts the hair of James Royster at the Broad Street Barber Shop in Oxford in the early 1950s. Royster's wife, Carmena, watches over son Jimmy and daughter Mary Frances. The couple had two more sons, Ricky and Larry. Mr. Royster was a successful farmer and father, while Mrs. Royster was known for her friendly smile and words of kindness. (Courtesy of Patsy Wells.)

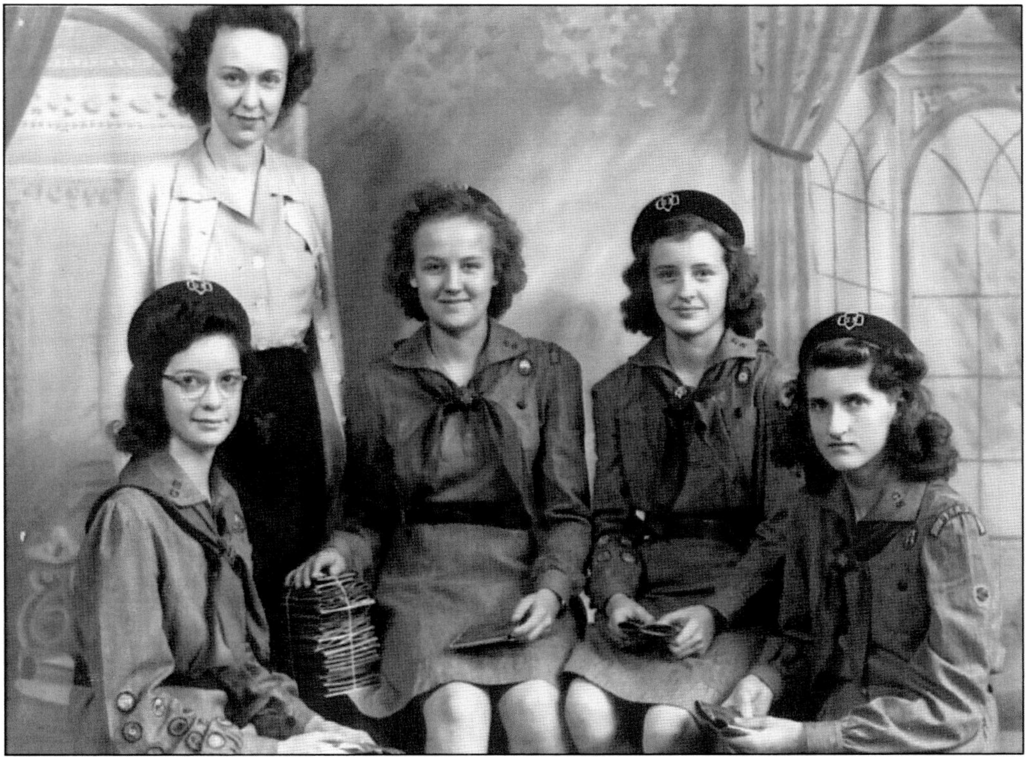

The Girl Scouts of Oxford contributed in many capacities during World War II. Among their efforts was a tin can drive. Nelly McFarland stands behind, from left to right, Lucy Royster, Dot O'Brien, Nancy Watkins, and Mariah Carroll. This gathering was in 1944. (Courtesy of Nelly McFarland.)

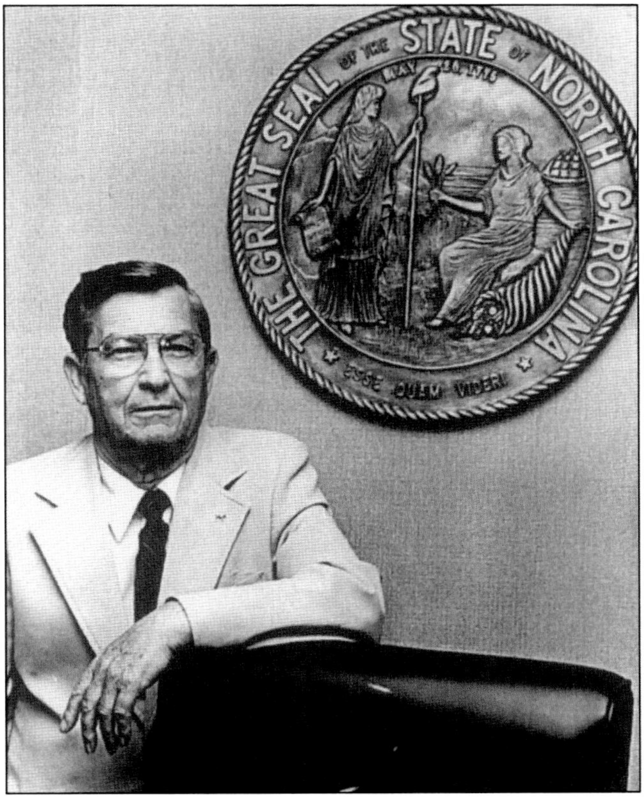

Billy Watkins was a lawyer in Oxford for 37 years. Watkins also served in the North Carolina State Legislature, receiving an award in 1981 as one of the ten outstanding state legislators in the United States. Watkins fought for education and agriculture and accomplished many great things for Granville County. When people of the area needed help and advice, "call Billy" was a common refrain. (Courtesy of Mary Watkins Eason.)

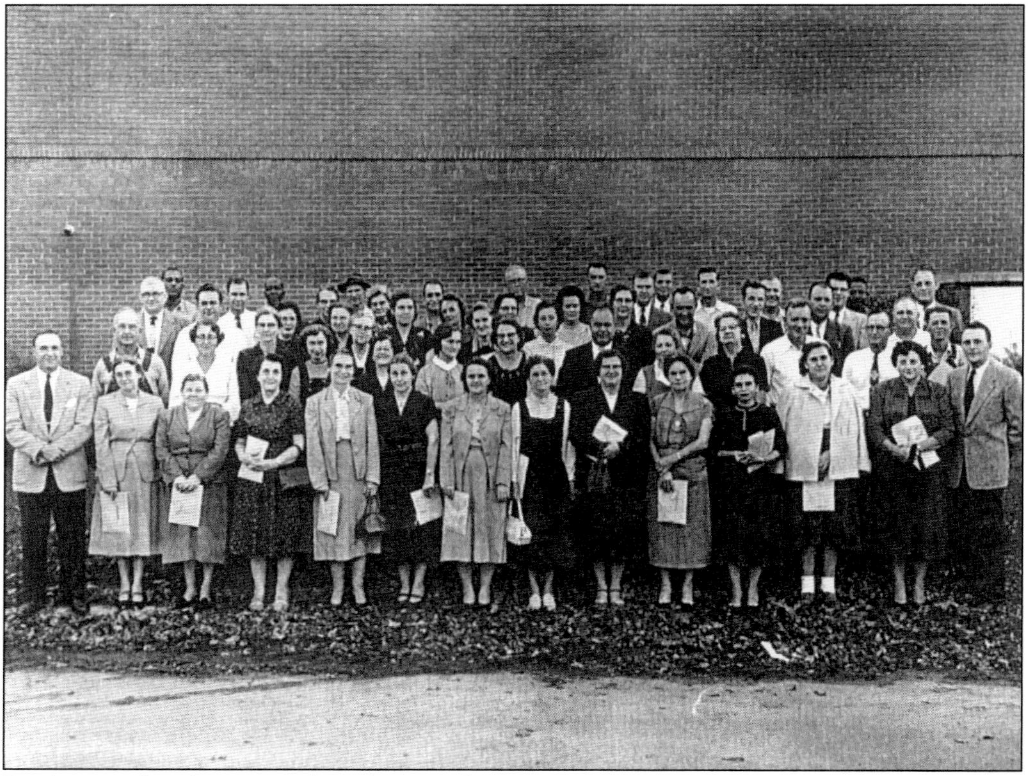

Employees of Burlington Mills gather together outside the plant in the mid-1930s. (Courtesy of Barbara Wilkerson.)

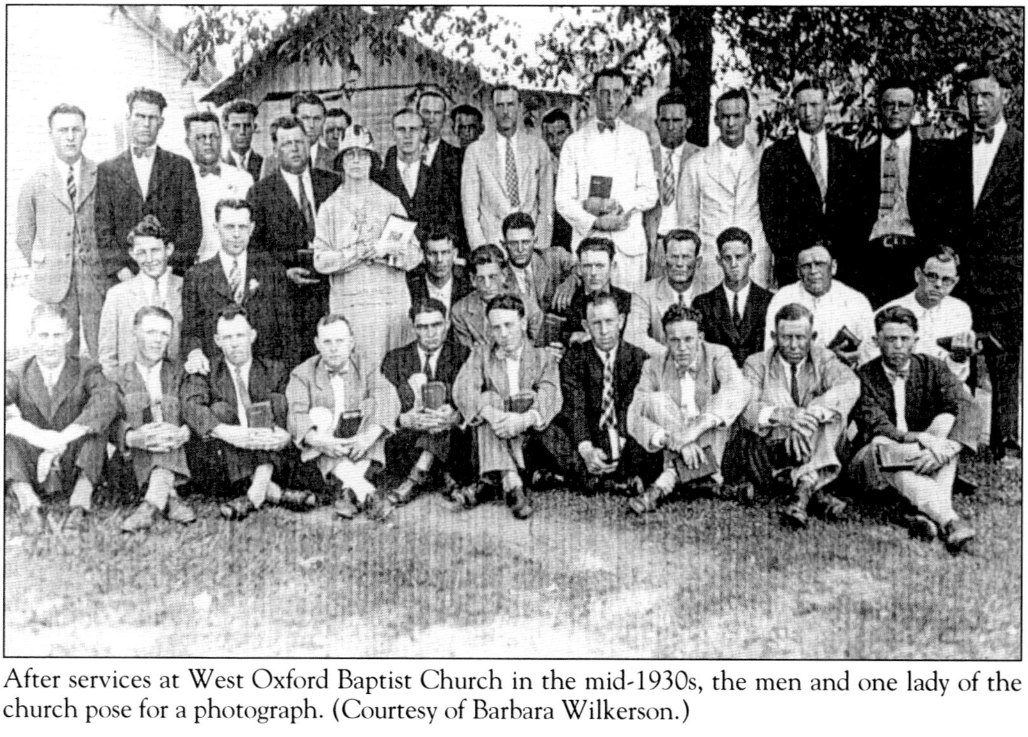

After services at West Oxford Baptist Church in the mid-1930s, the men and one lady of the church pose for a photograph. (Courtesy of Barbara Wilkerson.)

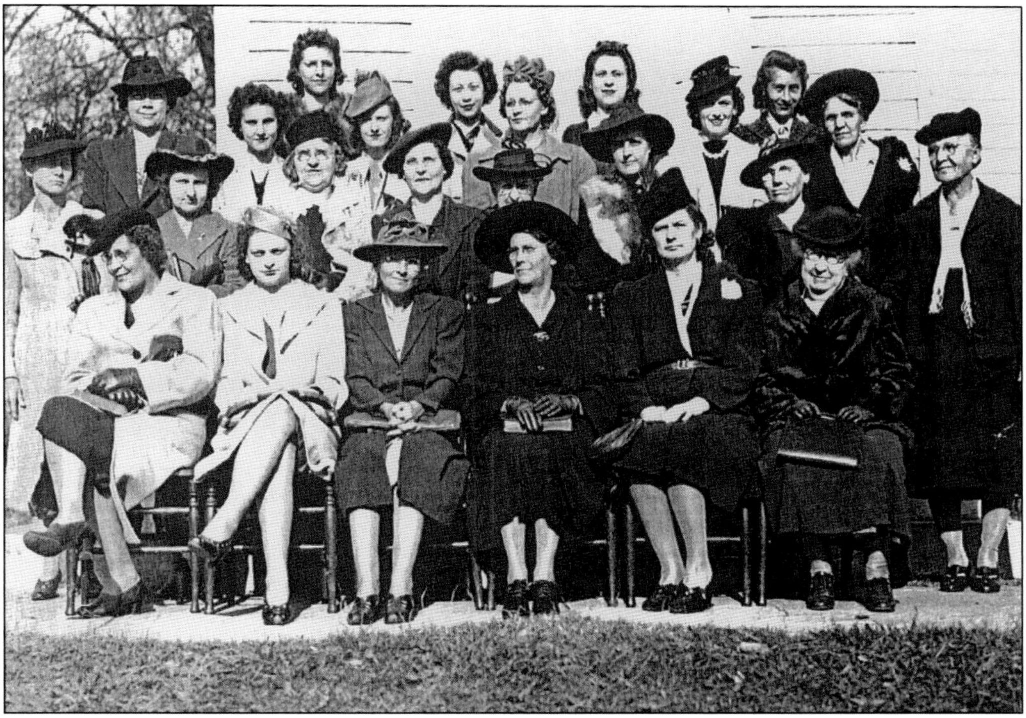

Ladies gather for a photograph at West Oxford Baptist Church in the mid-1930s. (Courtesy of Barbara Wilkerson.)

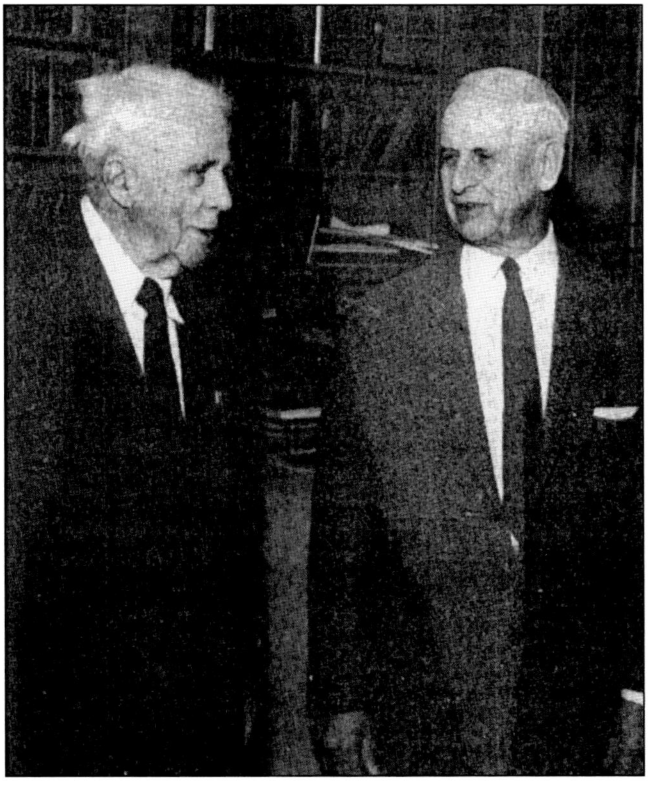

Richard Thornton, on the right, confers with Robert Frost, on the left, in the library in Oxford. Granville County has had many famous visitors, but not many as prominent as this great poet. "Stopping by the Woods on a Snowy Evening" and "The Road Not Taken" are to be enjoyed over and over. Mr. Thornton was a publisher of books and the Richard Thornton Library in Oxford is named for him.

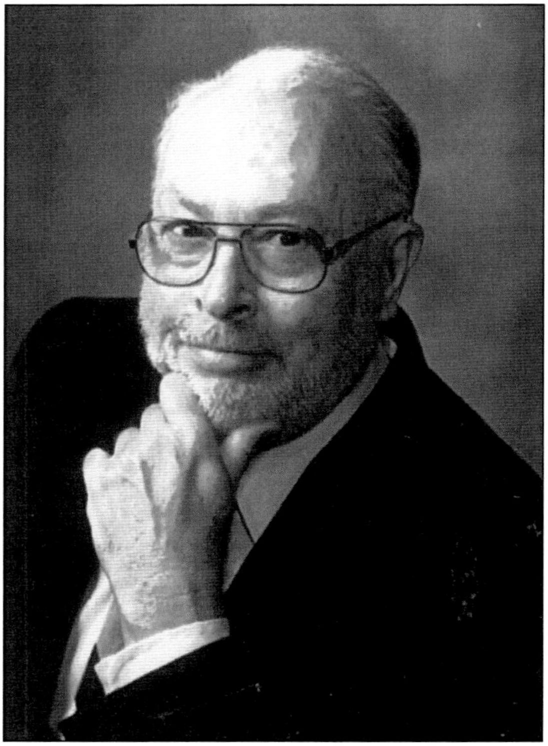

Do you enjoy *The Andy Griffith Show?* If you are like millions of other Americans, you have spent hours watching this program based around small town life in our state. The man pictured here is Harvey Bullock, born in Oxford; he wrote many of the episodes for the *Andy Griffith Show*. Mr. Bullock, who now resides in California, also wrote for *The Love Boat*, *Gomer Pyle*, *The Doris Day Show*, and *The Flintstones*, among many others. (Courtesy of Joe Haskins.)

President John F. Kennedy and James Webb of Oxford walk together after exiting an airplane in Florida. Mr. Webb played a pivotal role in man walking on the moon in 1969. Administrator of our nation's space program from 1961 to 1968, James was the son of J.F. Webb, a longtime superintendent of Granville County schools and for whom J.F. Webb High School is named.

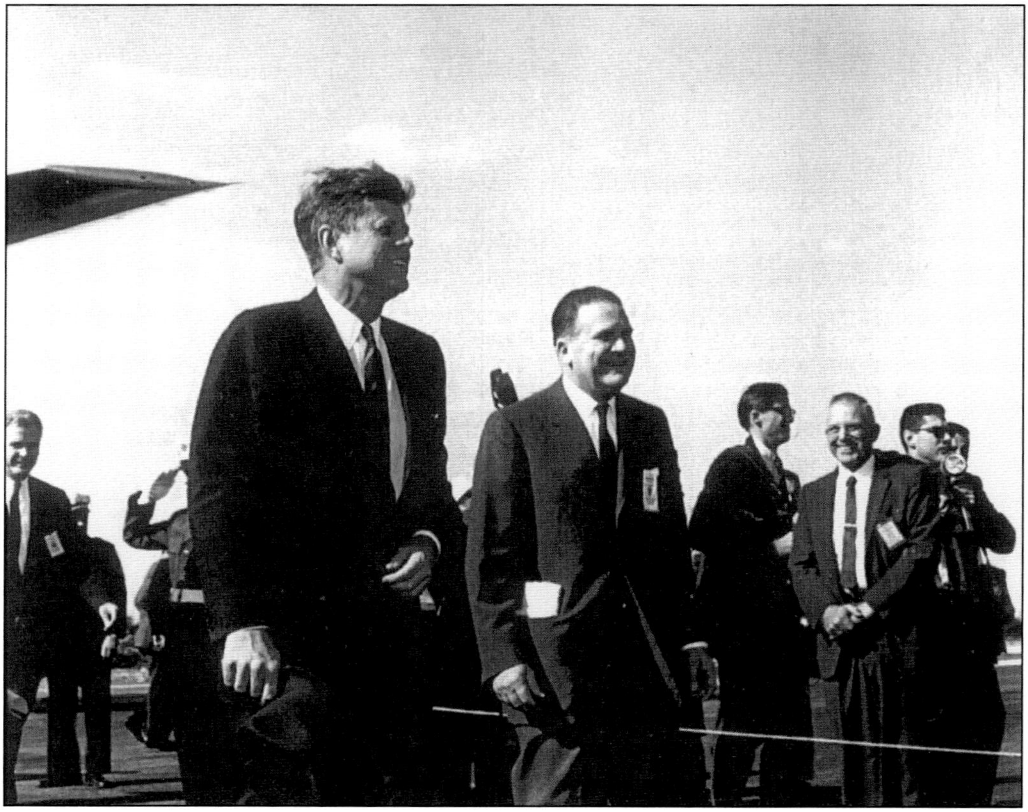

A graduate of Oxford High School, Ferebee Taylor later attended Harvard and was awarded a Rhodes Scholarship to attend Oxford University in England. Taylor was also awarded the Bronze Star and two commendations for his service as an office in the navy during World War II. From 1972 to 1980, Taylor served as chancellor of the University of North Carolina at Chapel Hill. (Courtesy of Ferebee Taylor.)

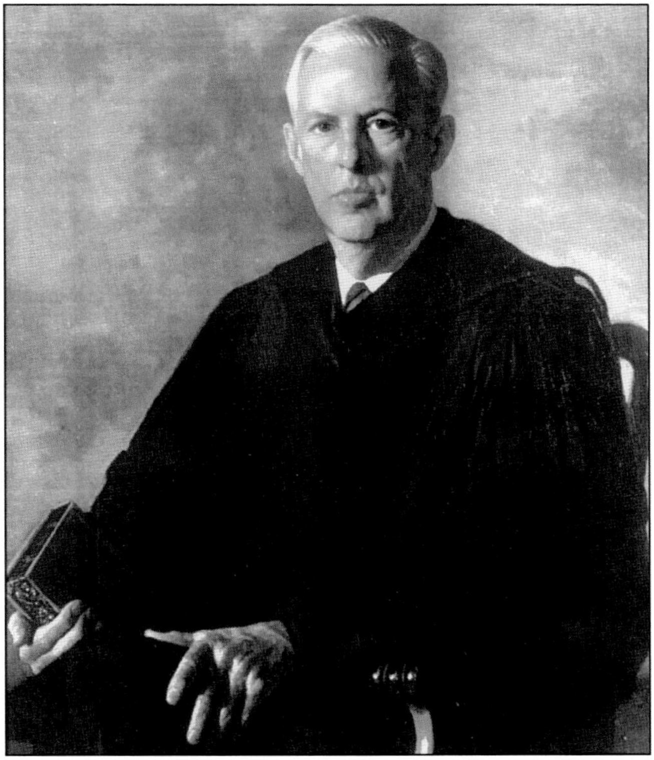

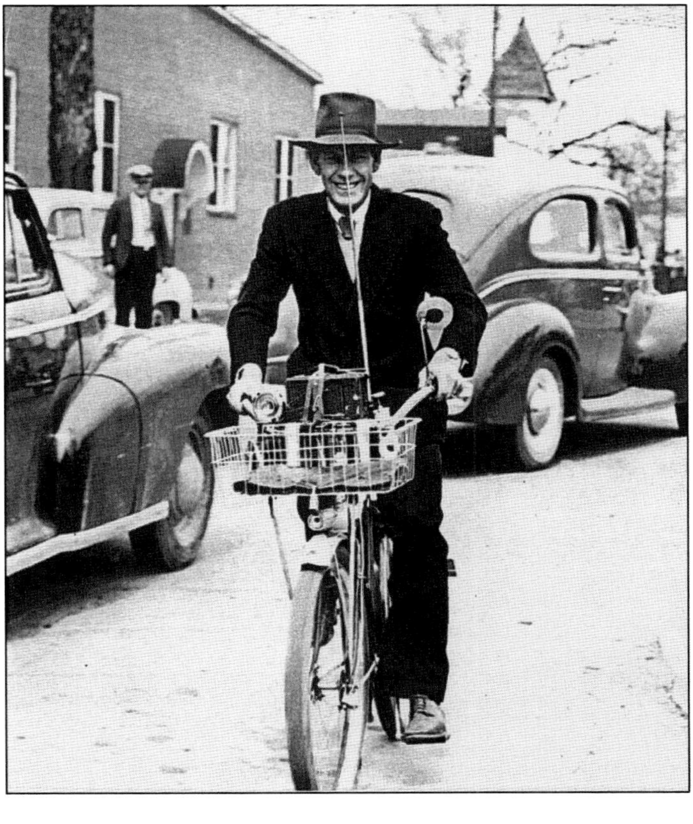

Thurston Newton is shown riding the streets of Oxford on his bicycle in the early 1950s. Mr. Newton was quite a fixture around town, always flashing a smile; he was well liked by town residents.

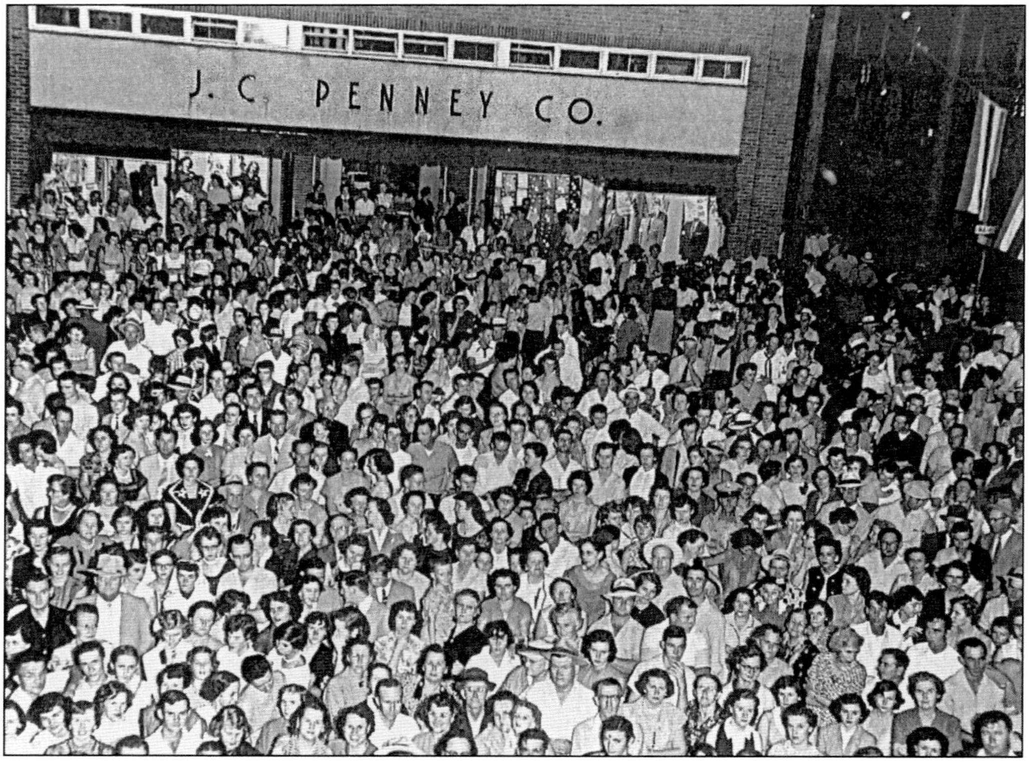

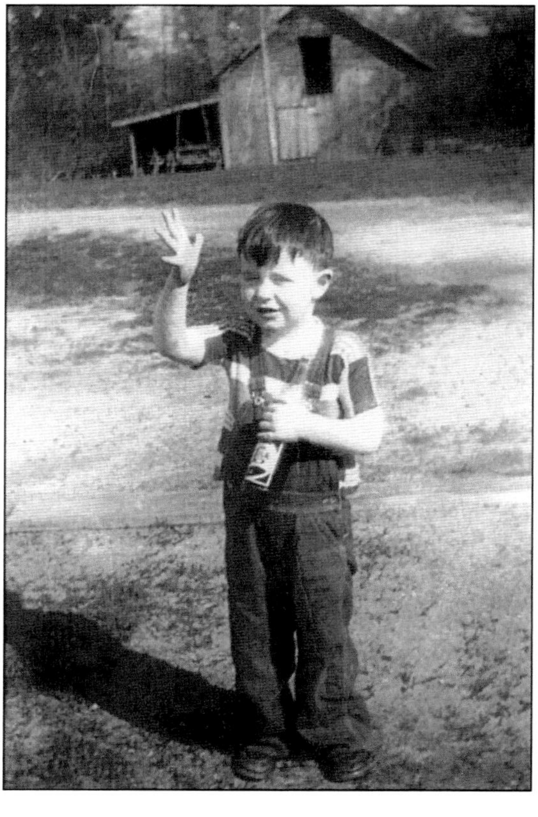

A huge crowd is assembled in Oxford in this picture from the 1950s. The J.C. Penney store can be seen in the background. (Courtesy of Bobby and Nancy Blackwell.)

Do you recognize this friendly looking young fellow from the 1950s in Providence? This is Al Woodlief, the present mayor of Oxford. Mayor Woodlief has devoted many years of service to his hometown of Oxford as mayor, radio station operator, and city commissioner. Mr. Woodlief's love of Oxford comes through in his conversation.

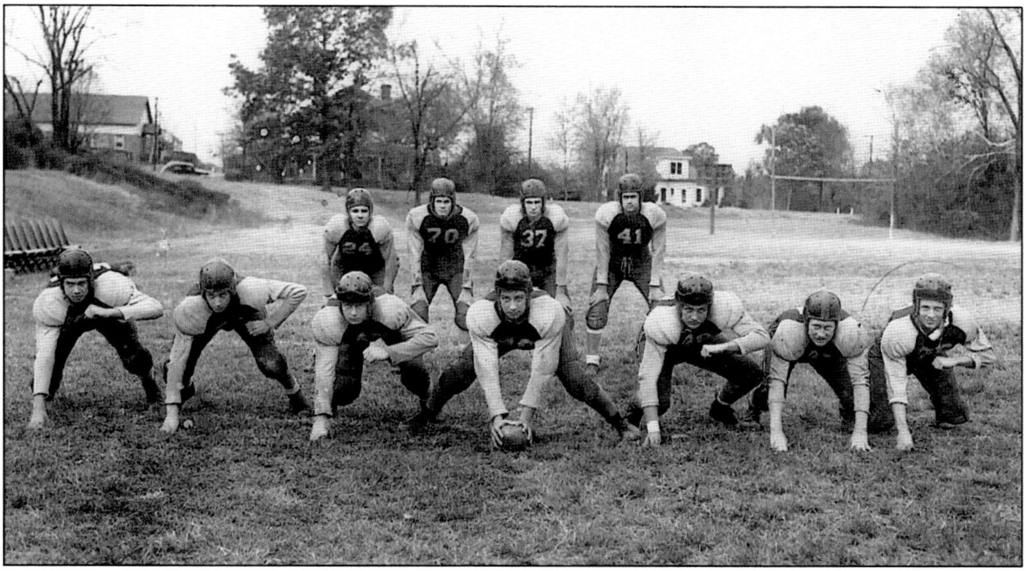

The 1945 Oxford High School football team outscored its first five opponents 133 to 18, including Mebane 33 to 0. Bill Frazier was the biggest player at 195 pounds and next was Paul Walters at 190 pounds. (Courtesy of Liz Falkner.)

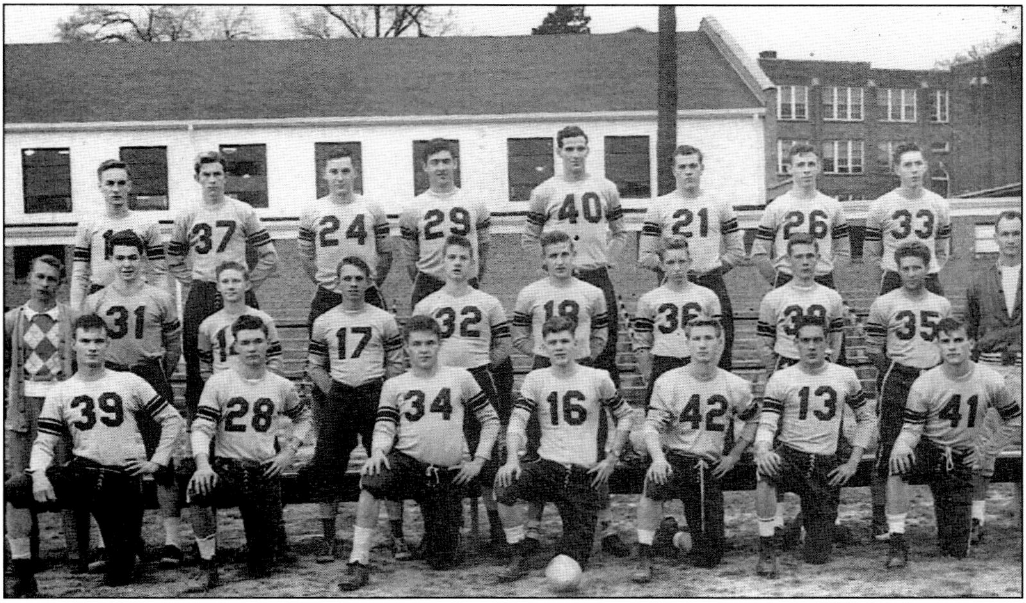

In 1949, the Oxford High School football team outscored its opponents 256 to 46, beating its first five foes 138 to 13. Among the victims were Erwin (40 to 6) and Durham County (26 to 0). From left to right are (front row) Hinnant Suitt, John Parham, Harold Currin, Gene Seabolt, Nat Burwell, Doug Currin, and Ralph Blalock; (middle) John Boyd (manager), Sidney Cutts, Albert Clay, Dick Young, Dan Jones, Joe Bryan, Jackie Jones, Ralph Blackwell, Norris Cole, and R.C. Culton (coach); (back) E.V. Strother, Alex Hancock, Roy Beard, Ed Meadows, Thomas Chappell, Sam Finch, Eugene Woodlief, and Howard Critcher. Harold Currin later became influential in the lives of the county's young people, offering sports and recreational opportunities for many youth under his leadership. Ed Meadows went on to play in the National Football League after an All-American career at Duke University.

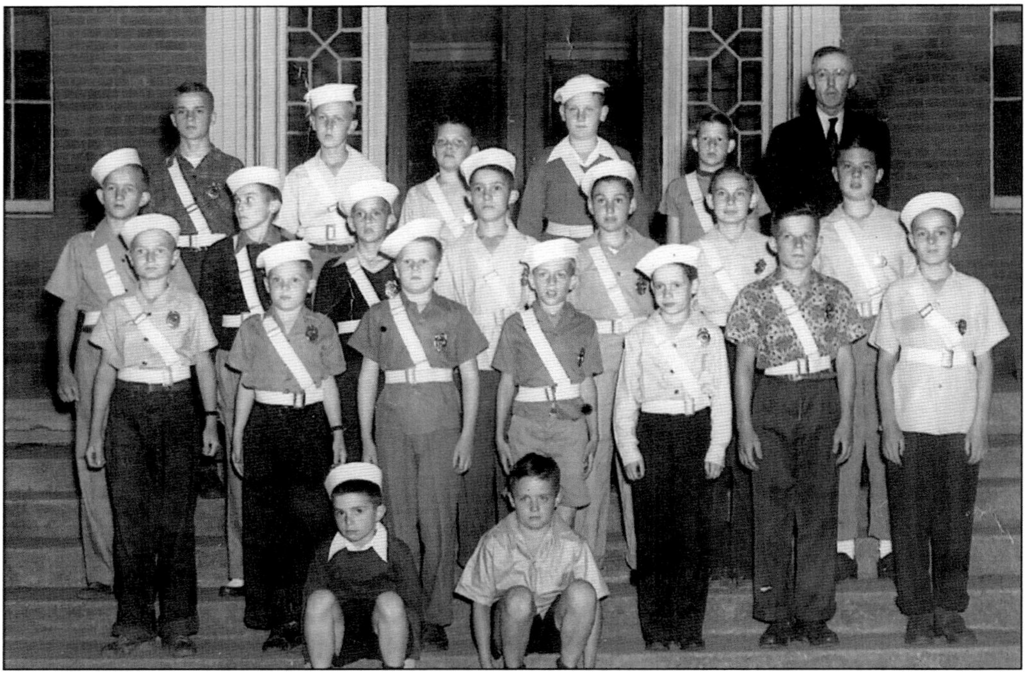

The C.G. Credle School Boy Safety Patrol is dressed and ready for work in this 1947 picture. (Courtesy of Catherine Noblin.)

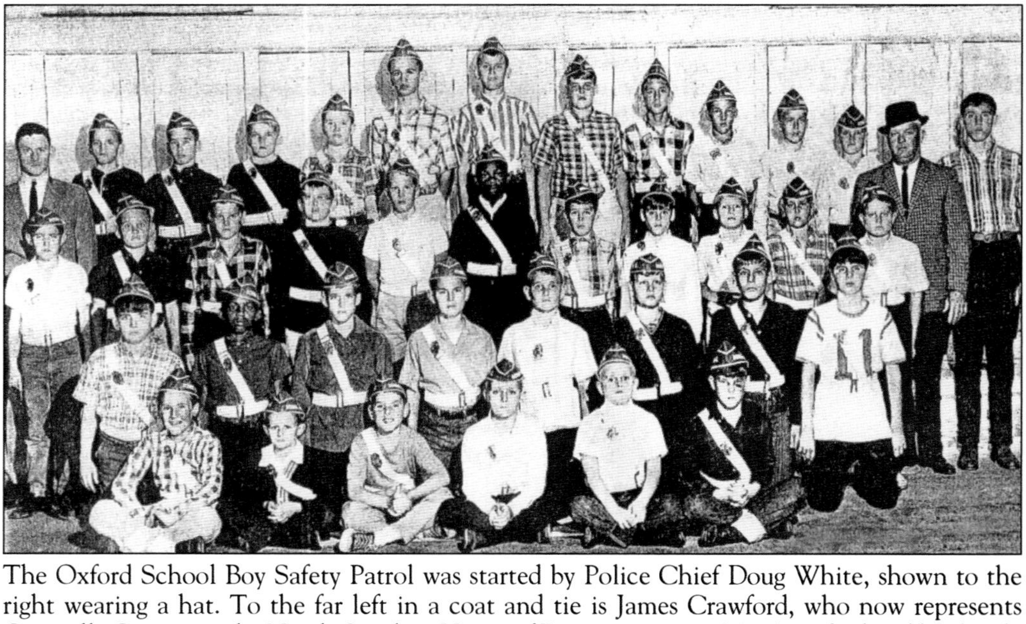

The Oxford School Boy Safety Patrol was started by Police Chief Doug White, shown to the right wearing a hat. To the far left in a coat and tie is James Crawford, who now represents Granville County in the North Carolina House of Representatives. Mr. Crawford and his family have made many contributions to Granville County and the area. This picture is from 1965. (Courtesy of Opal White.)

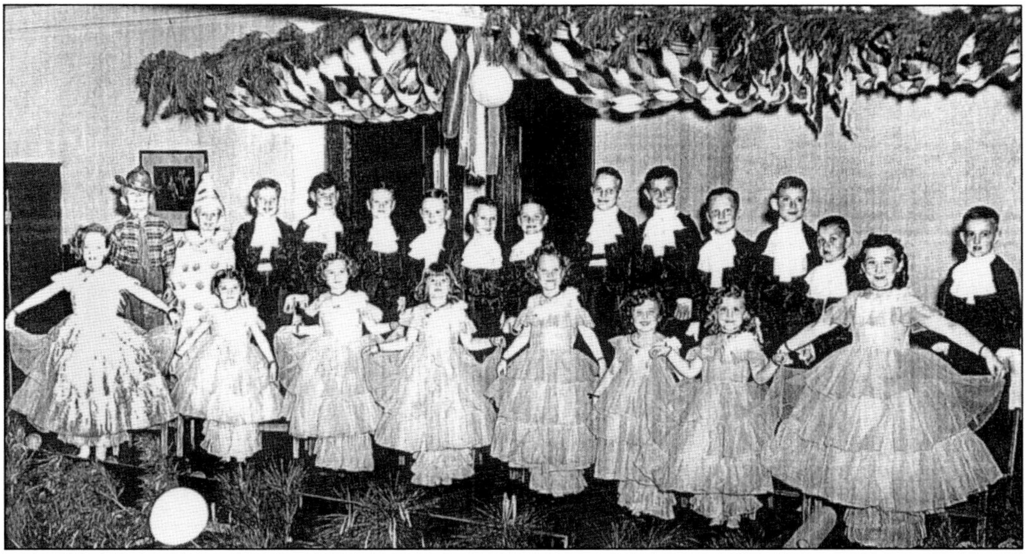

A play is performed at the Lewis Street School in Oxford in 1949. Among the girls are Elizabeth Bullock, Donnie Briggs, Carolyn West, Carolyn Almond, Carol Woodlief, and Mary Oakley. Among the boys are Grady Mangum, Ed Mangum, Billy McGee, J.D. Owens, James Bullock, Billy Daniel, Bobby Dickerson, W.D. Dillehay, Phil Preddy, Bobby Stroud, Ray Dickerson, Steve Dickerson, and Roger Taylor. (Courtesy of Carol Sharron.)

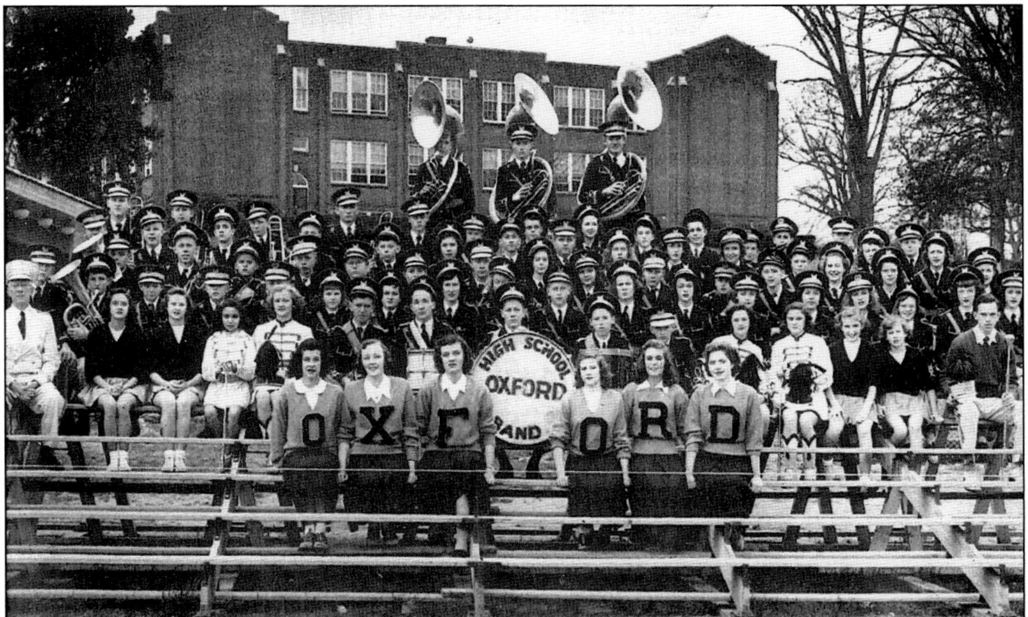

The Oxford High School Band is assembled in this 1949 picture.

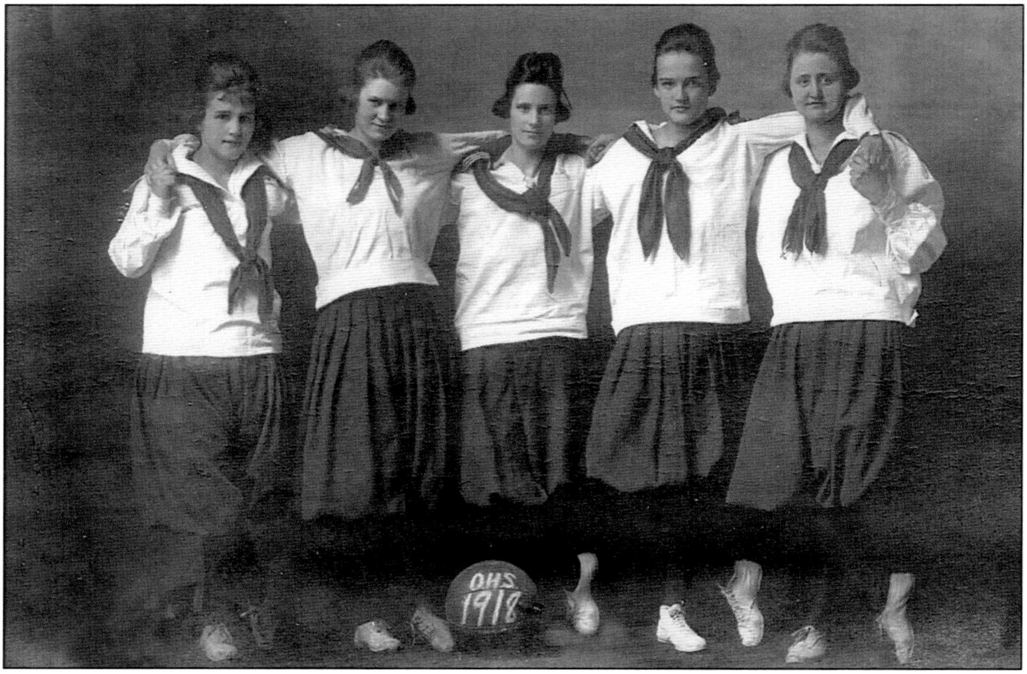

From left to right, Lula Smith, Charlotte Carroll, Ruth Parham, Sudie Crews, and Johnnie Peed are members of the 1918 Oxford High School Basketball Team. (Courtesy of William Adcock.)

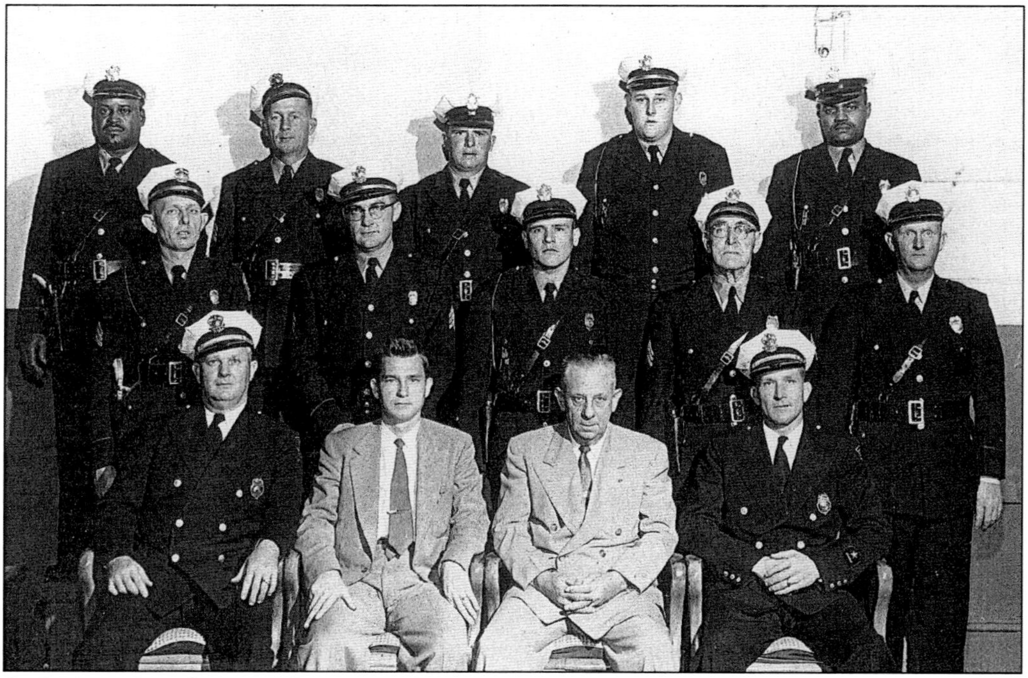

Oxford's police force in the 1960s, from left to right, are (front row) Chief Doug White, Billy Watkins, Will Mitchell (mayor of Oxford), and Nathan White; (middle row) Nick Carnell, Doug Barker, James Bray, Will Strickland, and John Tippett; (back row) George Barnett, Charlie Woodlief, Herbert Grissom, Taylor Jackson, and Hamp Moss. (Courtesy of Opal White.)

Two

CREEDMOOR

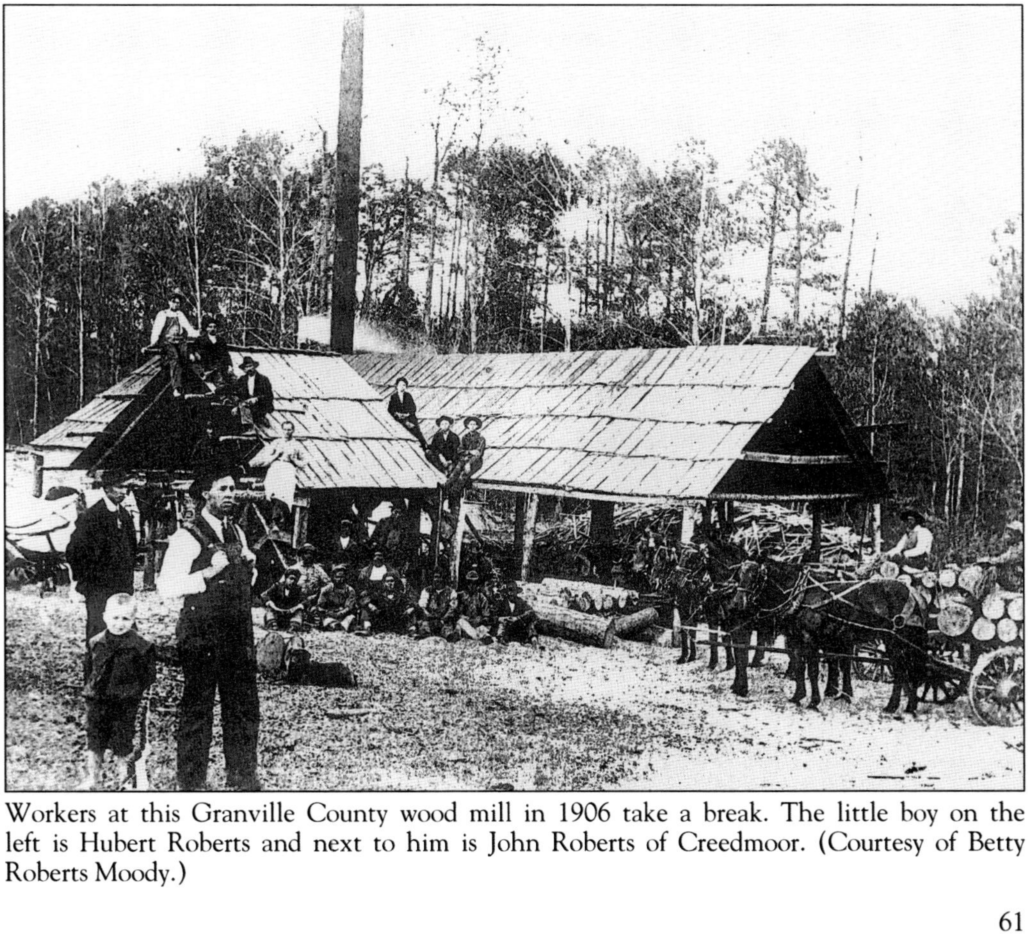

Workers at this Granville County wood mill in 1906 take a break. The little boy on the left is Hubert Roberts and next to him is John Roberts of Creedmoor. (Courtesy of Betty Roberts Moody.)

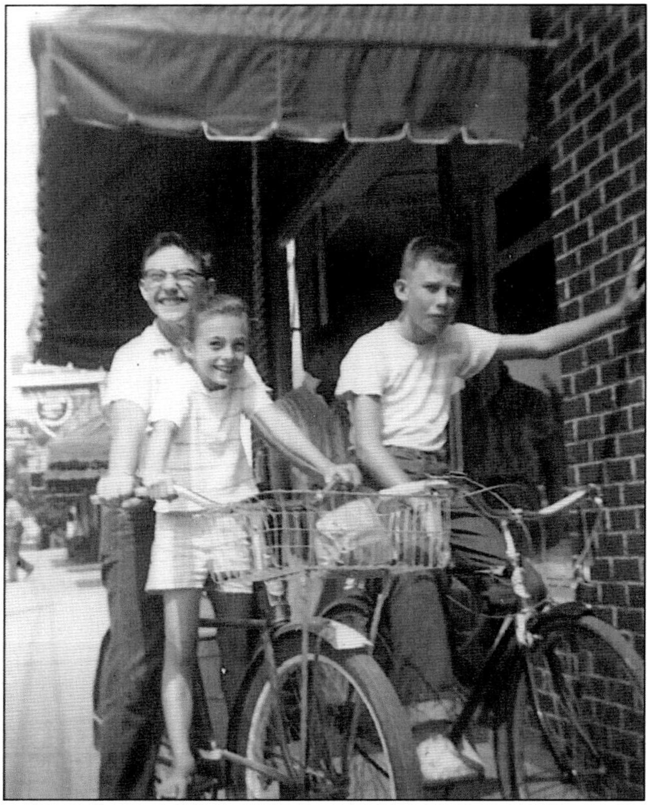

Riding down Creedmoor's Main Street in the 1950s, these young people seem to be enjoying themselves.

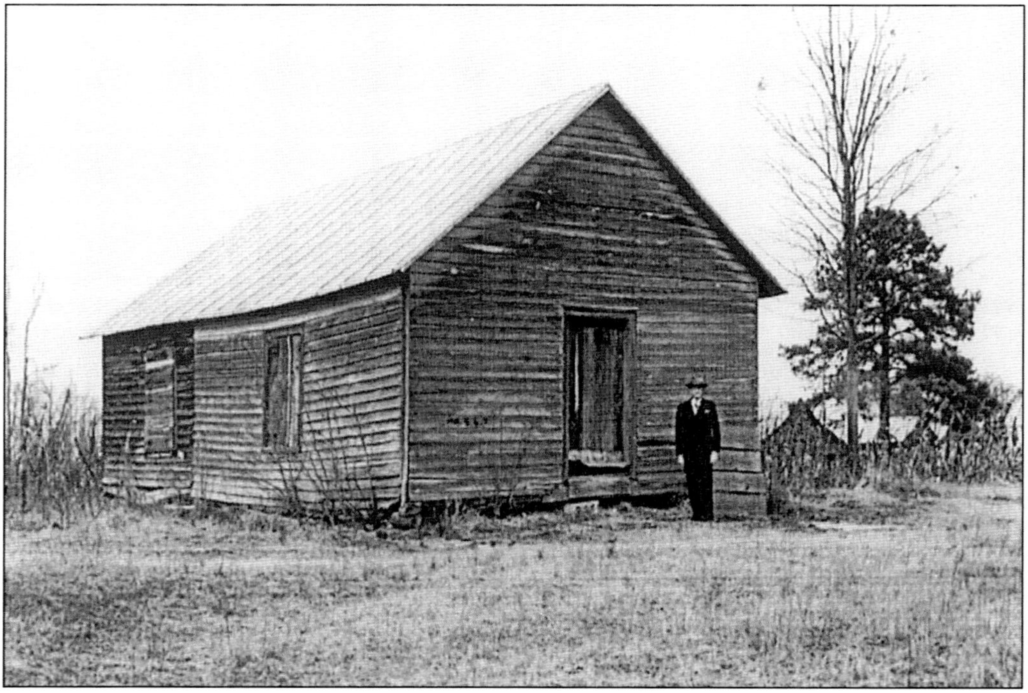

Robert Aiken stands in front of Molly Hill School in the early 1960s. Aiken had attended this school in the late 1800s. (Courtesy of David Rogers.)

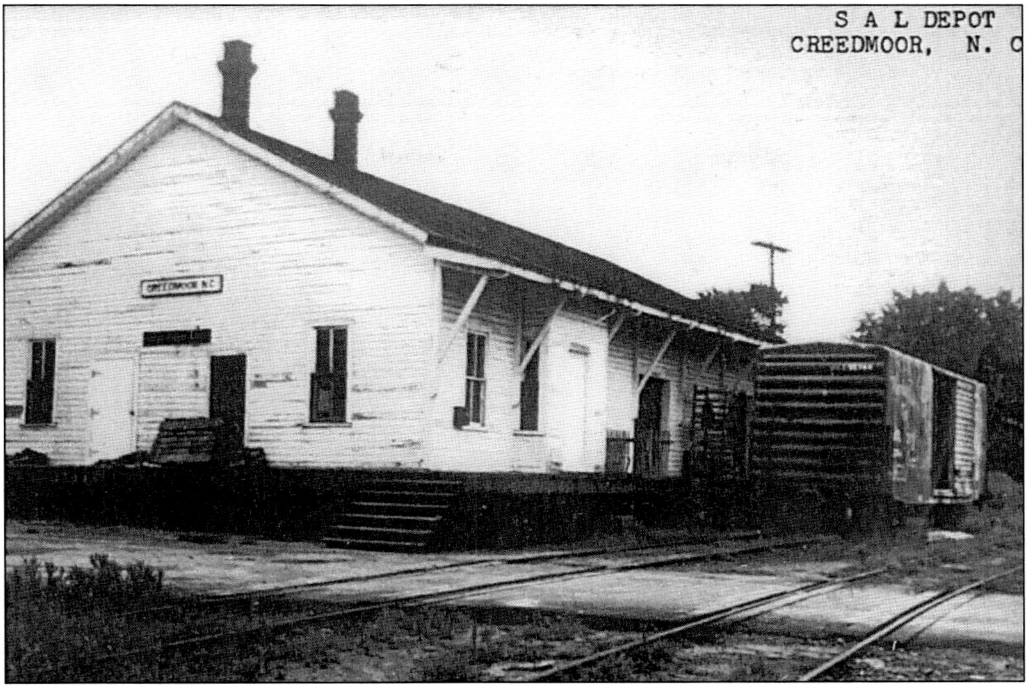

The Creedmoor Railroad Depot is shown in the 1940s.

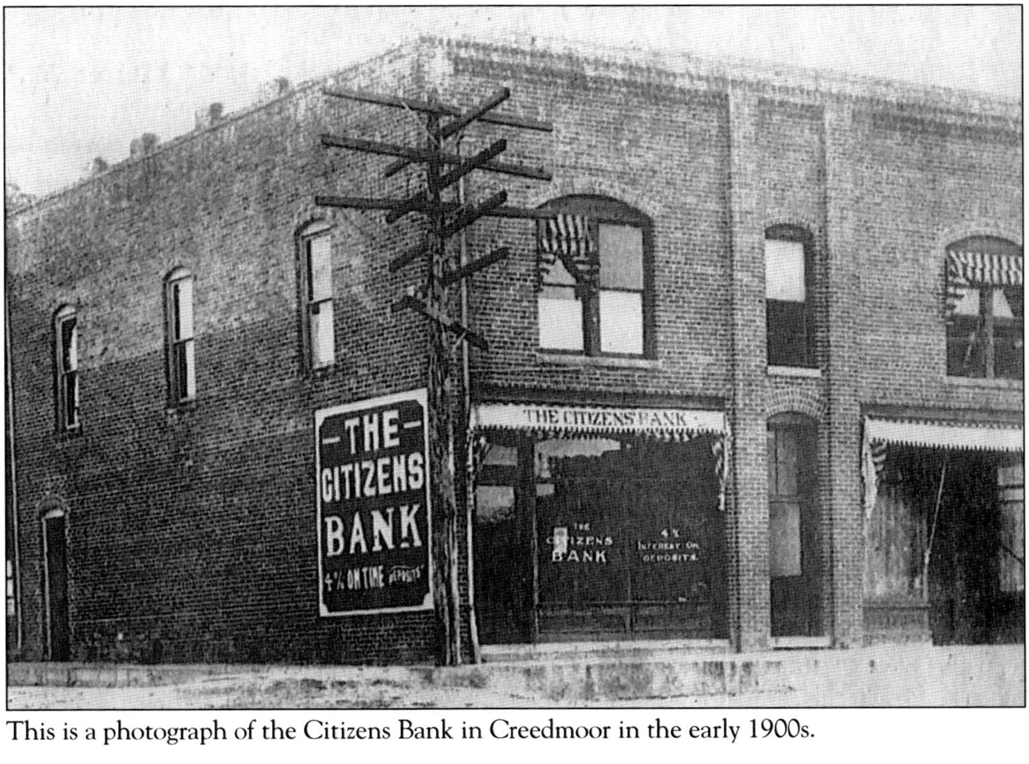

This is a photograph of the Citizens Bank in Creedmoor in the early 1900s.

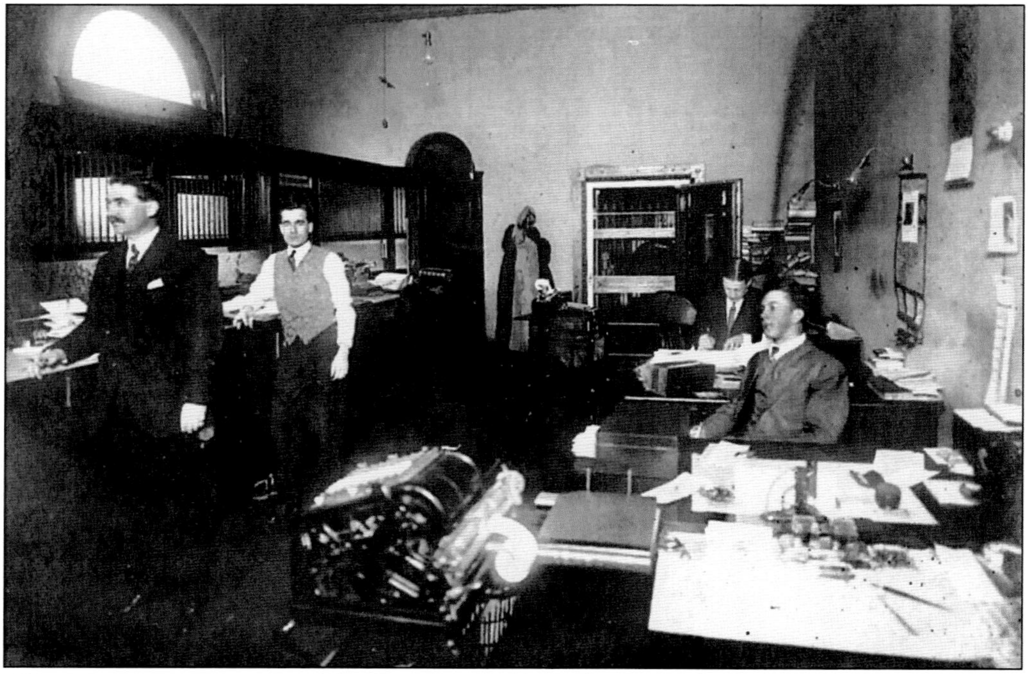

Above is an interior view of the First National Bank of Creedmoor during the early 1900s. (Courtesy of Mary Harris.)

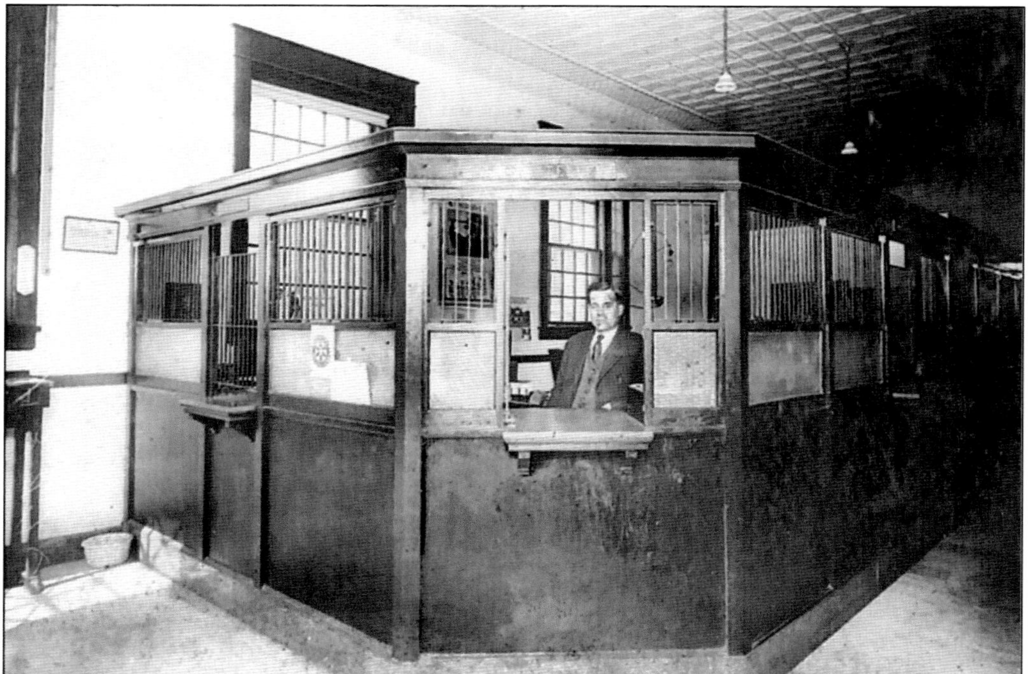

J.P. Harris is shown at work in the First National Bank of Creedmoor in the early 1900s. Mr. Harris's banking career spanned from 1907 to 1981—the longest tenure of any banker in North Carolina. Mr. Harris was chairman of the board for Union National Bank and built Oxford's first theatre, the Orpheum, with E.G. Crews in 1911. (Courtesy of Mary Harris.)

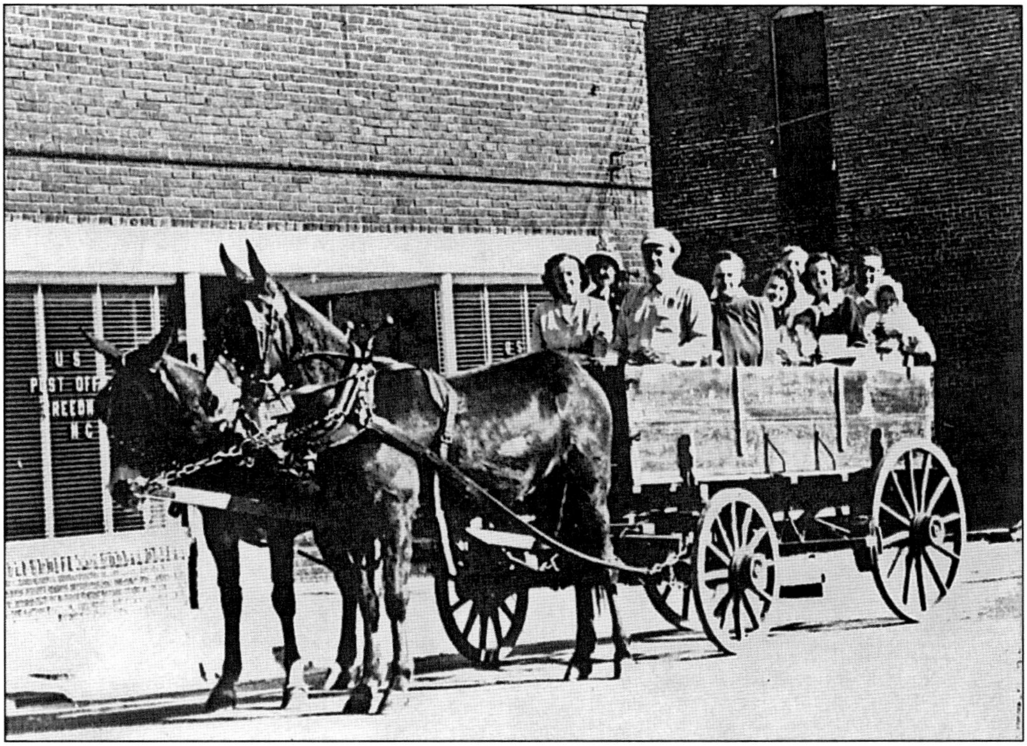

A wagon load of people pass the old Creedmoor post office. (Courtesy of David Rogers.)

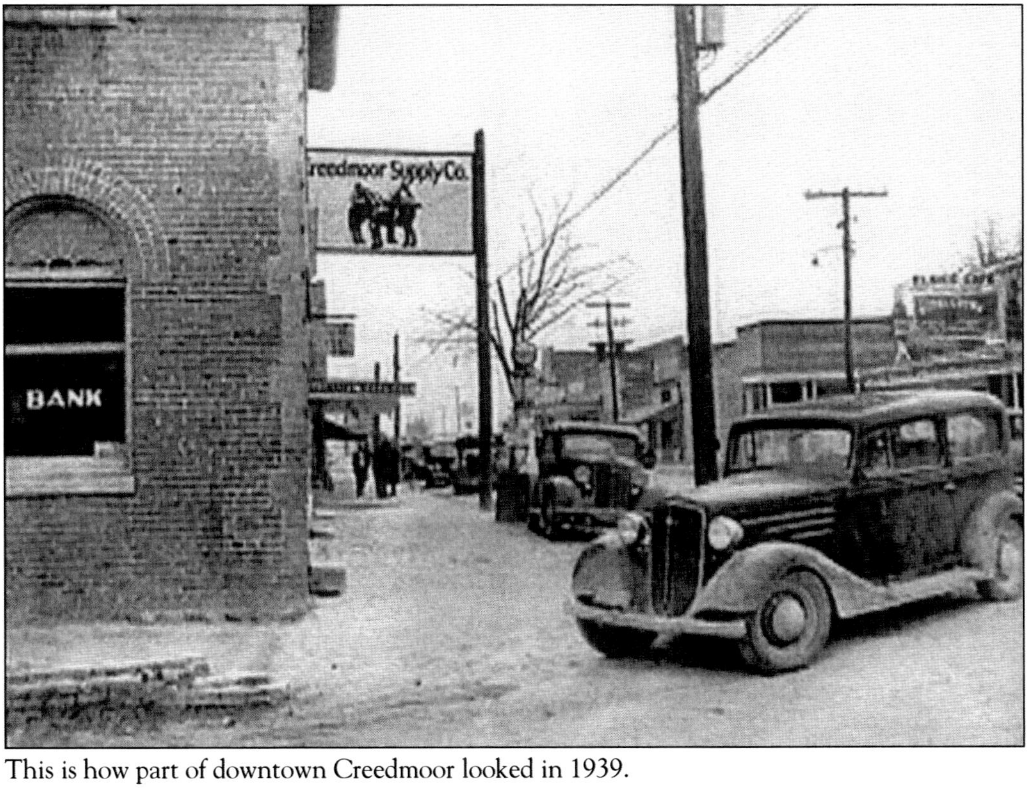

This is how part of downtown Creedmoor looked in 1939.

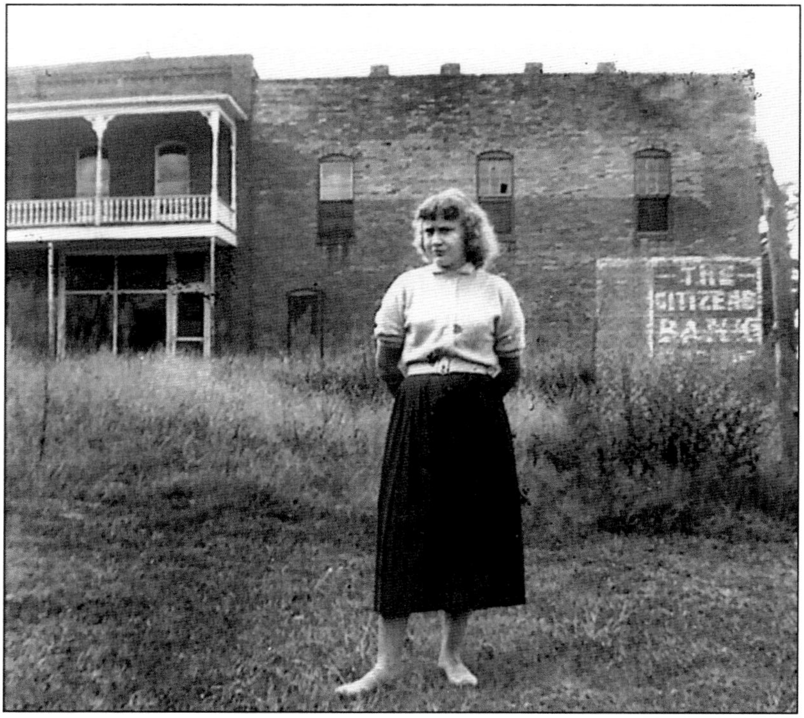

Nellie Brame stands in front of the Hotel Granville in Creedmoor during the 1950s. (Courtesy of Nellie Brame.)

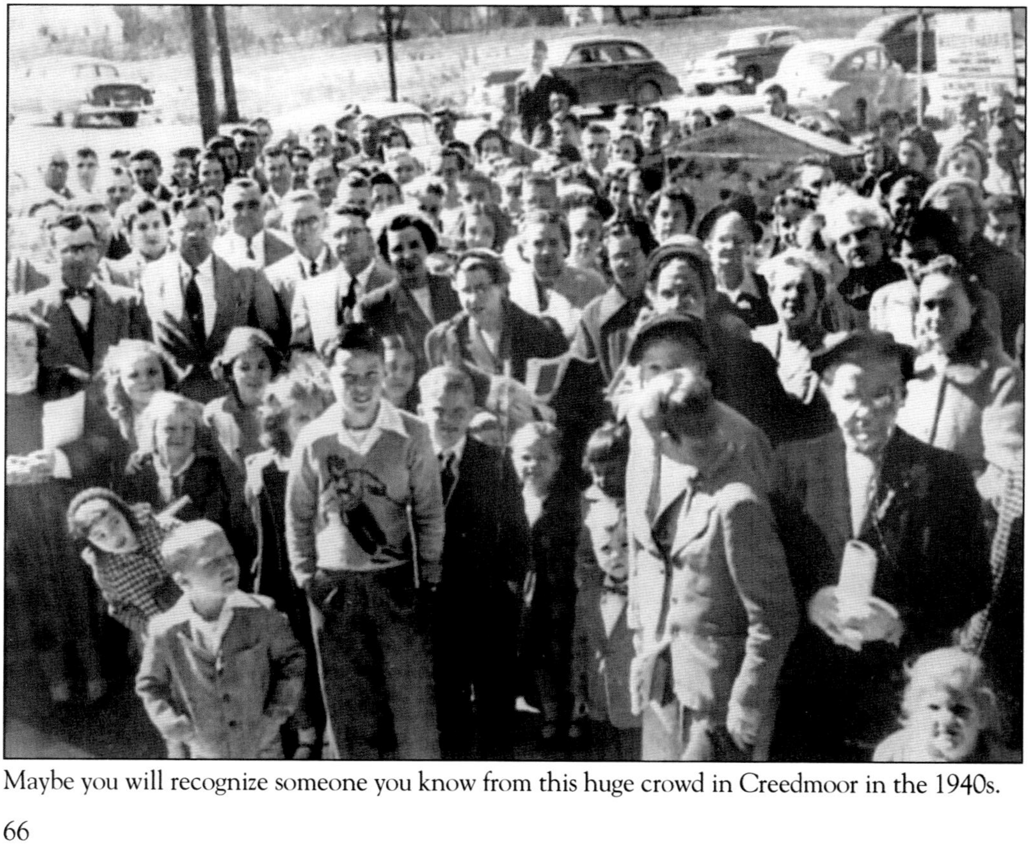

Maybe you will recognize someone you know from this huge crowd in Creedmoor in the 1940s.

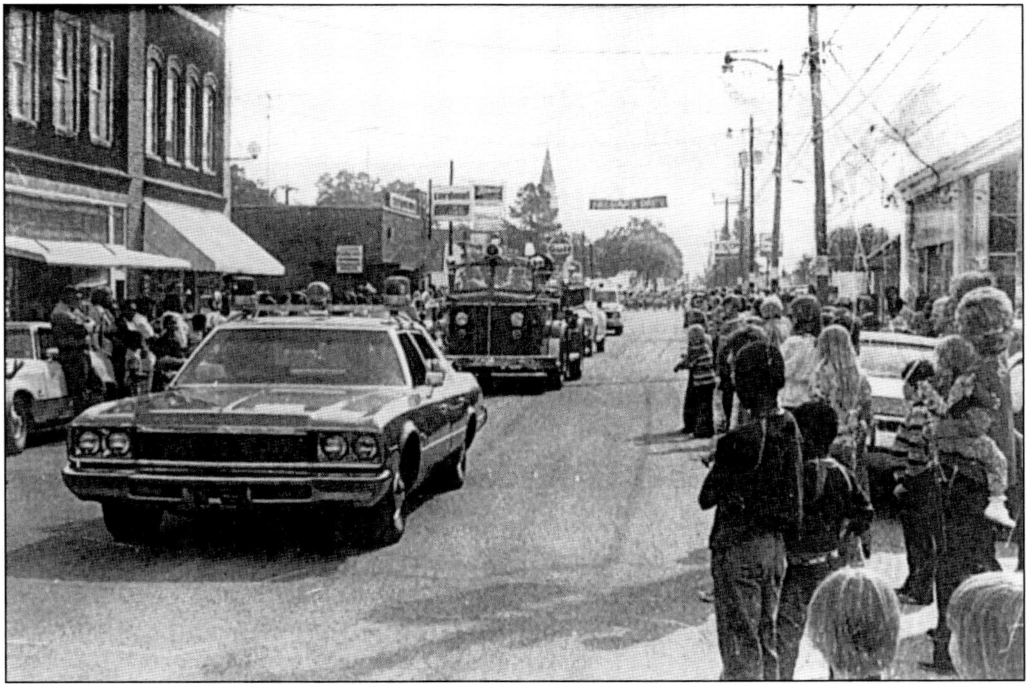

A Fireman's Day Parade rolls down Creedmoor's Main Street in 1970.

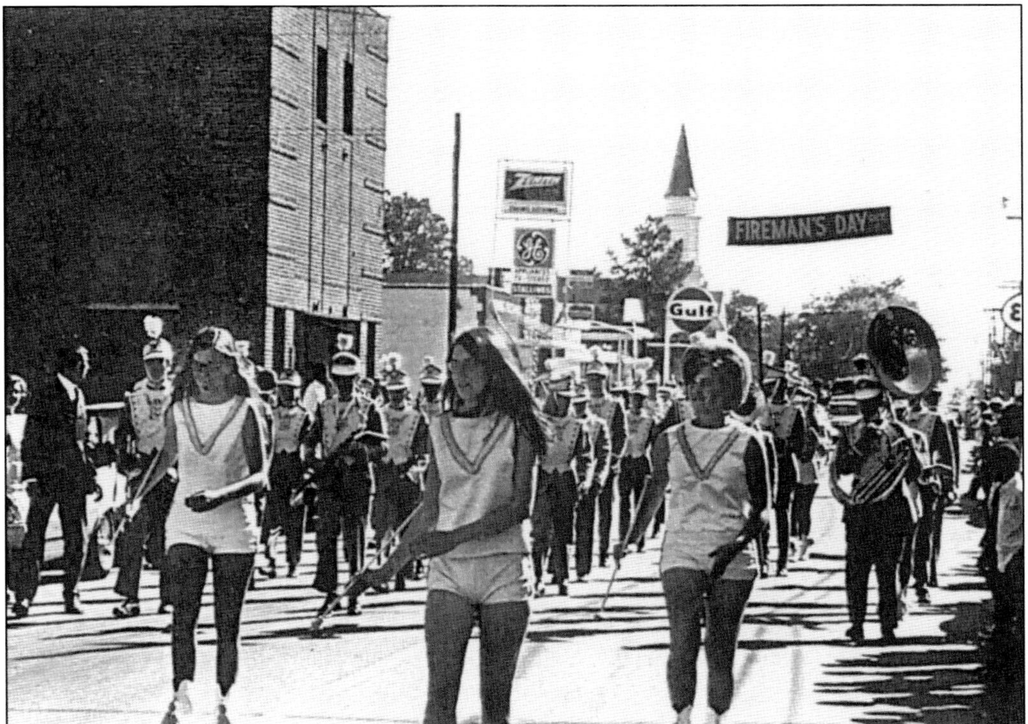

Festive music is in the air in 1970 as the South Granville High School band parades down Main Street in Creedmoor. (Courtesy of David Rogers.)

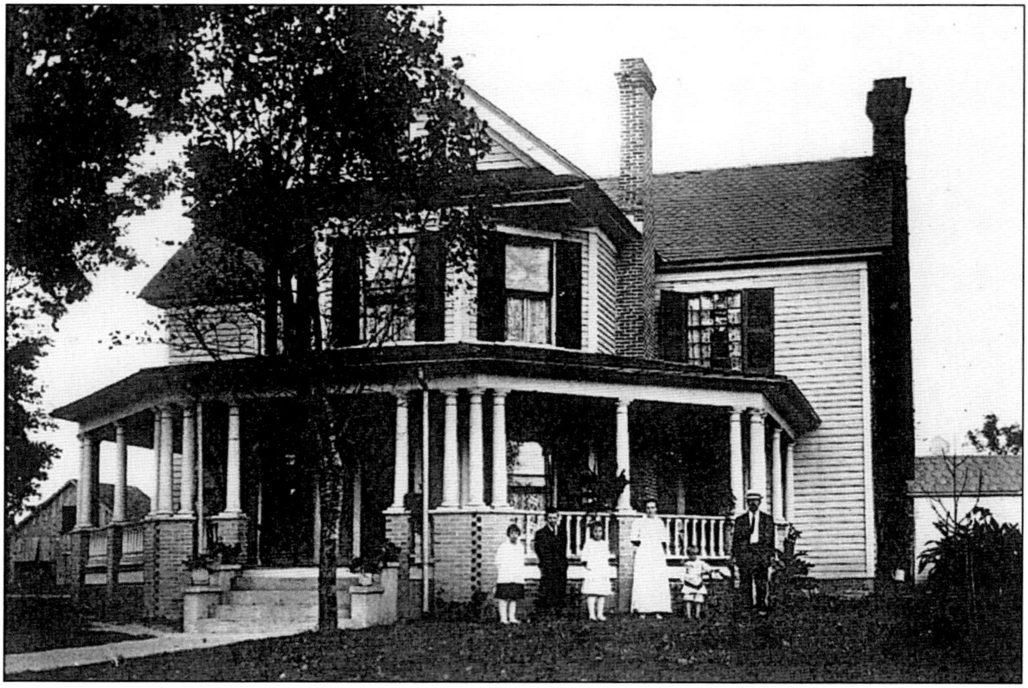

The Lyon family gathers outside the Lyon house in Creedmoor in the early 1900s. The Lyons were a founding family of Creedmoor. This beautiful old house stands on Elm Street. (Courtesy of David Rogers.)

Com I. 5 NC Calvary
7 miles below Richmond
Tuesday May the 15 th/64

Dear Brother & Sister. It is great pleasure to me when I can have the oppotunity of writing to you all. These lines leave me well & hope they will find you all enjoying the same. I, Saml, I have had a hard time Since I saw you last. we have been marching & fighting every day since we left Louisburg with the exception of 4 or 5 days. we fought the yankees from the Rapidan with in 3 miles of Richmond. it was cavalry. I don't know the number but I think about 8000 & 30 cannon. we never had more than half that number of men & no cannon atal until we got to Richmond. There we got 4 cannon & some reinforce<u>ments</u> so circuard [scared] they had to leave. if our force had been a little stronger we could of captured them every one. They only had just one way to get out. lost from our Regt. only 3 wounded. one I suspect is dead. he was shot senter through the boddy. it looks like the yankees is cutting talligraph lines to Richmond. I under stand the yankees have cut all the railroads running from Richmond & understand old Lee gave them a bad floging at Spotsylvania CH [Courthouse] on Friday last. They are fighting at Drunia bluf yesterday. I could heare the firing plane all day. I think they are making the Strongest effort to get to Richmond that ever have made but I tell you they will leave a great meany of their men behind in the road stroad [strewed] with thir dead now as far as they have come. They say they are going on to Rich[mond] but I think they will have a hard road to travel. but the great fear is that they will cut off our supplies. I think if they make a big offensive if anything ain't needed it is rain & if they ever do entend to do any good let them come now with 3 days rations & thir guns, on thir horses to Stop thet Rading party that is Cut[t]ing of[f] Gen Lees Suplices. The Sitty [city] battalian met them & was so much Ceard [scared] to infileth [?] they kild as meny of our men as they did the yankees & then run. Gen [James B.] Gordon was leding them when he was wounded. his arm has been amputated. The brave Gen. Stuart was kild near the Sitty when leading a charg. He lived about a day and a night after being wounded. we stopt heare to rest a day or too. both men and horses are broke down.

Your Brother CC Wheeler

Christopher Columbus Wheeler, who lived in the Creedmoor area, served in the Civil War. In a battle near Reams Station, south of Petersburg, Virginia, his horse was shot and fell on his leg, causing amputation. The sacrifices and hardships these soldiers endured are evident in this letter.

These men were members of the Creedmoor Lions Club in 1948–1949. (Courtesy of Nellie Brame.)

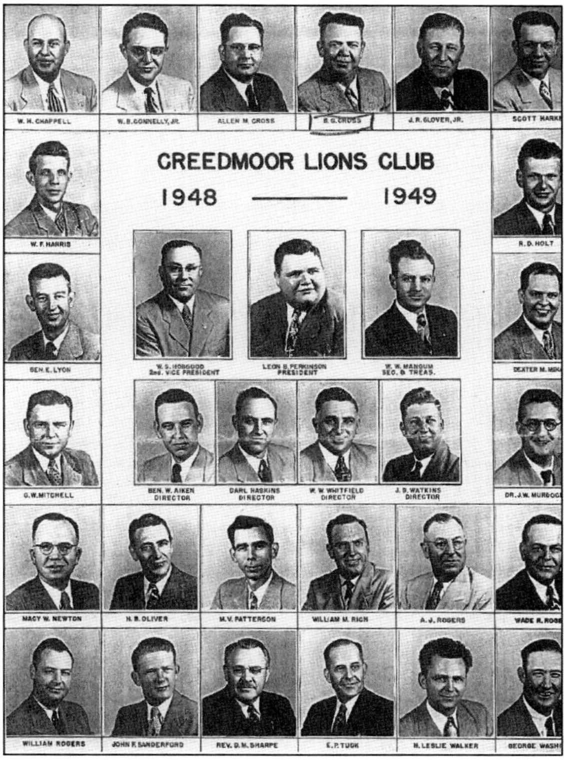

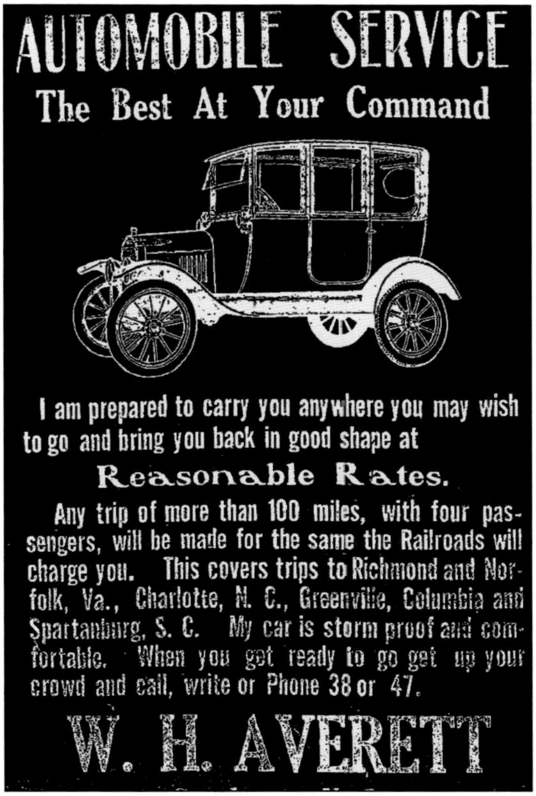

This is an advertisement for a taxi service in Creedmoor that appeared in 1918.

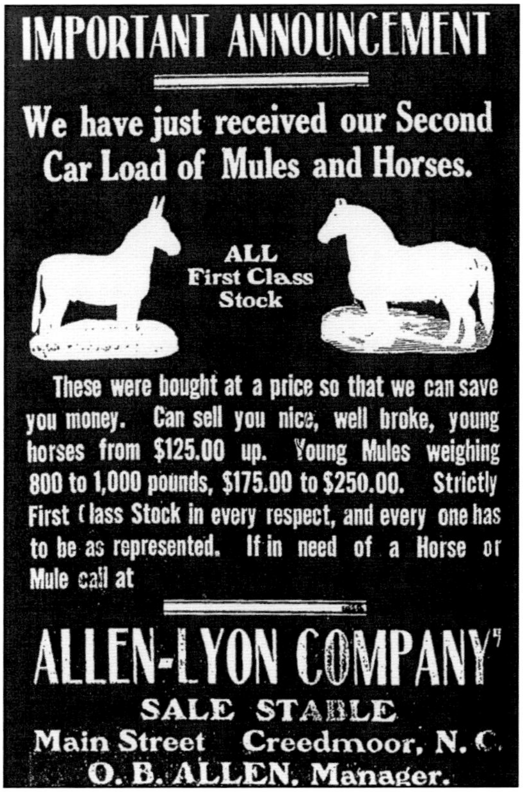

Creedmoor was once known as one of the leading mule trading centers in the world. This is an advertisement that appeared in the *Creedmoor Times-News* in 1918. (Courtesy of *Creedmoor Times-News*.)

This is Harry Coleman, a reporter for the *Mebane Enterprise*, in 1967. Mr. Coleman is well known around Granville County as the owner of the *Butner-Creedmoor News*. (Courtesy of *Butner-Creedmoor News*.)

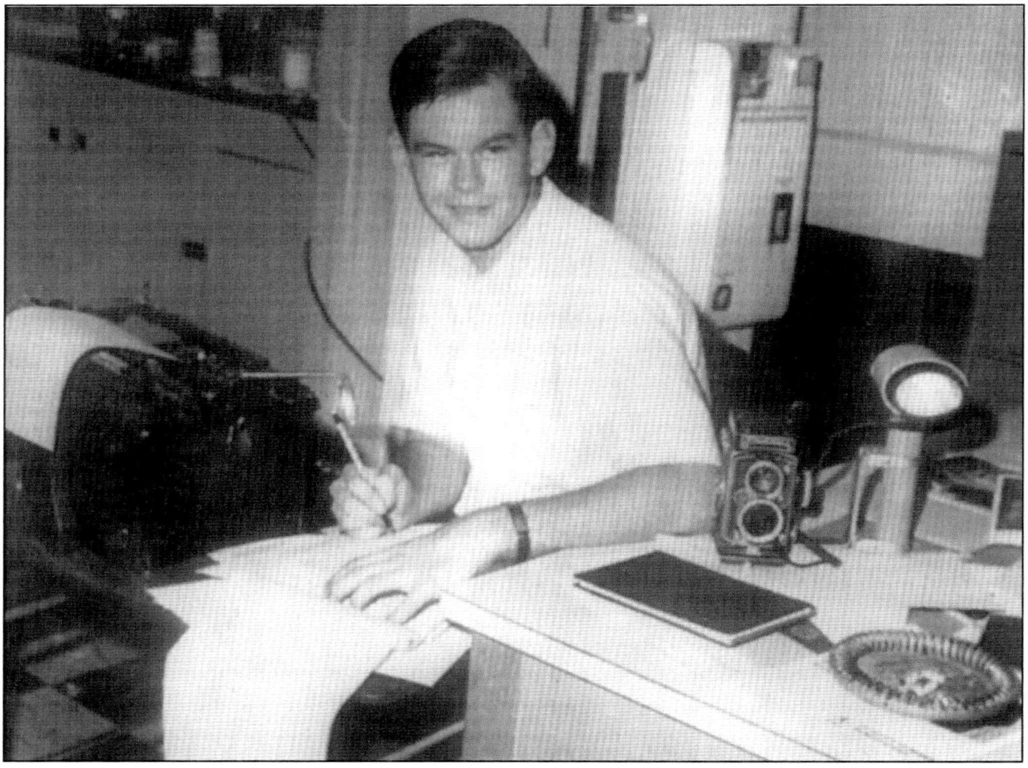

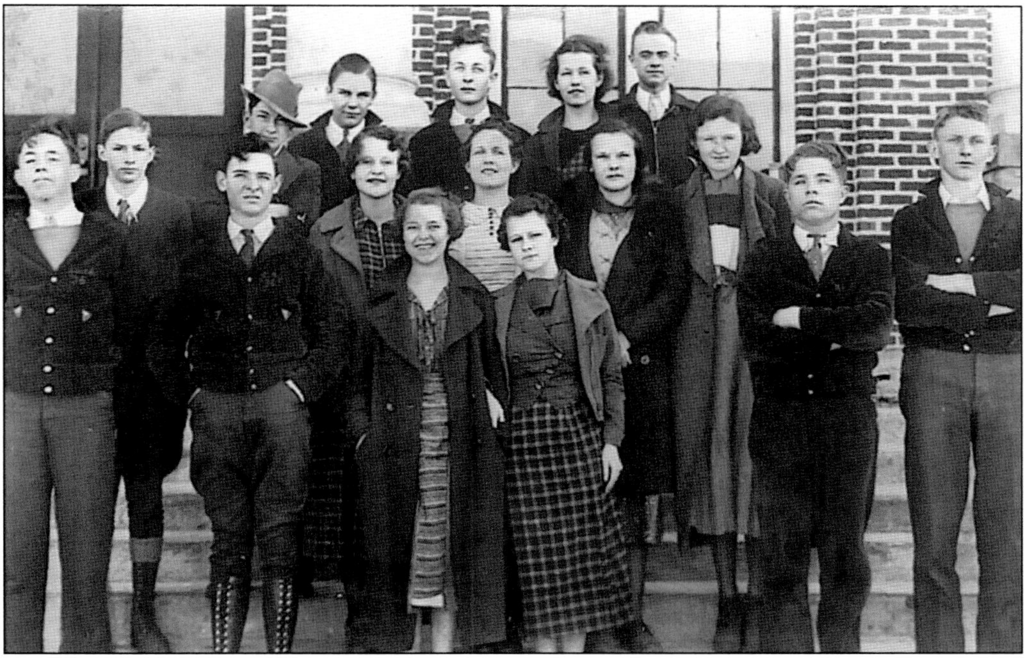

The Creedmoor High School Class of 1935, from left to right, are (front row) Rueben Johnson, Carmel Allen, Irene Goss, Florine Curl, Ray Sherron, and unidentified; (second row) Eugene Broughton, Virginia Dare Lyon, Vida Lee Peed, Catherine Curl, and Lou Ellen Green; (third row) Mitchell Allen, Thaxter Wheeler, Linwood Newton, Frances Wood, and Hugh Haskins. (Courtesy of Al and Josephine Lyon.)

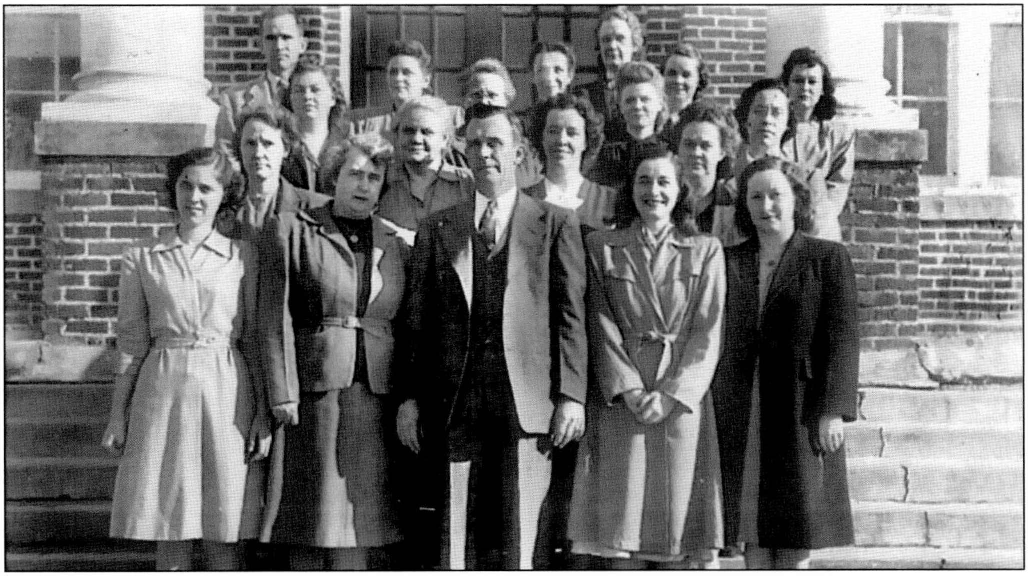

Faculty at Creedmoor High School in 1944, from left to right, are (first row) Ernestine McCluny, Josephine Newell, John Newell (principal), Catherine Bullock, and Marilyn Mangum; (second row) Marjorie Aiken, Annie Boyd Bullock, Margaret McIntosh, and Lucille Lyon; (third row) Josephine Hardy, Grace Cockerham, Gyla Dale Clark, and Margaret Wilson; (fourth row) Eva Catlette, Jane Thomas, Ollie Lyon, Minta Lula Pittard, and Roberta Goodwin. The man in the back is unidentified. (Courtesy of Al and Josephine Lyon.)

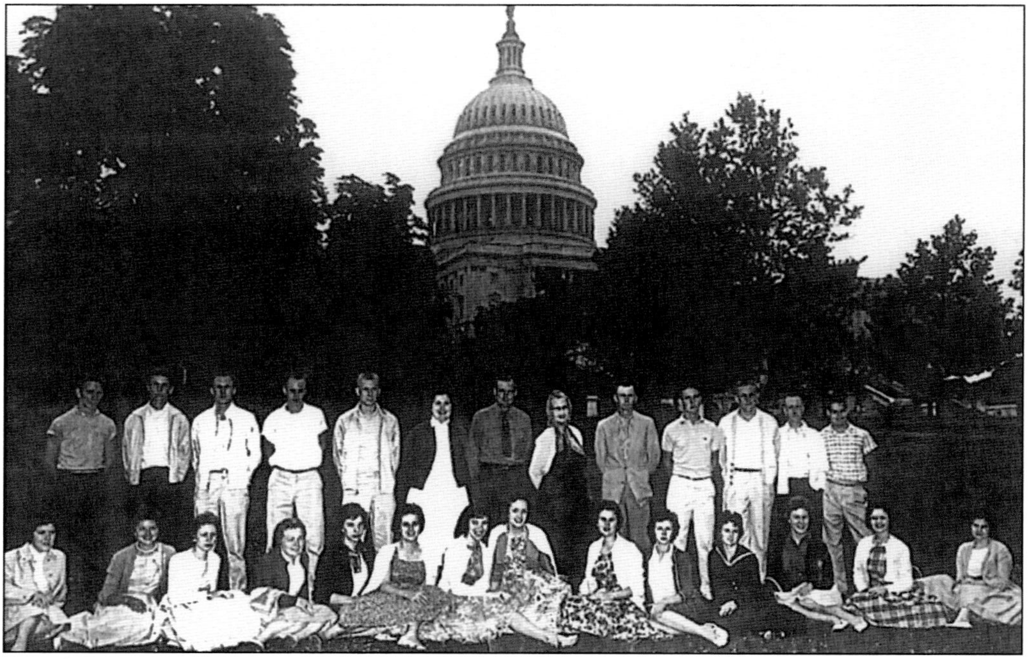

Creedmoor High School's Class of 1959 went on a trip to Washington D.C. The following are listed from left to right: (seated) Carolyn Crews, Margaret Jean Oakley, Mary Nell Aiken, Linda Green, Julia Ann Sherron, Linda Bennett, Martha Washington, Laura Sue Cash, Edith Newton, Judy Arnold, Rachel Fowler, Anne Ellington, Julianne Currin, and Lucy Parrott; (standing) Wayne Whitfield, Roy Bailey, L.A. Veasey, Stancil Roberts, Mac McCombs, June Crews, Irene Parrott, Al Lyon, Hal Crews, Jimmy Fleming, Andy Curl, and Ronald Prince.

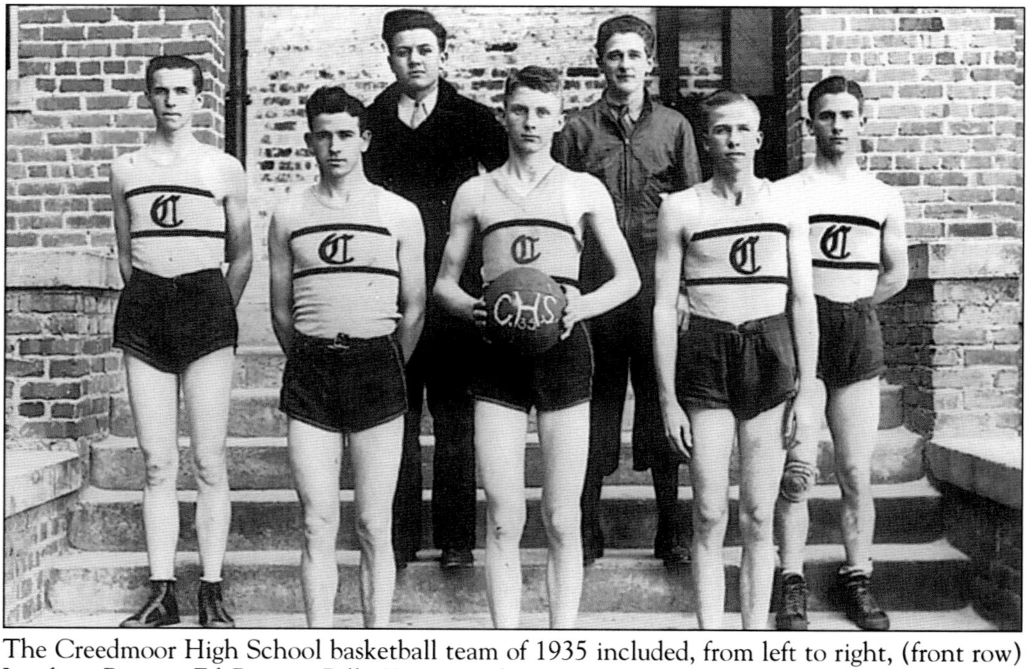

The Creedmoor High School basketball team of 1935 included, from left to right, (front row) Lambert Rogers, Ed Rogers, Billy Yates, Paul Hester, and Joe Hester. The two men not in uniform are unidentified. (Courtesy of Al and Josephine Lyon.)

B.G. Cross, shown here talking on the telephone, was the City of Creedmoor Fire Chief in 1951. (Courtesy of Nellie Brame.)

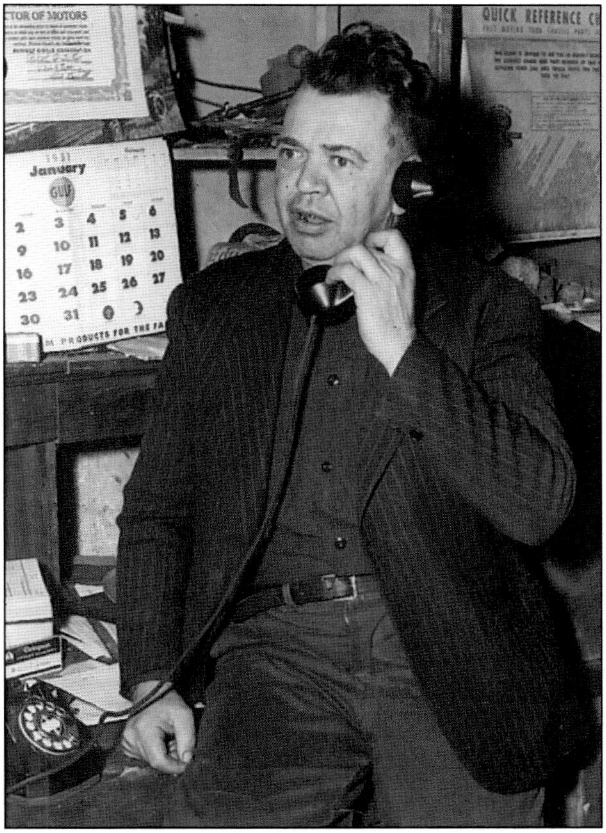

The Creedmoor High School band marches down Main Street in 1952. A Western Auto shop can be seen in the background. (Courtesy of June Cross.)

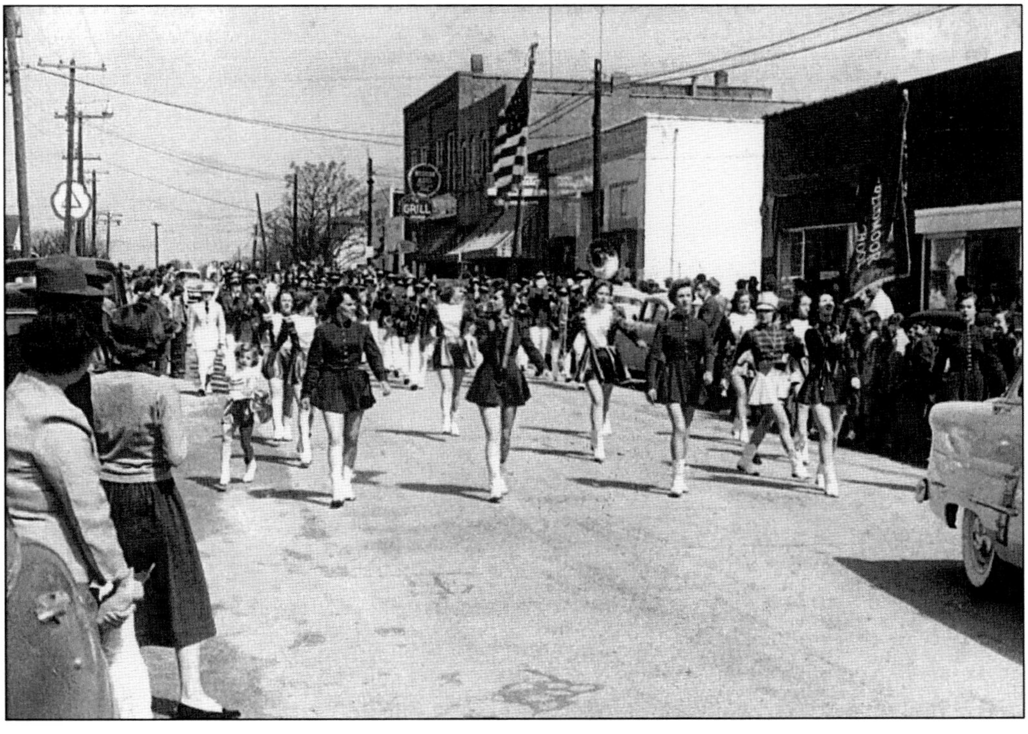

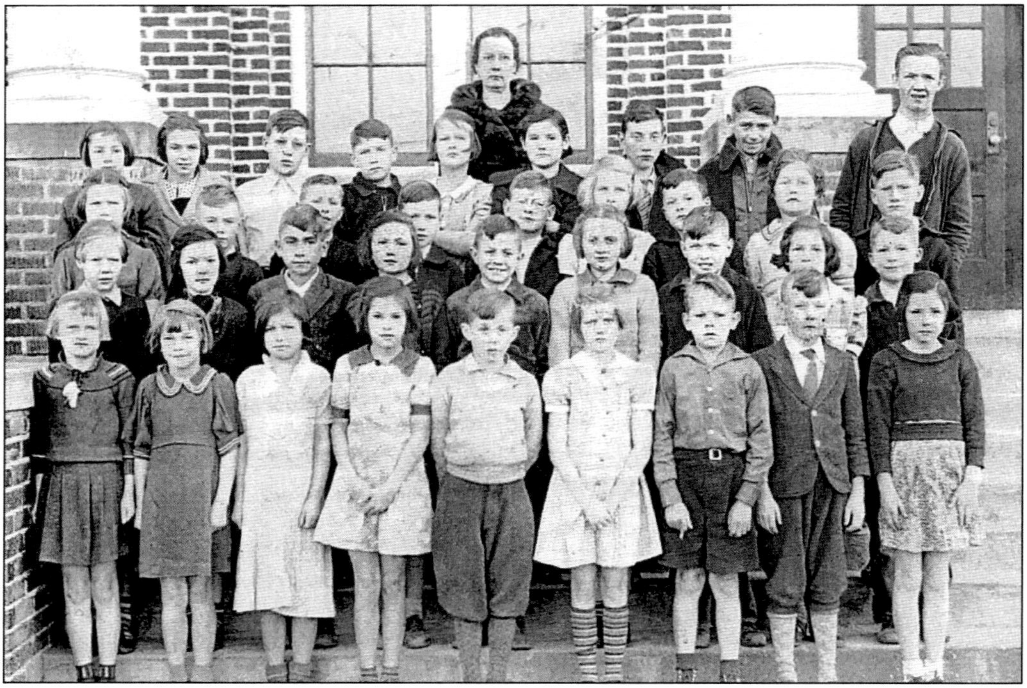

This is the fourth grade class of Creedmoor School during the 1937–1938 school year. (Courtesy of Betty Roberts Moody.)

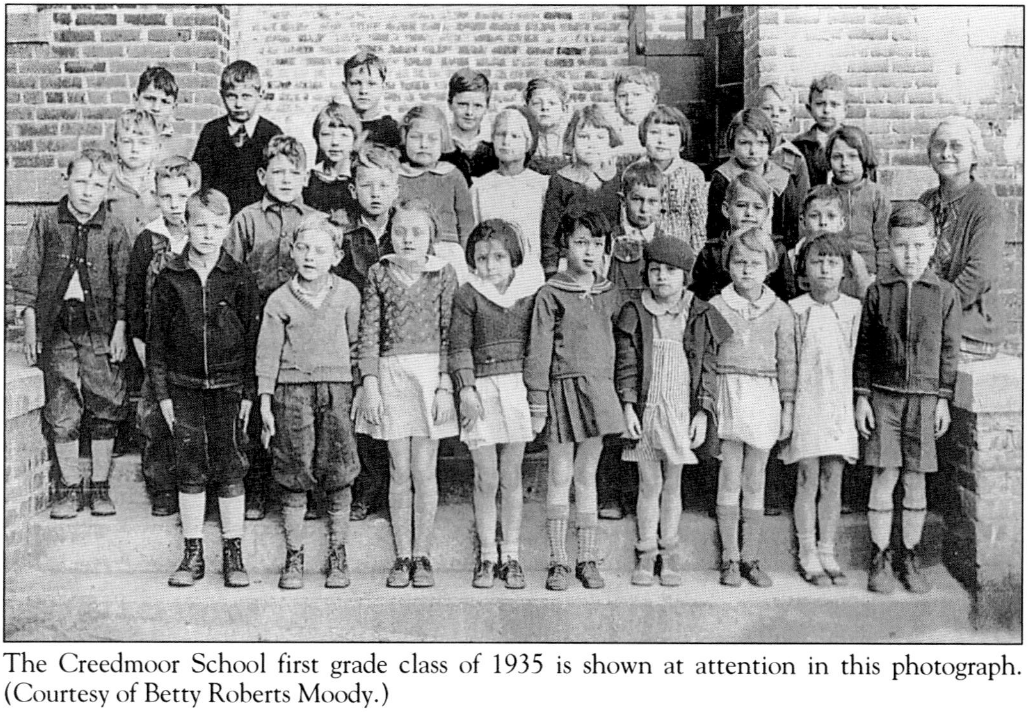

The Creedmoor School first grade class of 1935 is shown at attention in this photograph. (Courtesy of Betty Roberts Moody.)

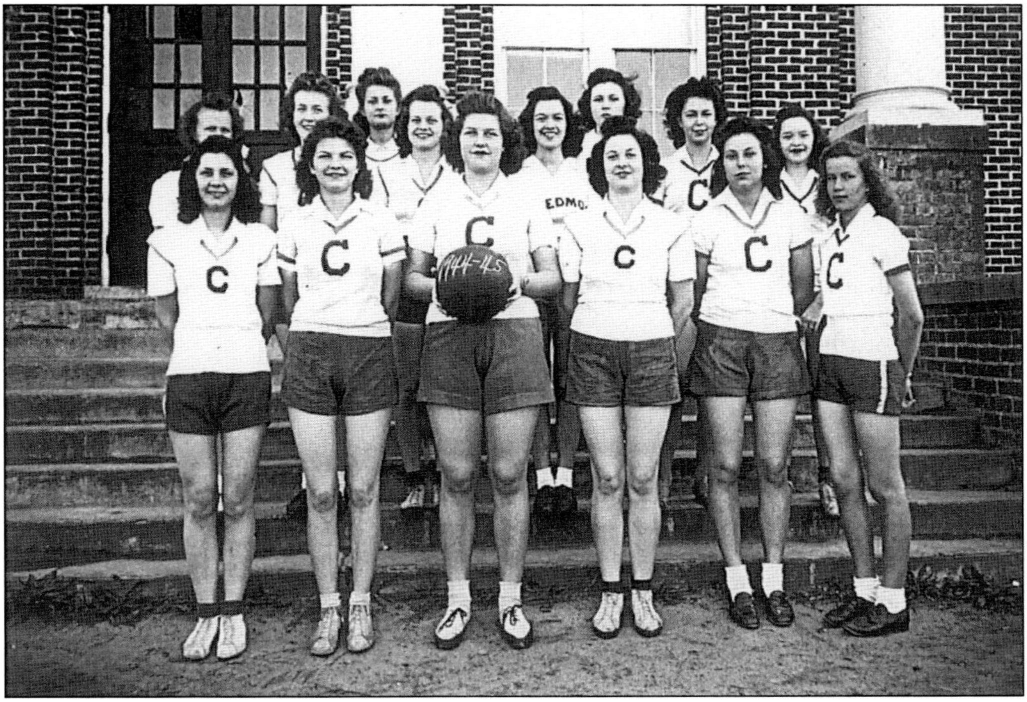

The 1944–1945 Creedmoor High School basketball team is ready for action. (Courtesy of Betty Roberts Moody.)

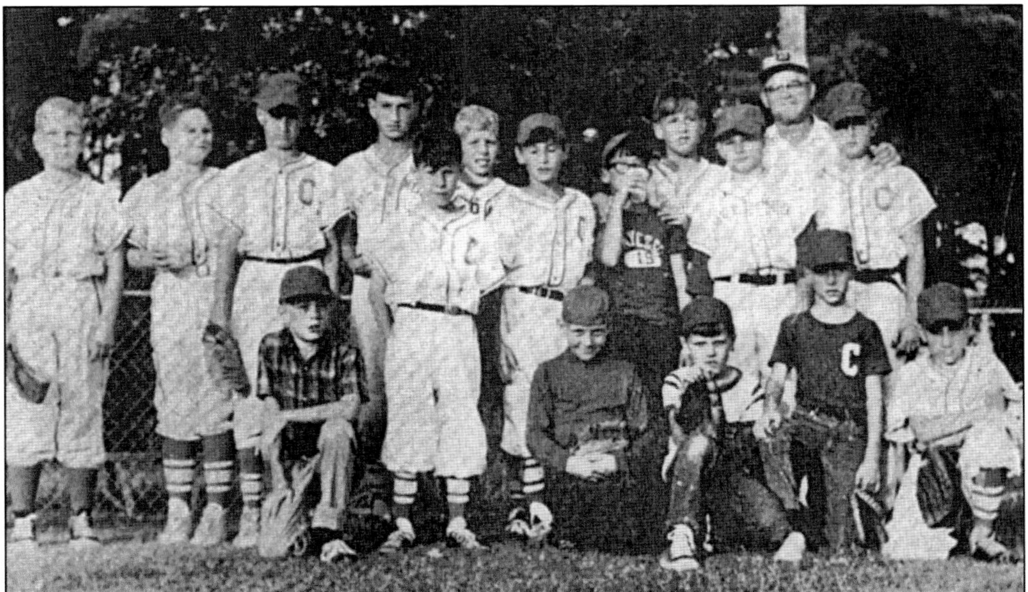

The Creedmoor ball field was named for Battle Roberts, who started the first little league team in Creedmoor in 1959 and was active in the South Granville Athletic Association until his death in 1982. Pictured from left to right are (kneeling) Neil Crews, Pat Robertson, Bryant Shearin, Rodney Washington, and Jimmy Mangum; (standing) David Yancey, Howard Hicks, Donnie Aiken, Ronnie Aiken, Dale Yancey, Joseph Peed, Ronnie James, Luke Steele, Tommy Whitt, Ray Kennedy, Battle Roberts, and Craig Whitfield.

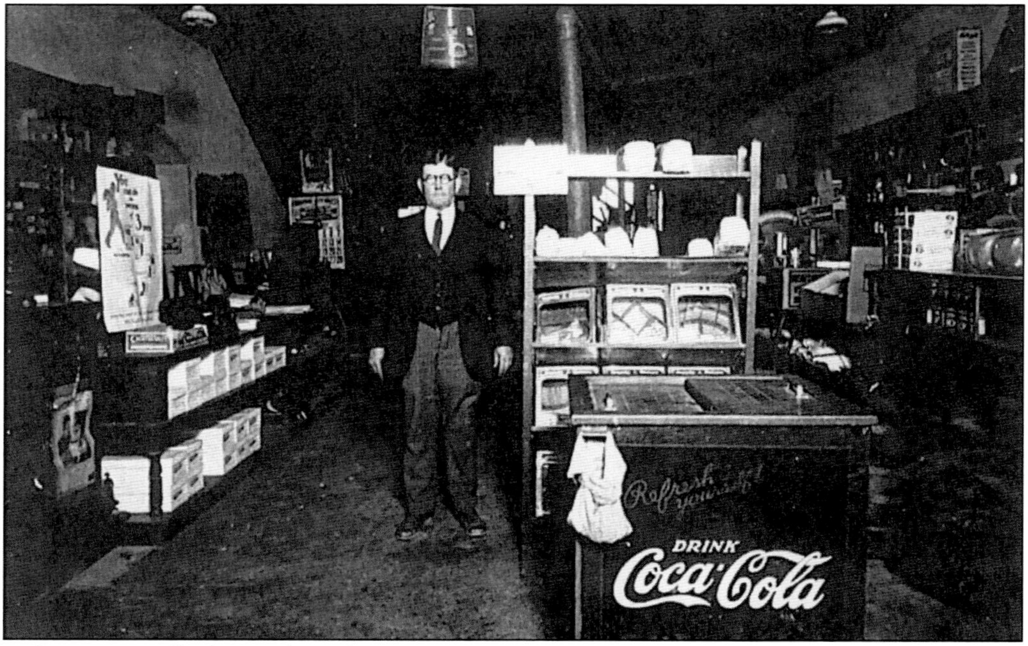

Hal Hester Bullock stands in his store, Bullock General Merchandise, in 1929. Bullock's store was located in the building that currently serves the *Butner-Creedmoor News*. (Courtesy of June Cross.)

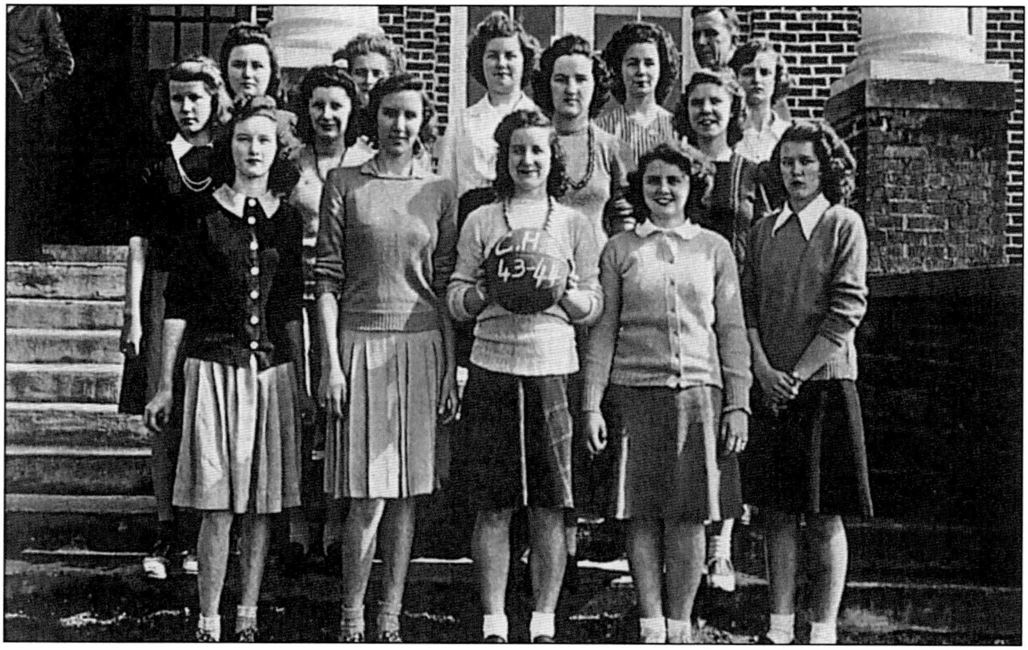

Although not dressed for basketball, these pretty ladies were members of the 1943–1944 Creedmoor High School basketball team. Shown, from left to right, are (front row) Carmen Pope, Helen Longmire, Wyleene Emory, Ozelta Cash, and Elizabeth Emory; (middle row) Patsy Emory, Laura Brinkley, Alene Keight, and Mary Frances Bullock; (back row) Elna Mangum, Mary Currin, Ann Rogers, Maxine Nevils, unidentified, and John Newell (principal and coach). (Courtesy of Helen Longmire.)

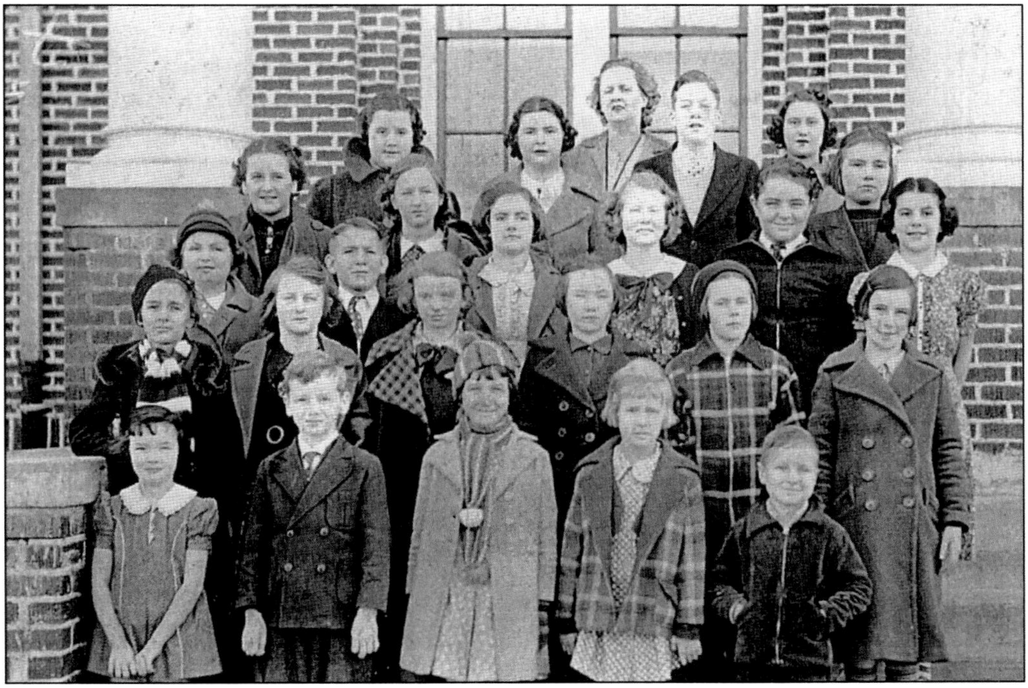

This is the 1938–1939 Creedmoor School music class. (Courtesy of Helen Davenport.)

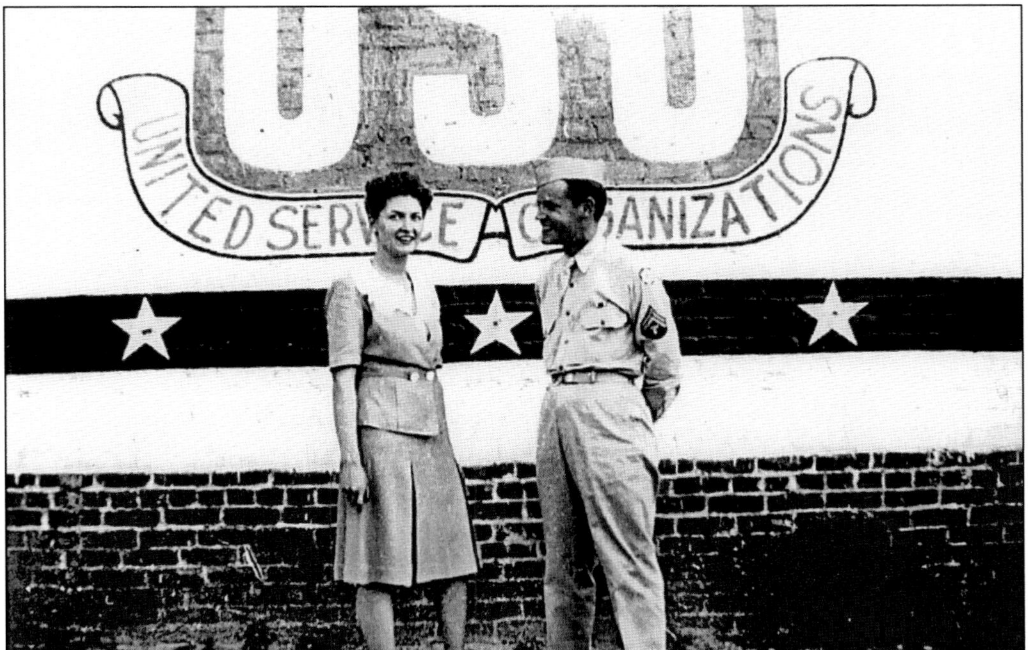

Billie Pope Weeks, who directed the USO (United Service Organizations) in Creedmoor during World War II, stands outside the building that now is occupied by the *Butner-Creedmoor News*. (Courtesy of David Rogers.)

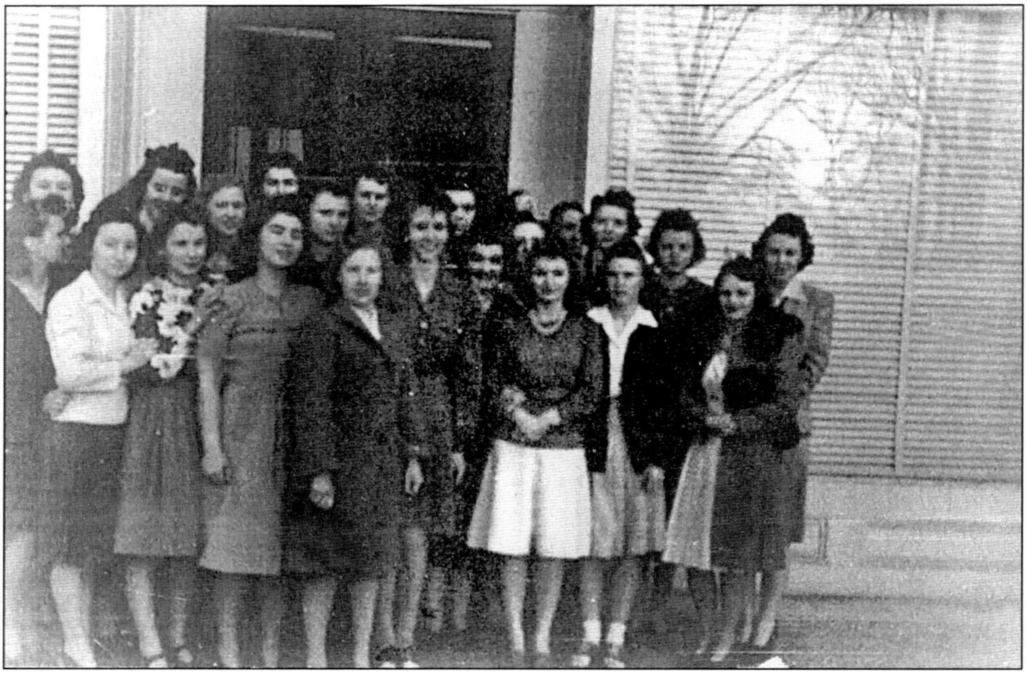

During World War II, with Camp Butner nearby, a USO Club was formed in Creedmoor. Shown are young women from the area who served as volunteers. (Courtesy of Billie Pope Weeks.)

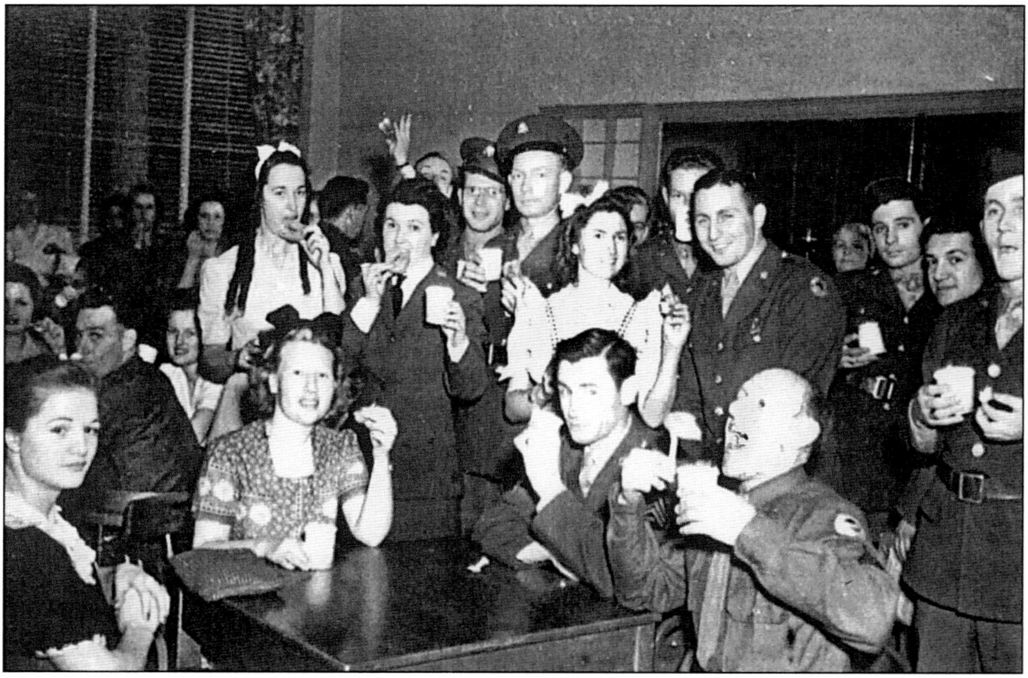

The soldiers from nearby Camp Butner and the USO volunteers seem to be having quite a good time at the USO Club in Creedmoor during World War II. The second lady from the left, sitting, is Arlene Mangum, directly behind her with the long hair is Mildred Bullock, and the lady with the bow in her hair is Billie Weeks.

John Rogers was a druggist in Creedmoor from 1914 into the 1940s. Here he is shown preparing another order.

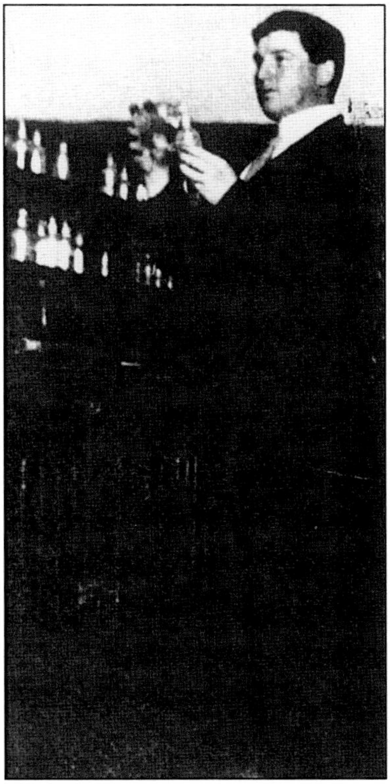

This log school was located in the Creedmoor area, near New Hope Church, in 1898. The school was on the farm of Dr. W.W. Cozart; his wife Emma was the teacher. Shown, from left to right, are (first row) Cooper Wheeler, John Currin, Thad Thomanson, Dee Lyon, and Walter Tingen; (second row) Ora Lyon, Sarah Currin, Nina Aiken, Olivia Beck, Bertha Beck, Lillian Aiken, Ola Thomanson, Rena Coley, Alma Thomanson, Lizzie Tingen, Betty Wheeler, and Buelah Tingen; (third row) Luther Tingen, Elva Tingen, Bessie Aiken, Alma Cozart, Mrs. Emma Cozart, Mabel Cozart, Viola Tingen, Viola Coley, and Lela Coley; (fourth row) Bernice Lyon, John Lyon, Robert Aiken, Elbert Aiken, Thaddeus Aiken, Tommie Aiken, and Avis Coley. (Courtesy of *Butner-Creedmoor News*.)

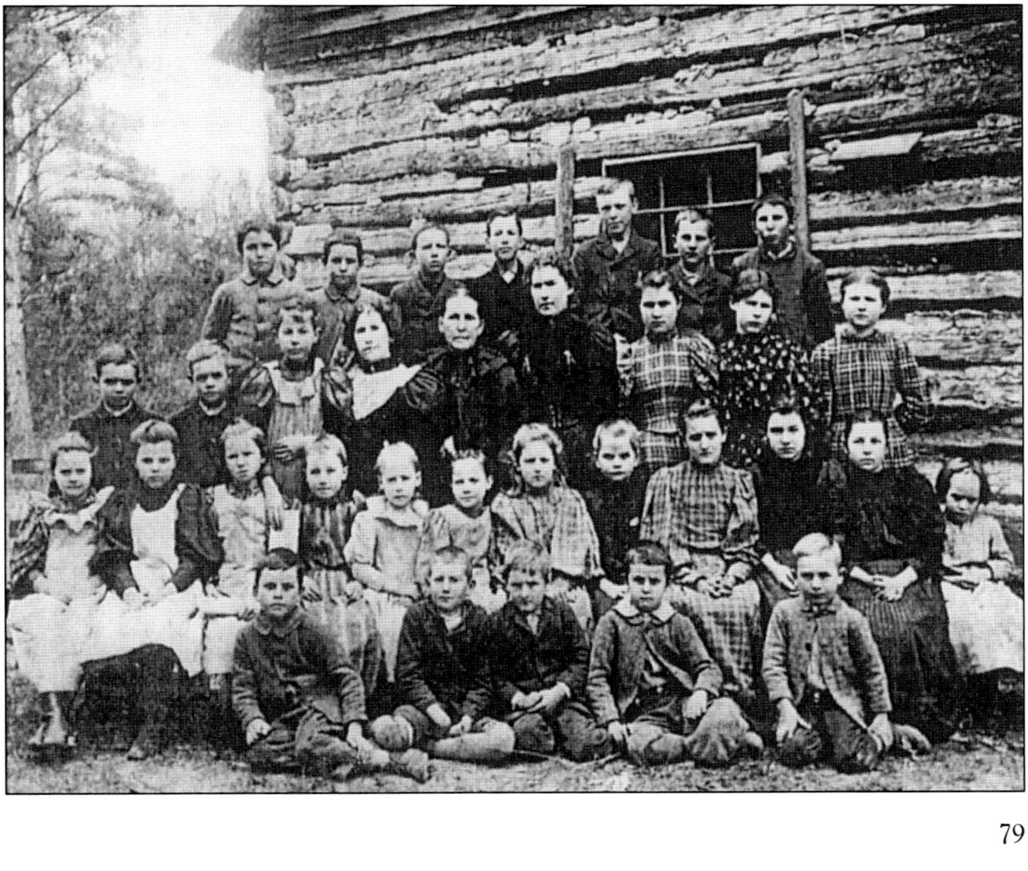

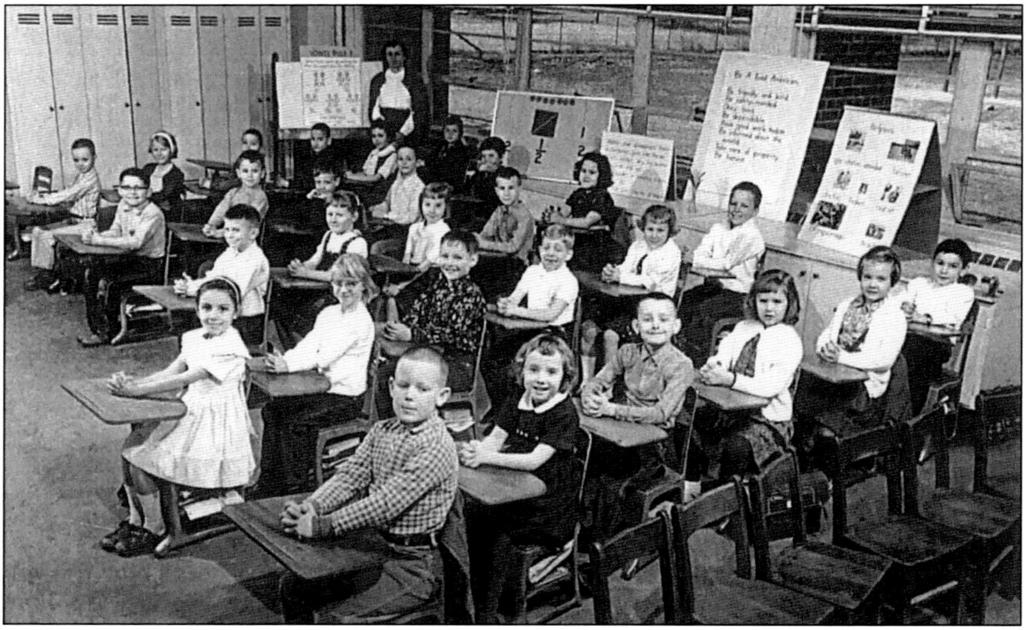

Teacher Carrie Suitt and her second grade class at Creedmoor Elementary School take a break from their rigorous academic schedule in 1963.

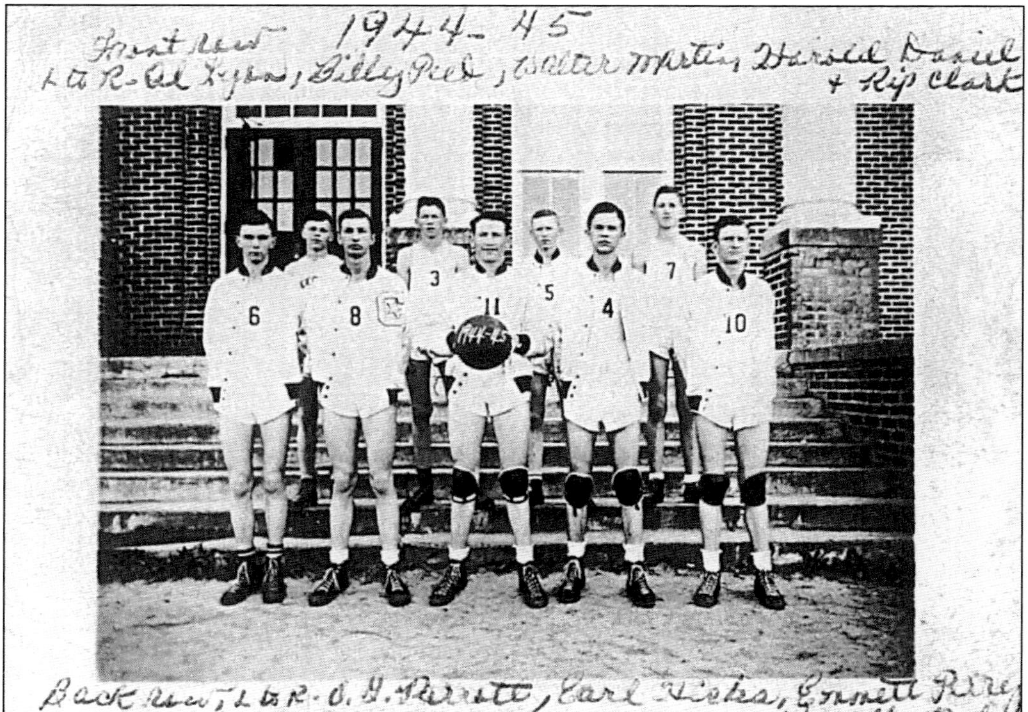

The boys from the 1944–1945 Creedmoor High School basketball team pose before a game. Pictured, from left to right, are (front row) Al Lyon, Billy Peed, Walter Martin, Harold Daniel, and Rip Clark; (back row) O.G. Parrott, Earl Hicks, Emmett Perry, and Harold Baker. (Courtesy of Al and Josephine Lyon.)

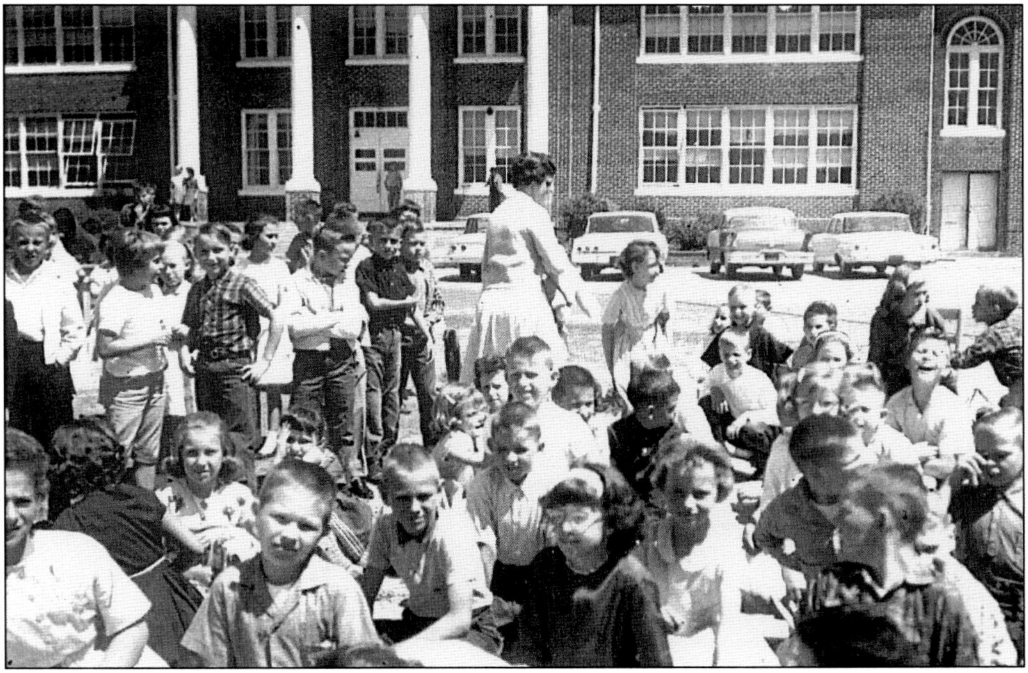

Students gather in front of Creedmoor High School in 1963. (Courtesy of Margaret Moss Cooper.)

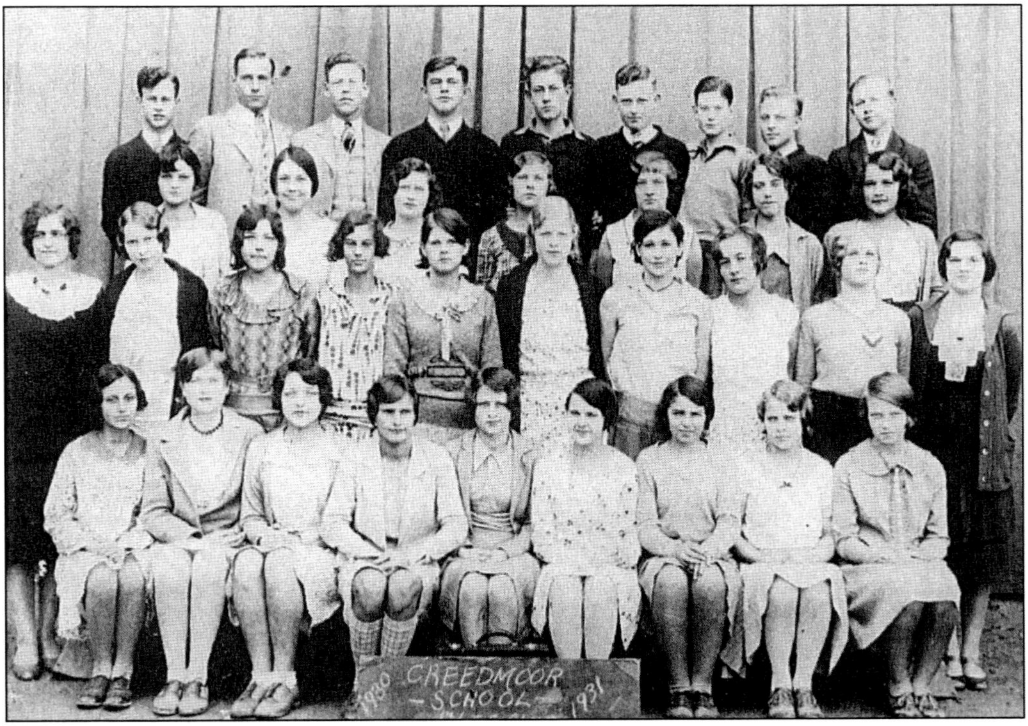

The Creedmoor School Glee Club from the 1930–1931 school year is shown in this photo.

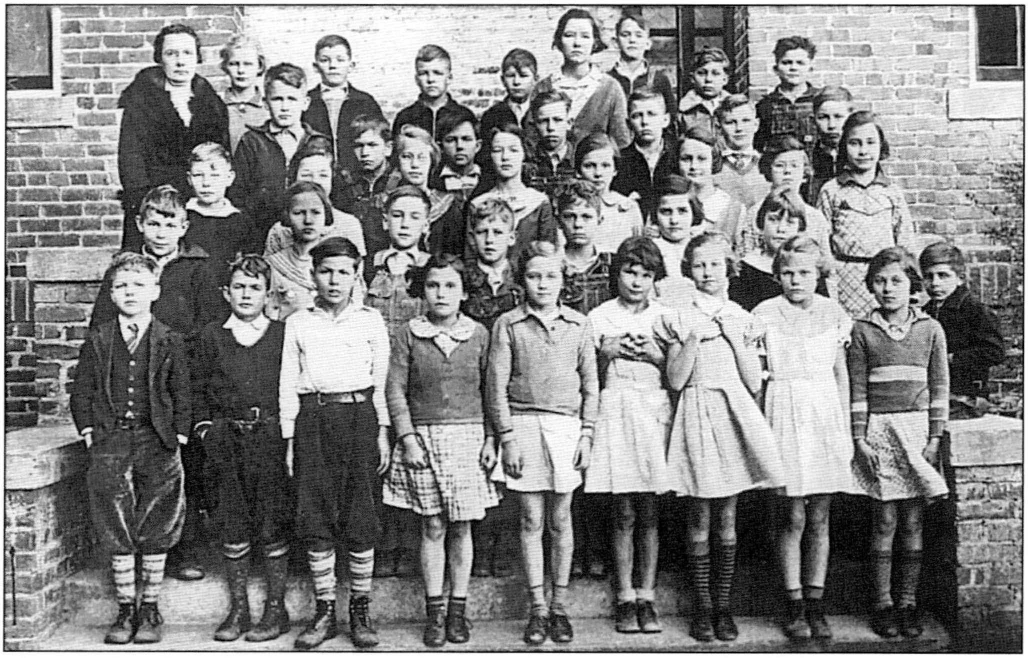

This is a fourth grade class of Creedmoor School in the early 1930s. (Courtesy of Margaret Moss Cooper.)

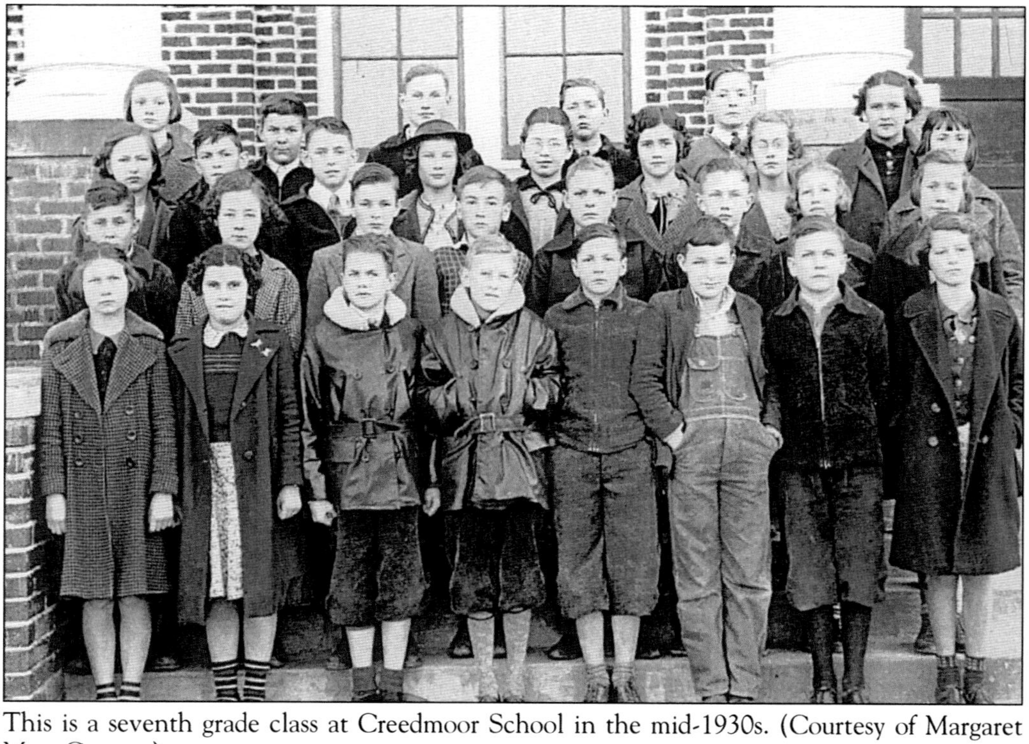

This is a seventh grade class at Creedmoor School in the mid-1930s. (Courtesy of Margaret Moss Cooper.)

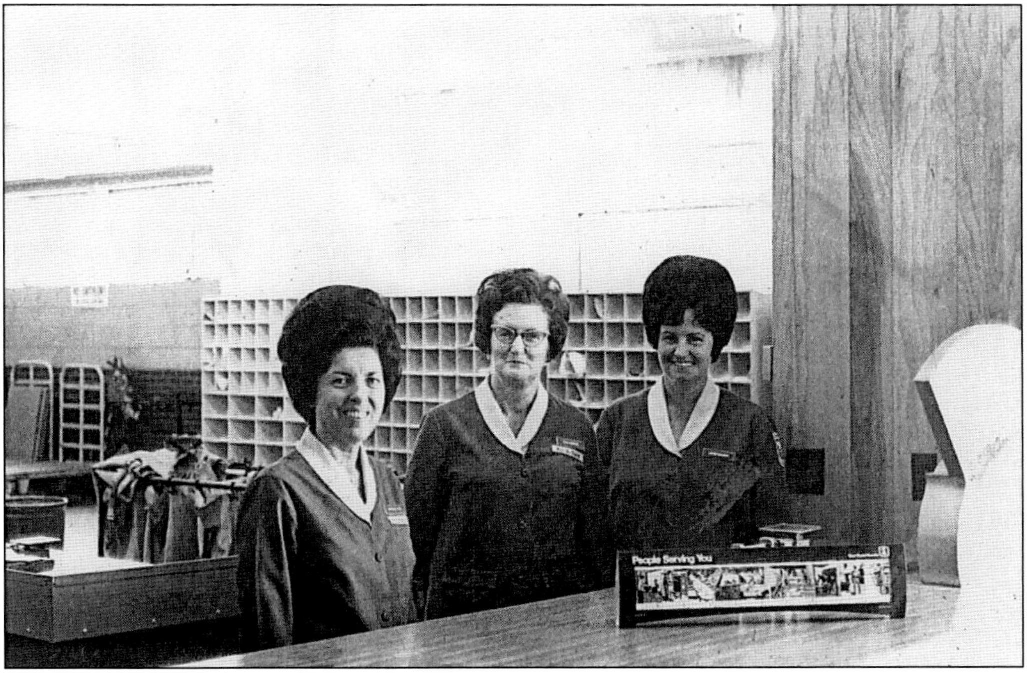

Employees at the Creedmoor post office look ready to serve customers in this picture from 1973. From left to right are Margaret Moss Cooper, Ella Mercer, and Sarah Mangum. (Courtesy of Margaret Moss Cooper.)

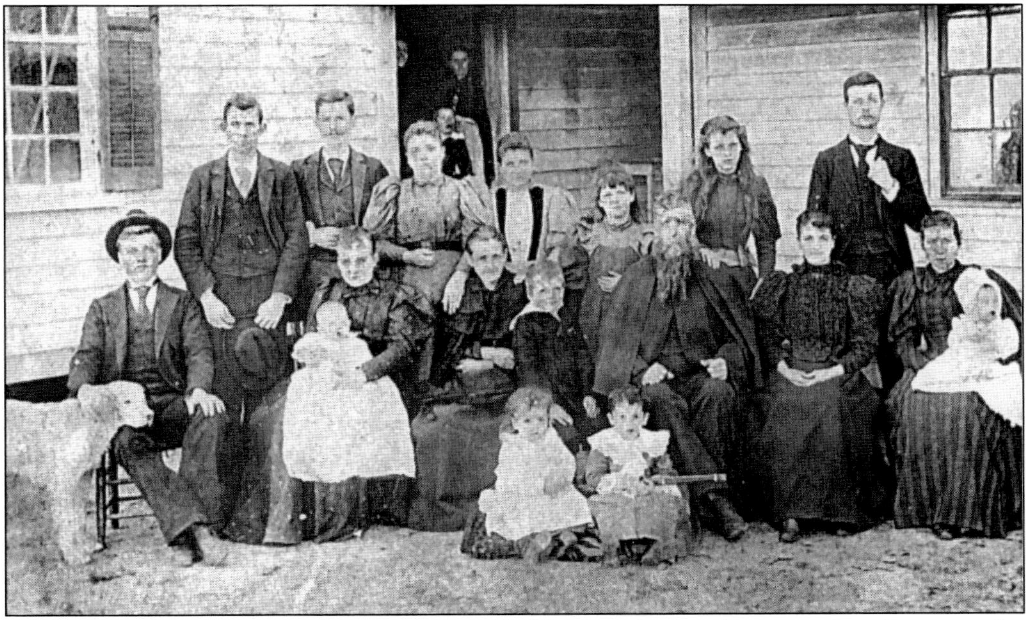

The family of William and Emma Mangum gather outside their home in Creedmoor in the late 1890s. The following are pictured, from left to right: (front row) Lois Winston and Johnny Rogers; (middle row) Elmer Mangum, Ilera Jones, Herbert Jones, Emma Mangum, Roy Mangum, William Mangum, Molly Rogers, and Annie Mangum; (back row) Henry Jones, Robert Rogers, Veola Rogers, unidentified, Clyde Hester, Nina Garner, and Sam Mangum. (Courtesy of David Rogers.)

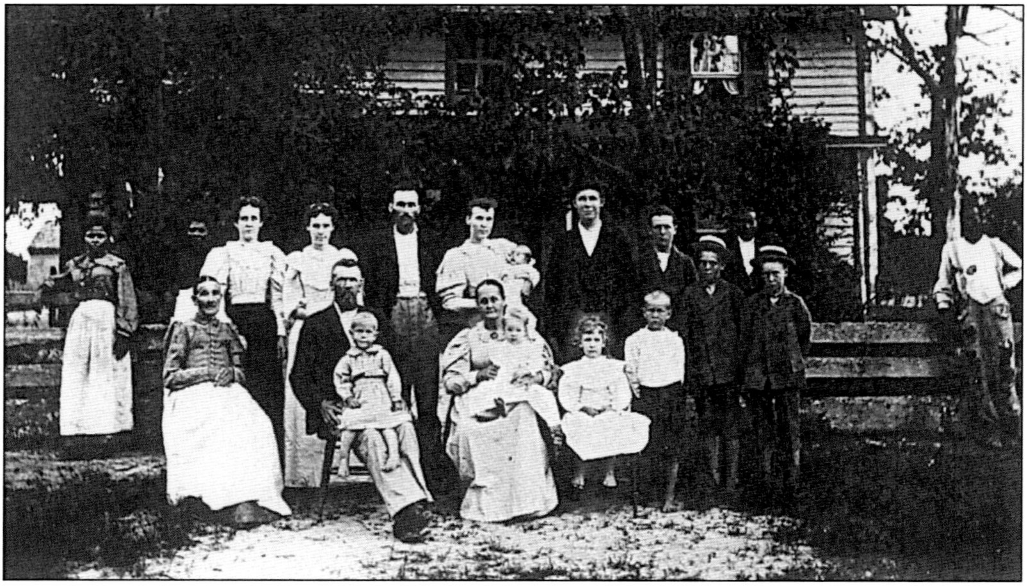

The Fleming family poses in front of their home in 1895. This house is located across the road from Bob's Barbeque. Pictured, left to right, are (front row) Eliza Fleming, James Fleming (holding Frederick Fleming), Cora Fleming (holding Cora Gertrude Fleming), Ziba Fleming, and Janadus Fleming; (back row) Eura Fleming, Kyle Fleming, Theodore Aiken, Viola Aiken, Roy Aiken, Tom Fleming, Augustus Fleming, James Fleming, and John Fleming. (Courtesy of David Rogers.)

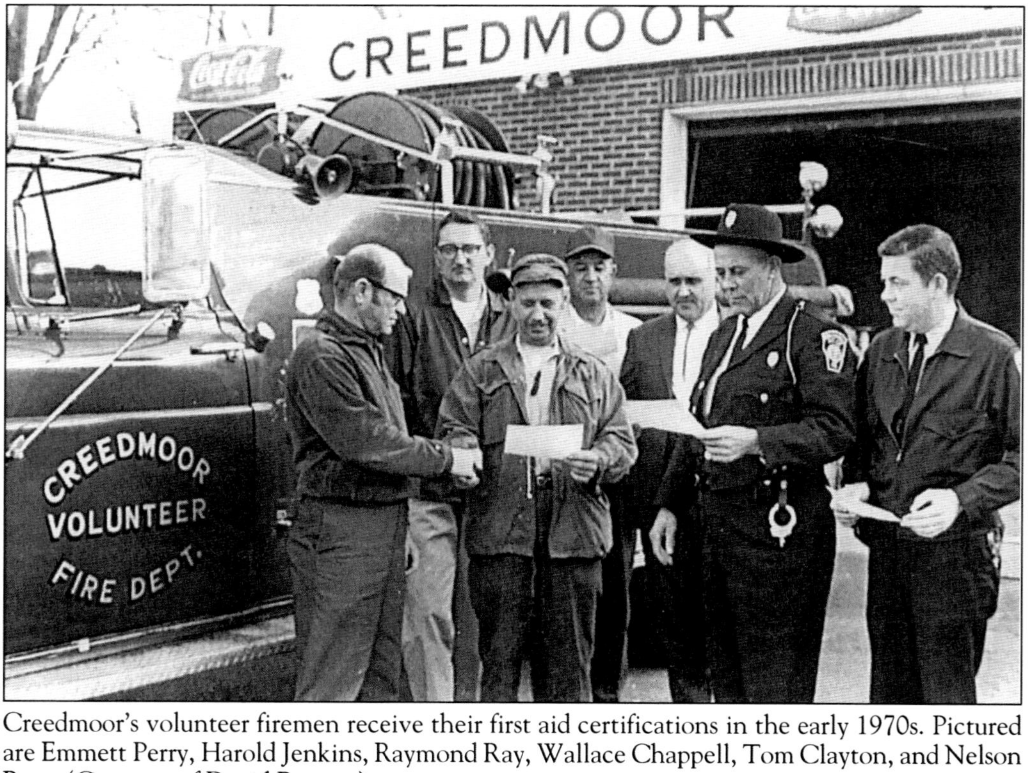

Creedmoor's volunteer firemen receive their first aid certifications in the early 1970s. Pictured are Emmett Perry, Harold Jenkins, Raymond Ray, Wallace Chappell, Tom Clayton, and Nelson Ross. (Courtesy of David Rogers.)

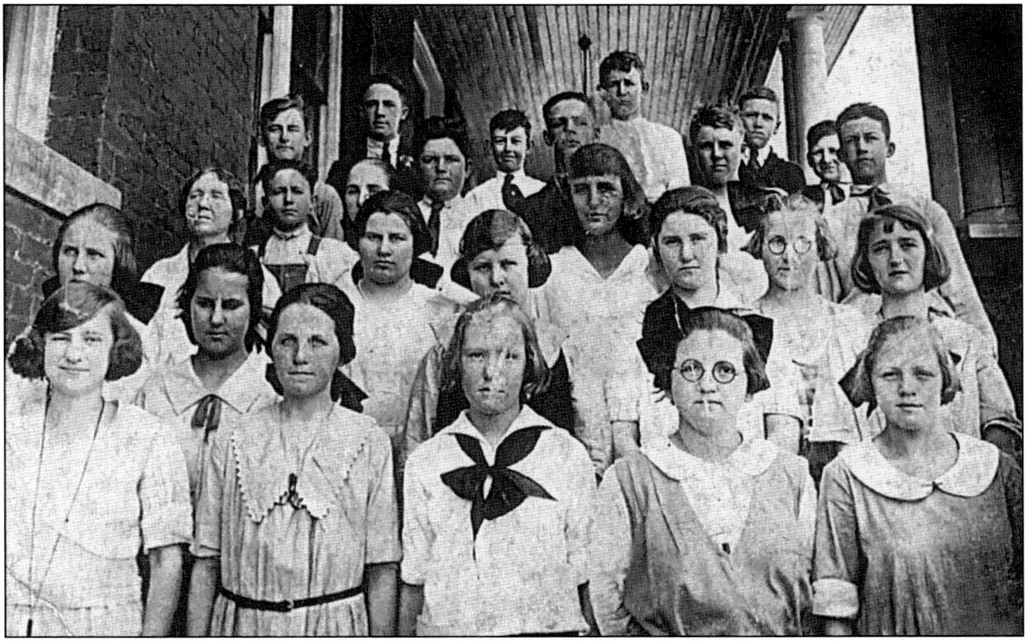

These are students of Creedmoor School in the 1920s. Pictured in no particular order are Ben Lyon, Lewis Daniel, Fred Aiken, Thomas Harris, William Green, Durward Fleming, Annette Whitfield, Ruth Keith, Frances Rogers, Charlene Haskins, Kathryne Lyon, Kathryn Bullock, Ethel Daniel, Marmie Leathery, Josie Chappell, Miss Ferguson (teacher), Frances Coley, Maggie Chappell, Lulie Hobgood, Onis Peed, Reed Crews, Lehman Bullock, Ronald Mangum, and Kenneth Woods.

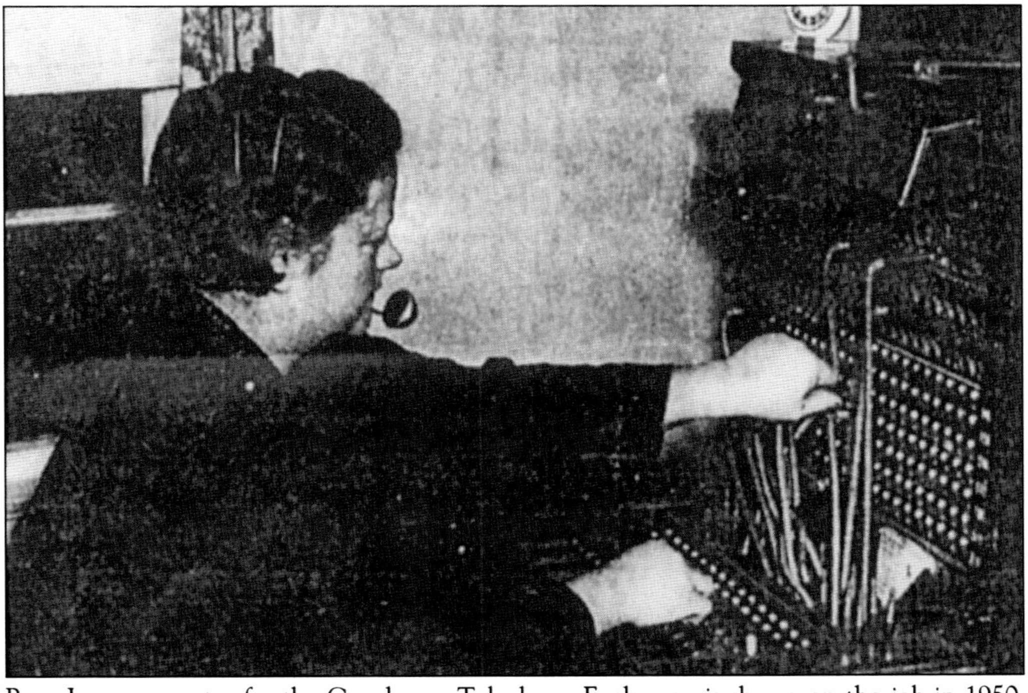

Rosa James, operator for the Creedmoor Telephone Exchange, is shown on the job in 1950. (Courtesy of David Rogers.)

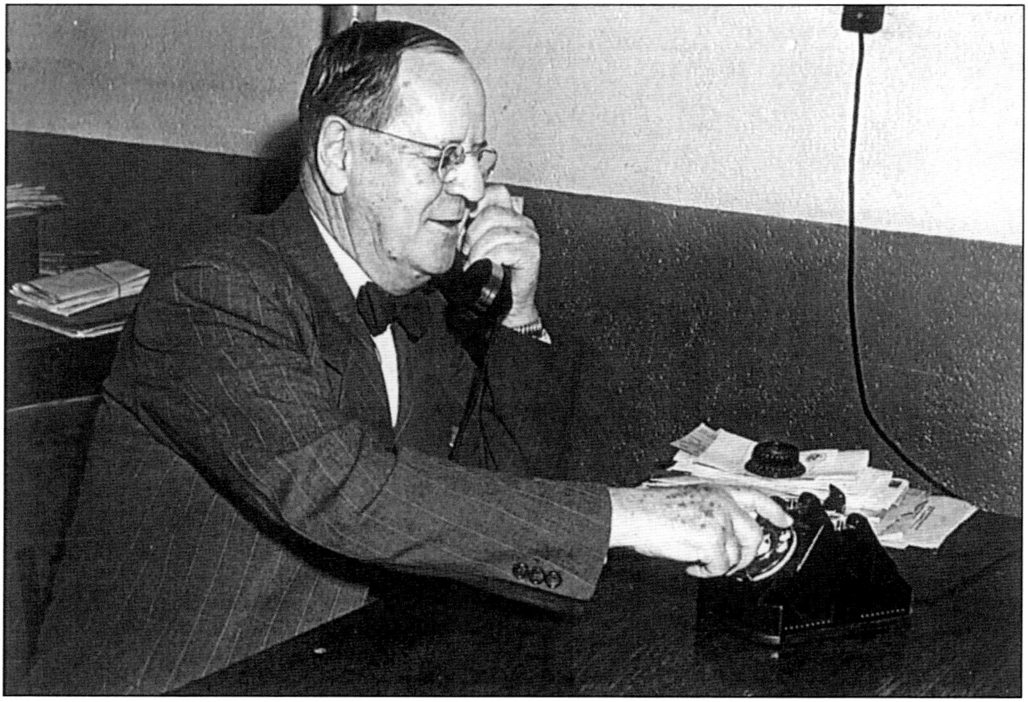

Mayor I.E. Harris of Creedmoor is placing the first direct call without the use of an operator at the Creedmoor Telephone Exchange in 1955.

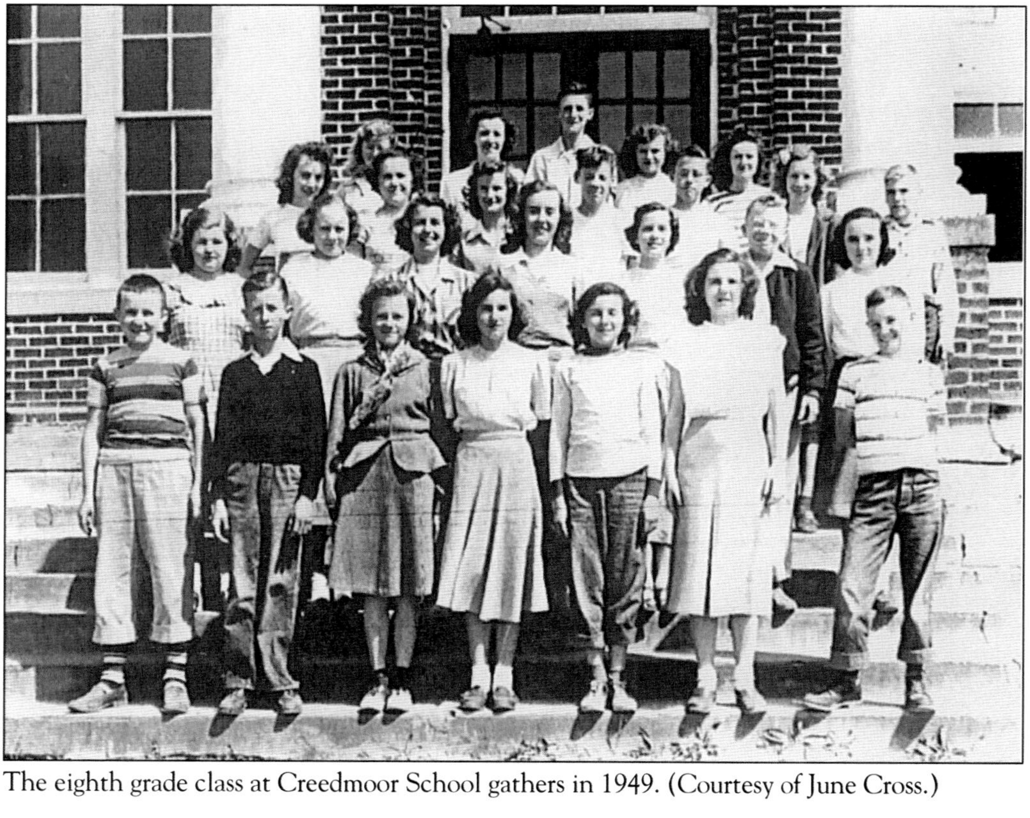

The eighth grade class at Creedmoor School gathers in 1949. (Courtesy of June Cross.)

Three

BUTNER

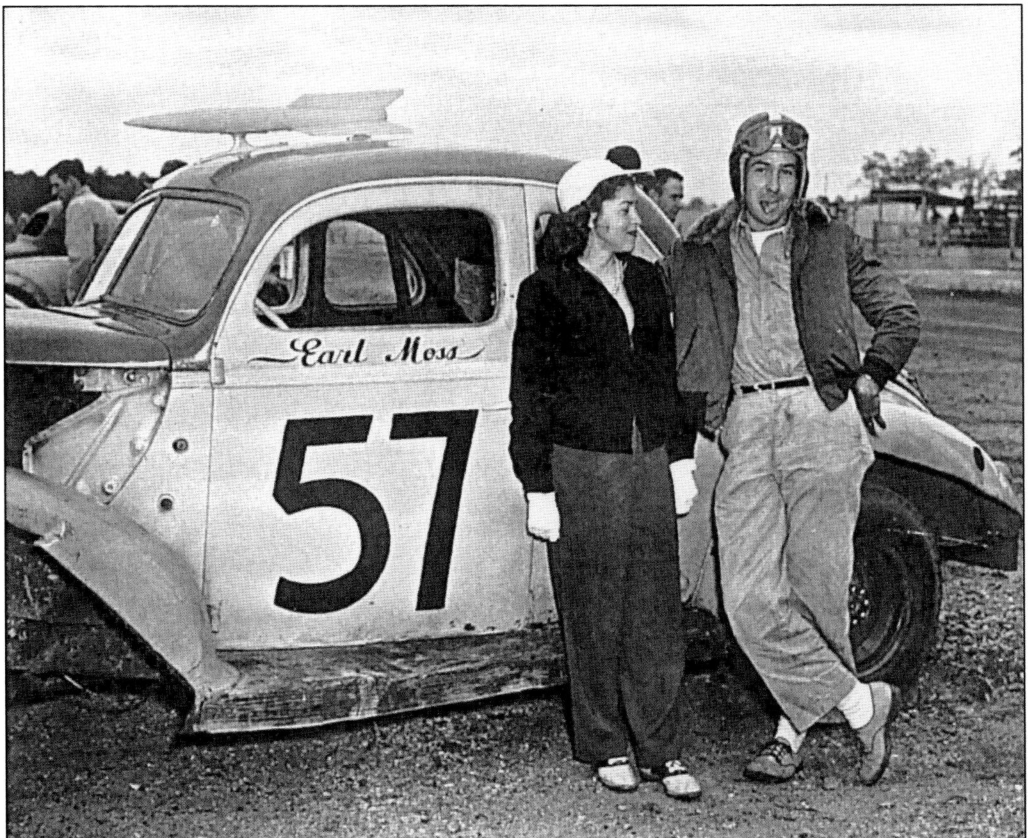

Margaret Moss Cooper stands beside her husband Earl Moss at Butner Speedway in the 1950s. Moss's racecar can also be seen. (Courtesy of Margaret Moss Cooper.)

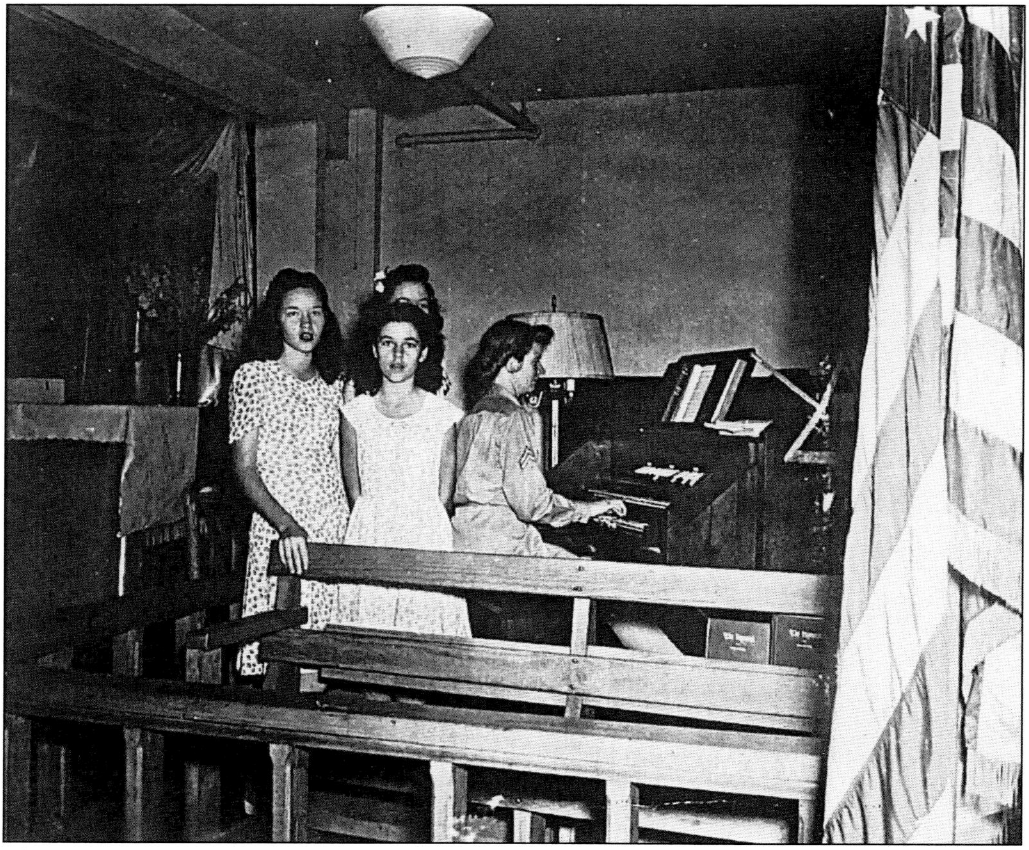

These young ladies are singing to Camp Butner soldiers in the hospital chapel in 1945. Pictured, from left to right, are Madeline Roberts, Joanne Roberts, Jean Burlington, and Betty Roberts (standing behind.) (Courtesy of Betty Roberts Moody.)

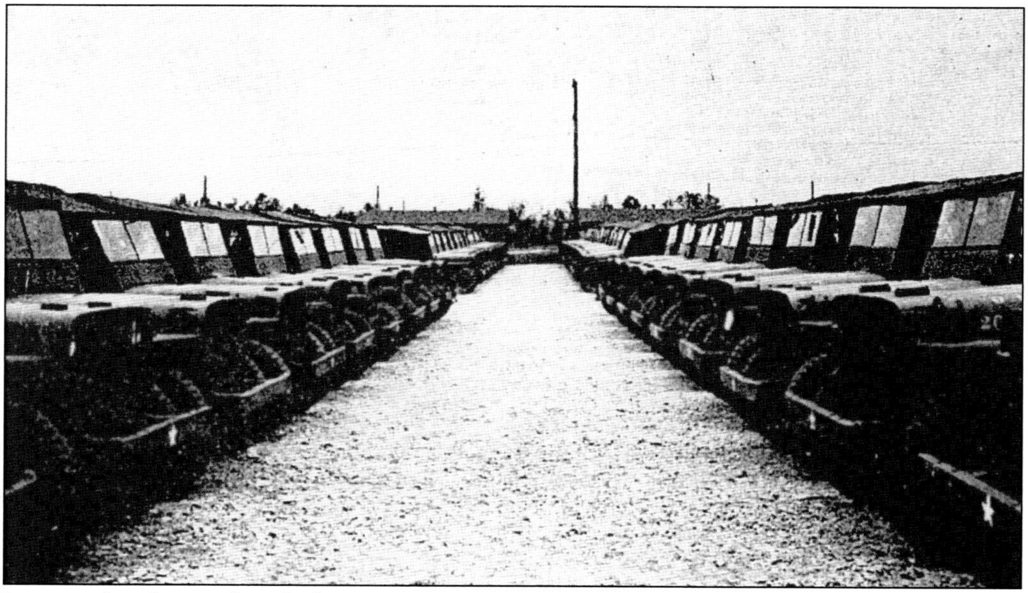

Jeeps are lined up and ready for service at Camp Butner.

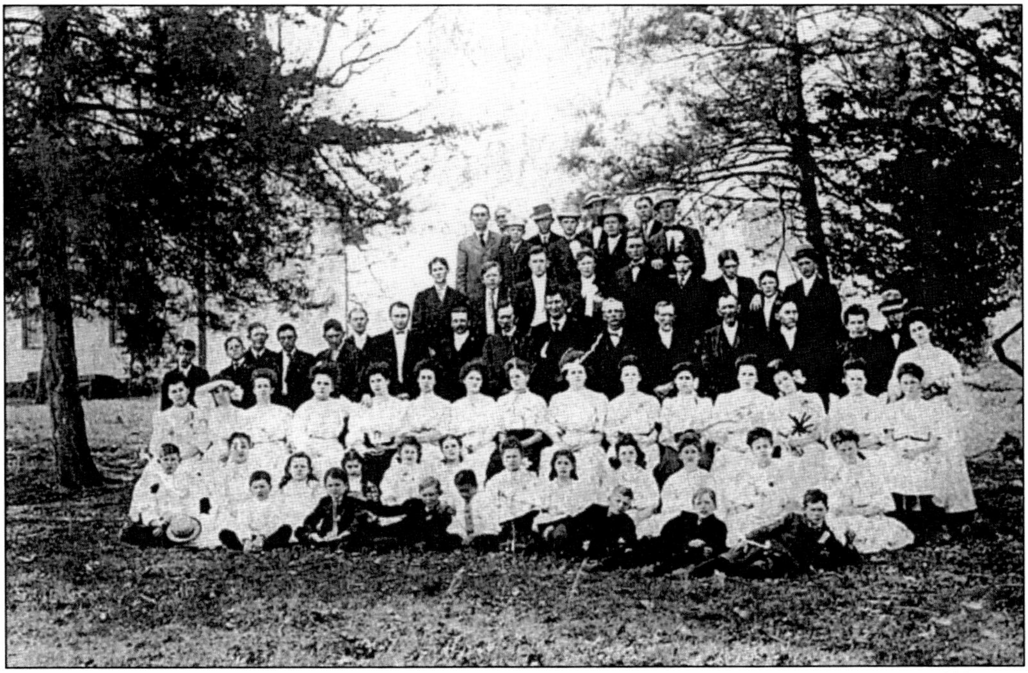

This is the Knapp of Reeds High School class around 1910. (Courtesy of Nellye Tunstall.)

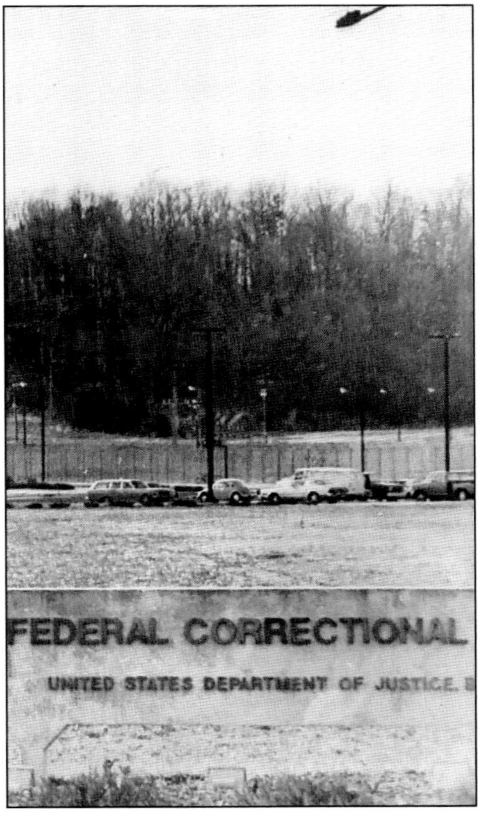

A helicopter can be seen at the very top of this picture. The helicopter is bringing John Hinckley, who had shortly before attempted to assassinate President Ronald Reagan, to the Federal Correctional Institution in Butner. The year is 1981. (Courtesy of Harry Coleman.)

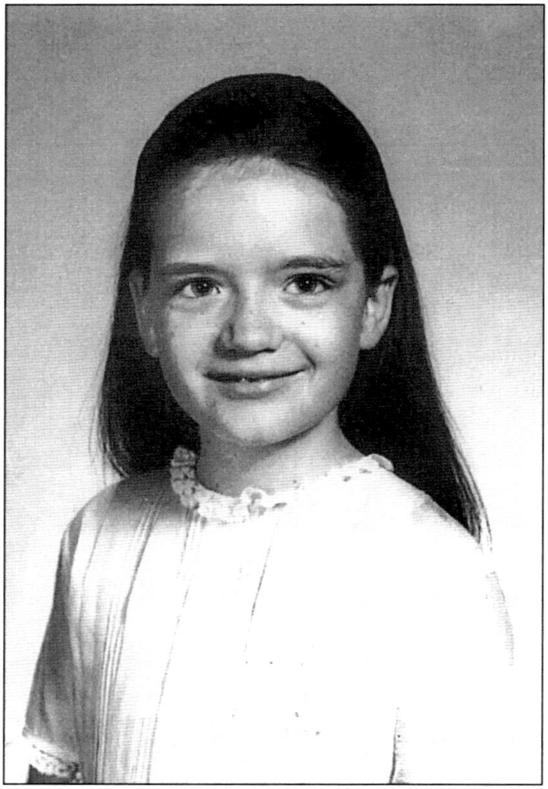

This little girl has grown up and has served Granville County as a teacher for the past 25 years. Beth Harward has been honored with many awards by her co-workers, parents, and students. She has been named Teacher of the Year at each of the schools where she has taught (Wilton, Hawley, and Butner-Stem Middle) and has represented Granville County on several state committees. Harward has positively influenced so many young lives mostly because she truly loves her students and wants them to succeed.

Contestants for the title of Miss Jet Motor Speedway, from left to right, are Bonnie Bowling, Susan Clayton, Norma Evans, Patricia Greene, Ann Springer, and Beverly Gibbs. This event took place in Butner in the 1960s. From all reports, the drivers were able to keep their eyes on the track enough to not cause any major mishaps.

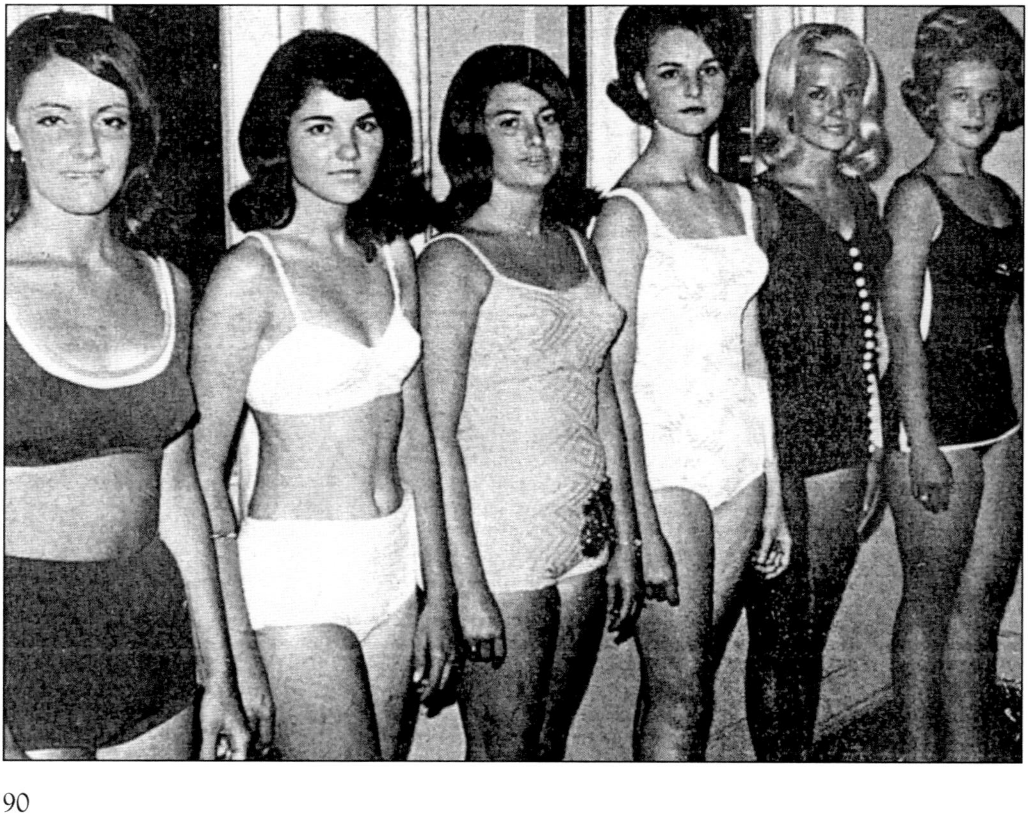

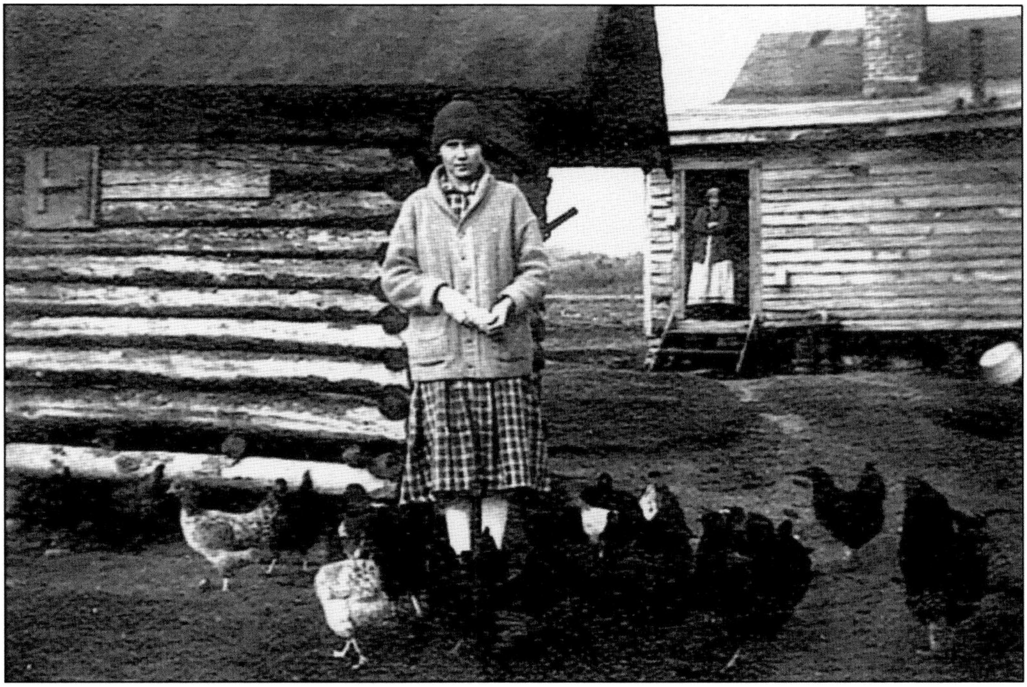

Alice Cross is shown feeding chickens at her home in Knapp of Reeds in the 1920s. This farm was taken by the government for the construction of Camp Butner. (Courtesy of Nellie Brame.)

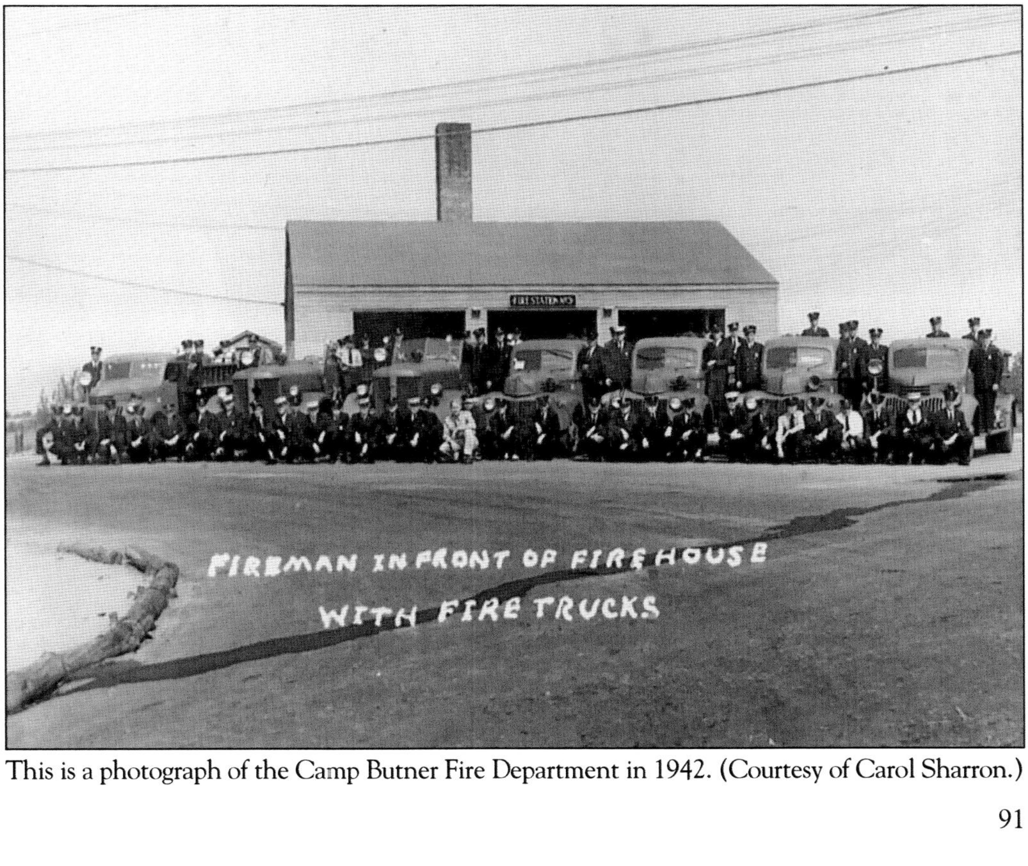

This is a photograph of the Camp Butner Fire Department in 1942. (Courtesy of Carol Sharron.)

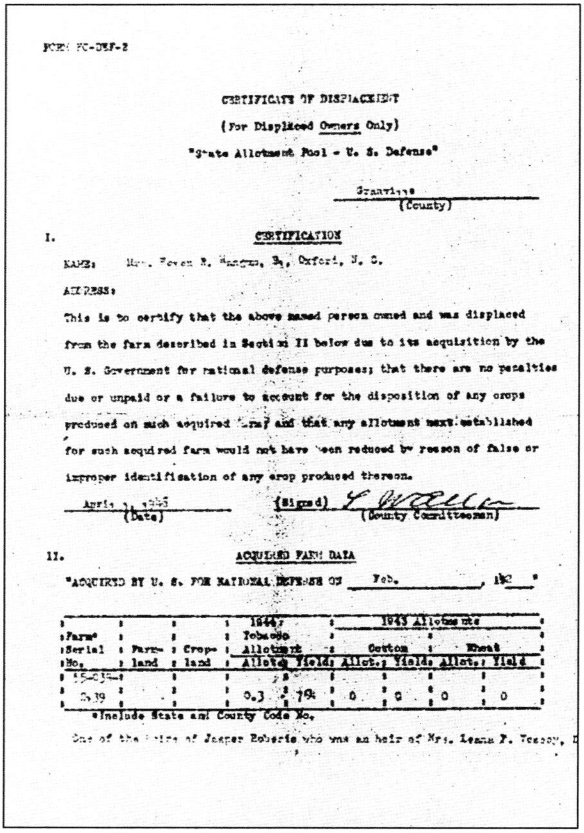

FORM FC-DEF-2

CERTIFICATE OF DISPLACEMENT

(For Displaced Owners Only)

"State Allotment Pool - U. S. Defense"

Granville
(County)

I. CERTIFICATION

NAME: Mrs. [illegible] R. Mangum, [illegible], Oxford, N. C.

ADDRESS:

This is to certify that the above named person owned and was displaced from the farm described in Section II below due to its acquisition by the U. S. Government for national defense purposes; that there are no penalties due or unpaid or a failure to account for the disposition of any crops produced on such acquired farm and that any allotment next established for such acquired farm would not have been reduced by reason of false or improper identification of any crop produced thereon.

April [illegible], 1943
(Date)

(Signed) [illegible]
(County Committeeman)

II. ACQUIRED FARM DATA

"ACQUIRED BY U. S. FOR NATIONAL DEFENSE ON Feb., 1942"

Farm* Serial No.	Farm-land	Crop-land	1942 Tobacco Allotment Allot.	1942 Tobacco Allotment Yield	1943 Allotments Cotton Allot.	1943 Allotments Cotton Yield	1943 Allotments Wheat Allot.	1943 Allotments Wheat Yield
35-039-039			0.3	794	0	0	0	0

*Include State and County Code No.

One of the heirs of Jasper Roberts who was an heir of Mrs. Leana P. Veasey, [illegible]

A certificate of displacement was issued to land owners who were uprooted by the establishment of Camp Butner. This one belonged to Helen Mangum. (Courtesy of Josh Mangum.)

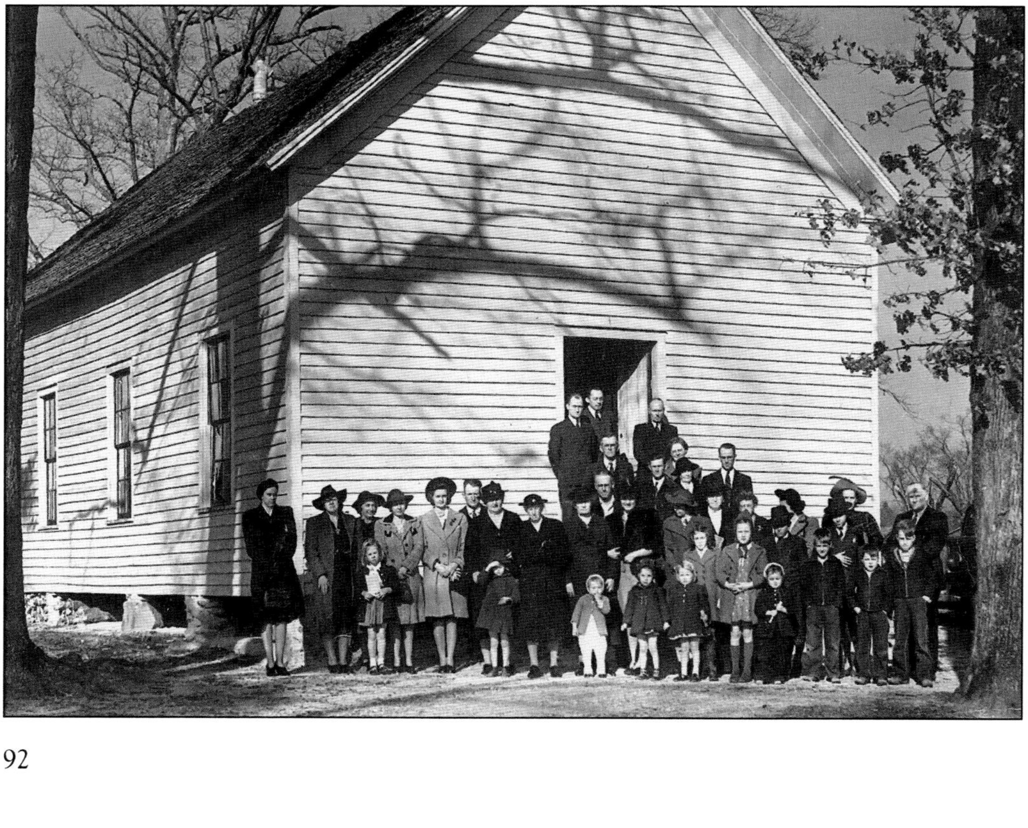

The Roberts Chapel congregation is shown in 1942. Those pictured include Cortez Veasey, pastor J.A. Lindsay, Lonnie Roberts, Ralph Jones, Mabel Jones, Lee Jones, Coy Luxton, Lucy Roberts, Russell Jones, Allie Glass, Kathleen Roberts, Dorothy Lawson, Lee Daniel, Lulu Veazey, Jeanna Veazey, Eunice Jones, Mildred Norris, Madeline Jones, Cora Sanford, Eva Perry, Page Roberts, Edna Luxton, John Roberts, Maude Roberts, and Ed Roberts. (Courtesy of Ada Lee Walker Cozart.)

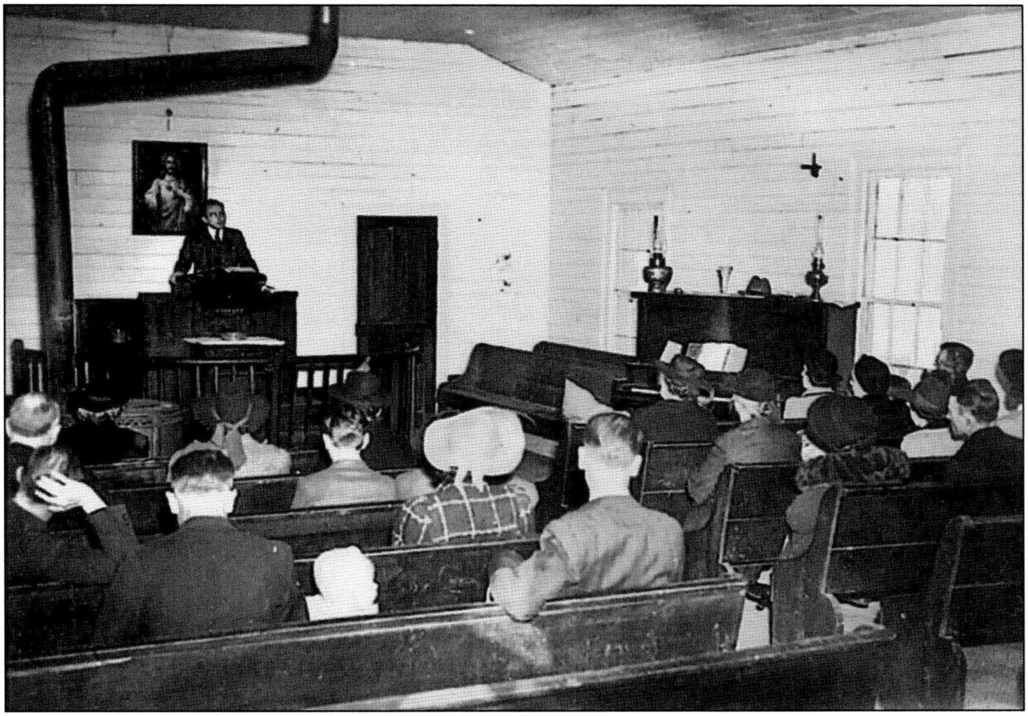

Roberts Chapel parishioners listen intently to their pastor in this photograph from the early 1940s. (Courtesy of Josh Mangum.)

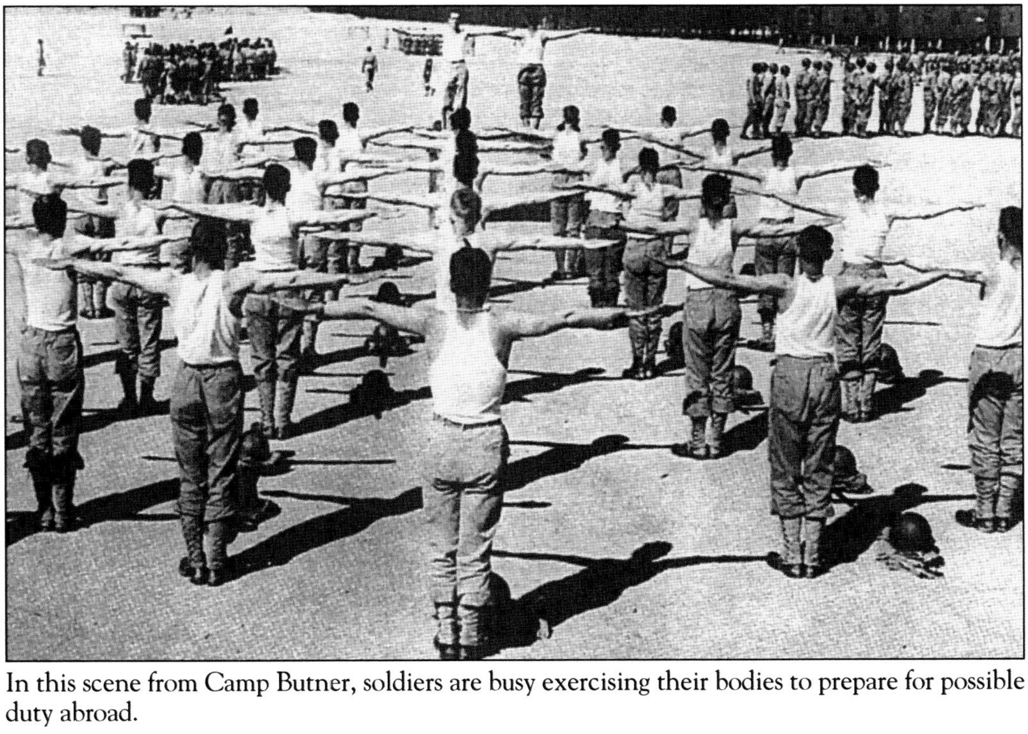

In this scene from Camp Butner, soldiers are busy exercising their bodies to prepare for possible duty abroad.

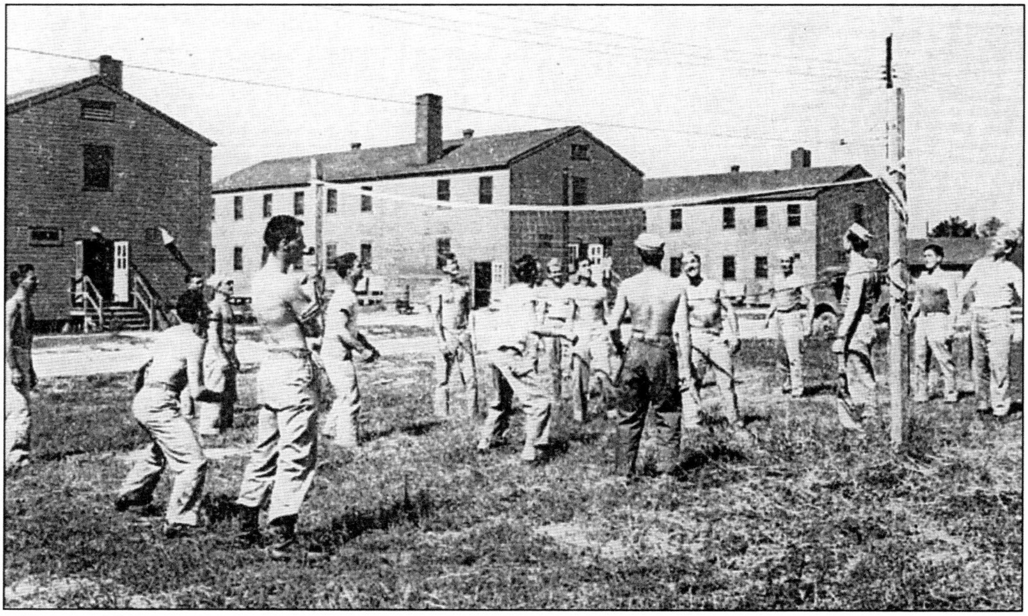

These soldiers are enjoying a game of volleyball at Camp Butner in the early 1940s. Camp Butner was built as a training center for our soldiers and to house prisoners of war after World War II started.

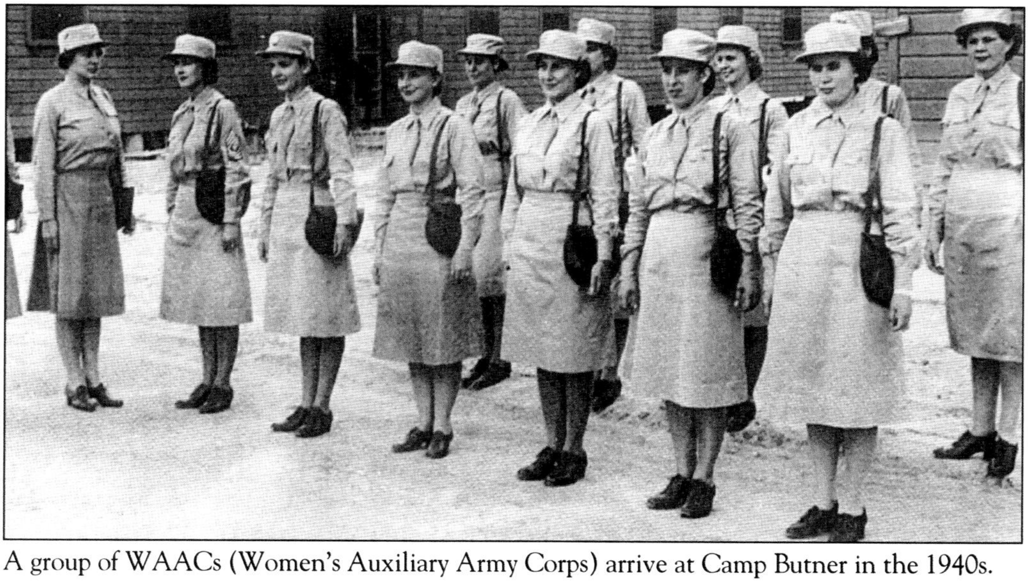

A group of WAACs (Women's Auxiliary Army Corps) arrive at Camp Butner in the 1940s.

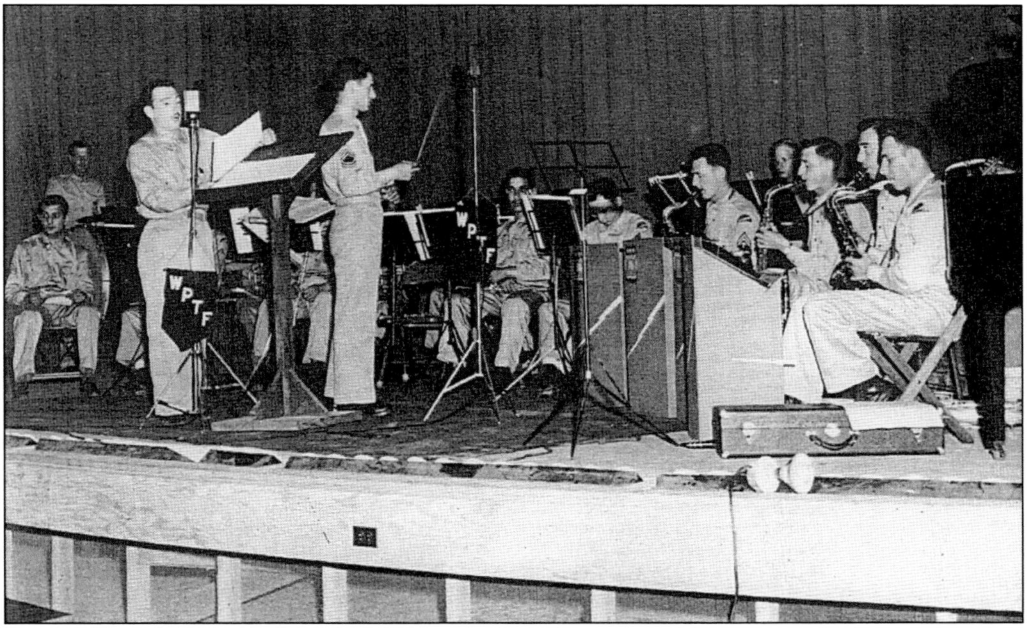

A group sings during Camp Butner's Radio Hour.

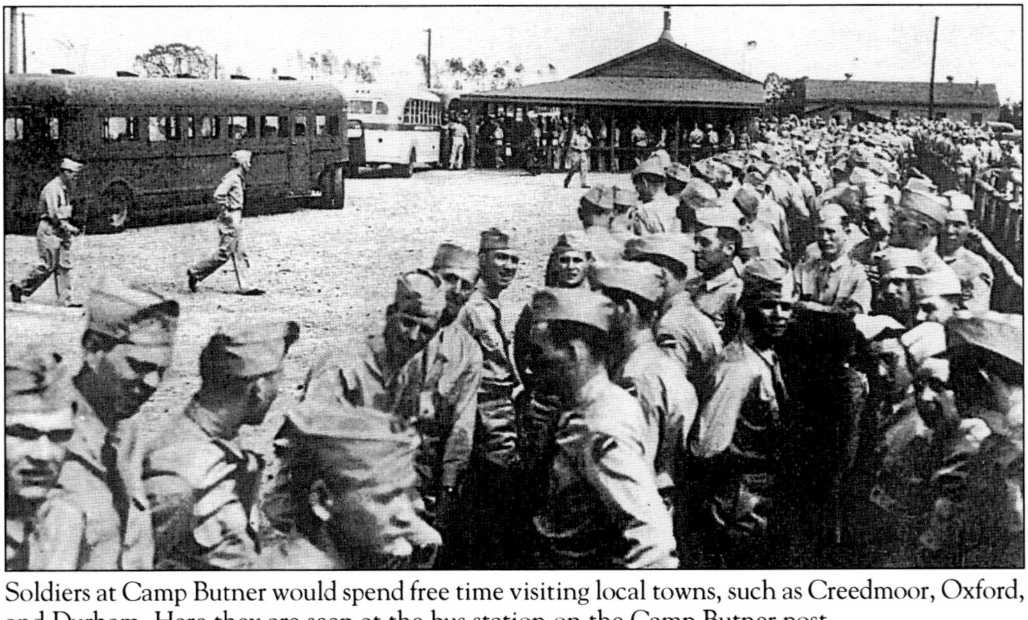
Soldiers at Camp Butner would spend free time visiting local towns, such as Creedmoor, Oxford, and Durham. Here they are seen at the bus station on the Camp Butner post.

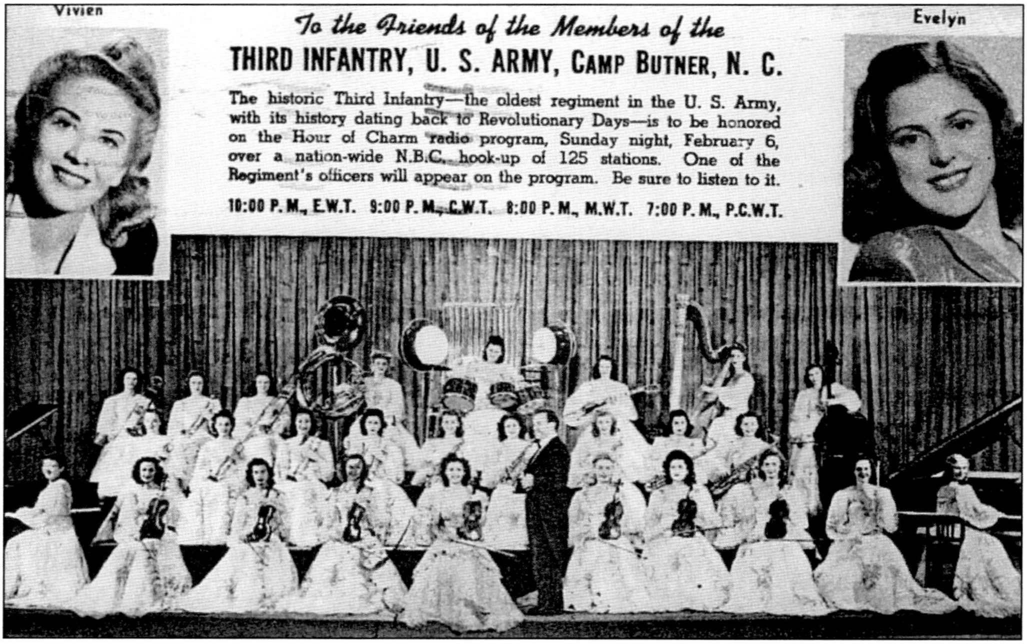

This is a postcard advertising the "Hour of Charm" radio program to soldiers at Camp Butner.

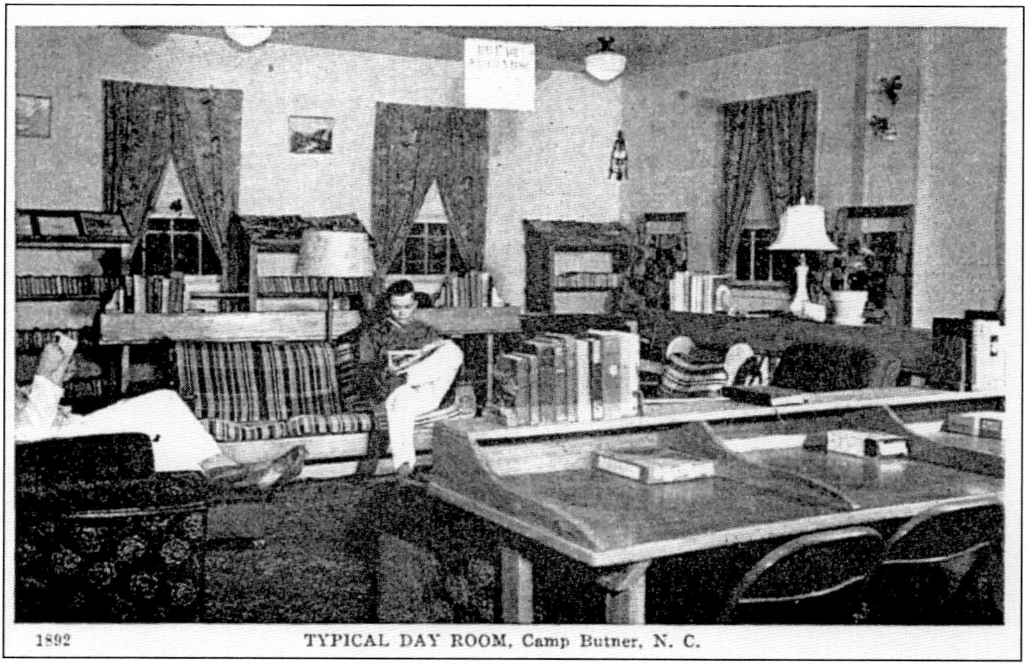

This photograph shows one of the lounge areas on the base at Camp Butner.

Four

Stovall and Bullock

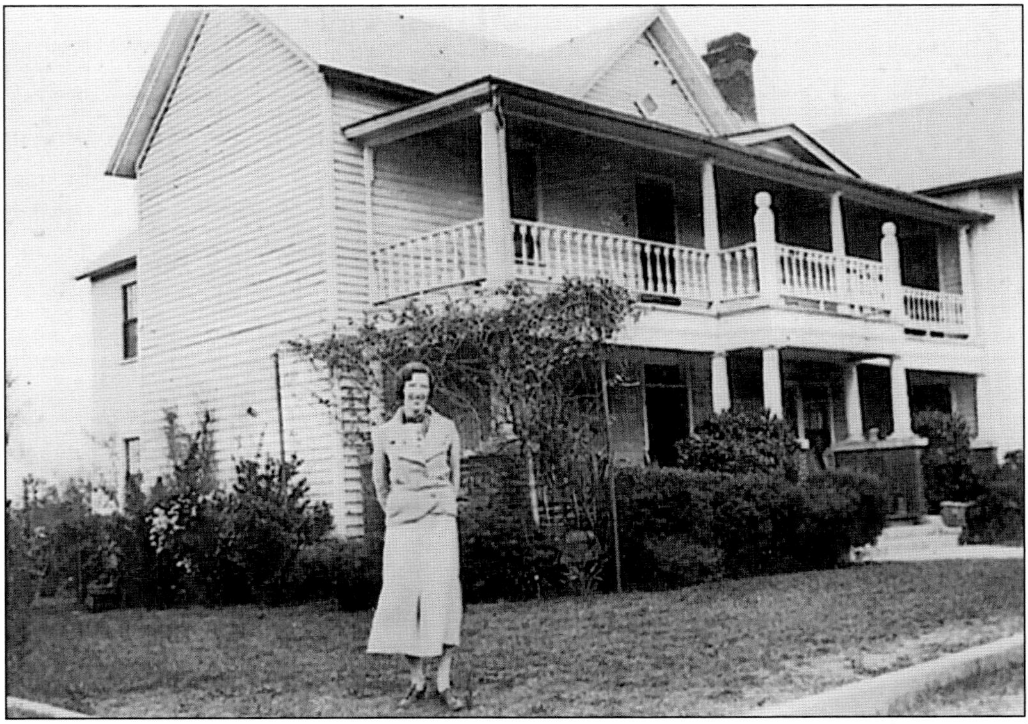

Rosa Lee Woodlief stands in front of the White Hotel in Stovall in 1934. (Courtesy of Nellie McFarland.)

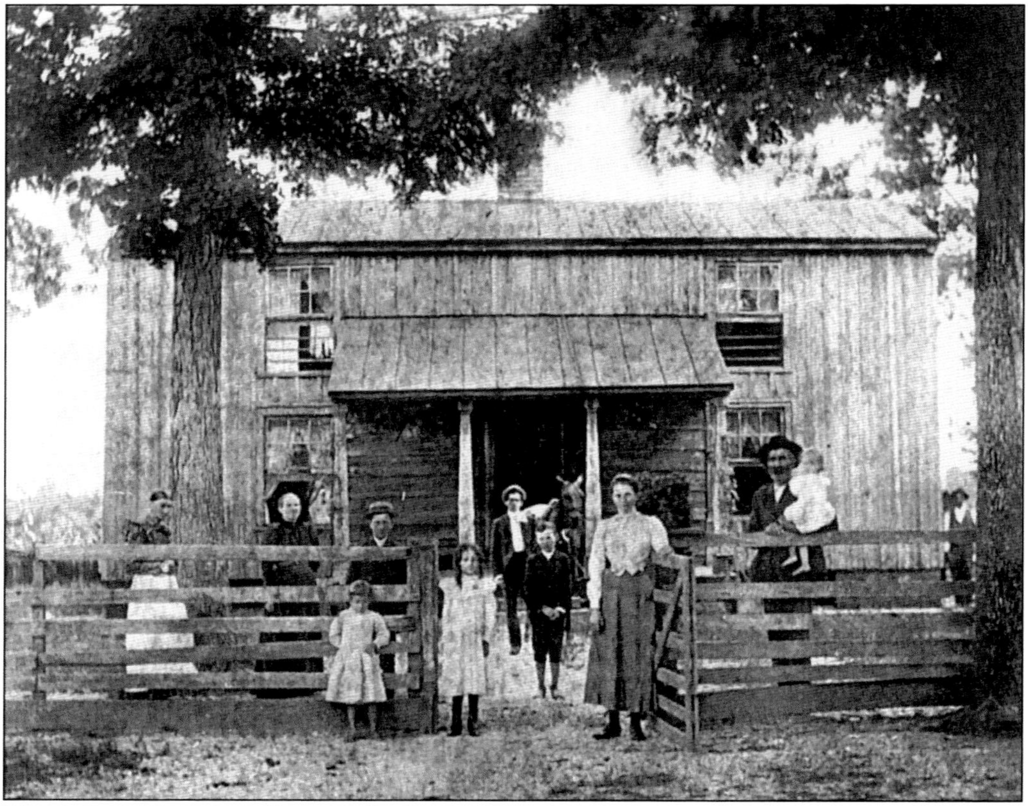

The Gill family of Stovall pauses for this picture taken in the 1890s. (Courtesy of Jean Gill.)

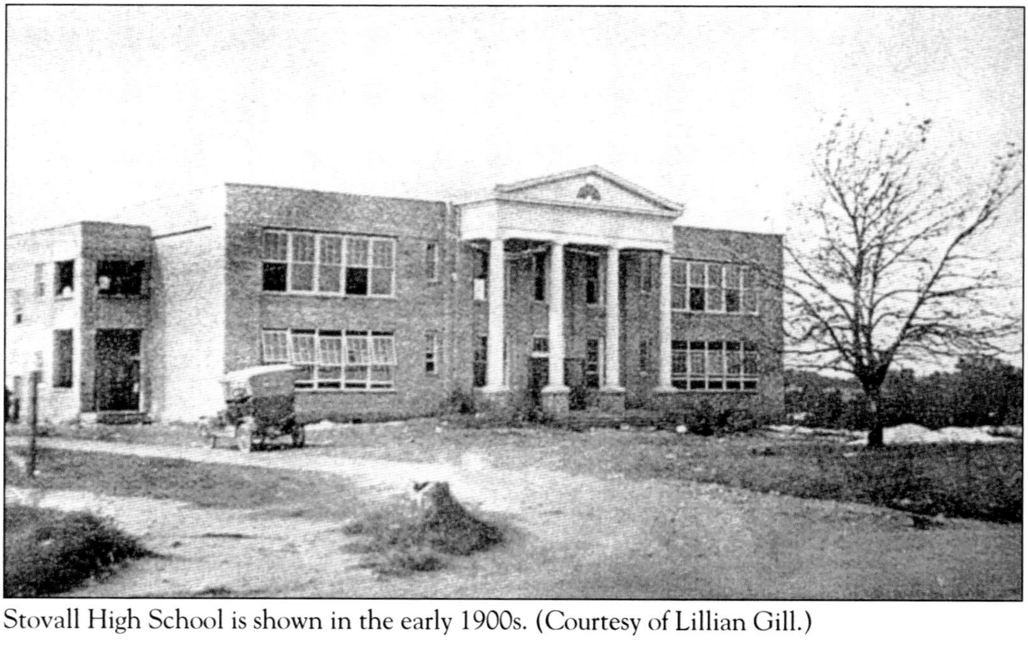

Stovall High School is shown in the early 1900s. (Courtesy of Lillian Gill.)

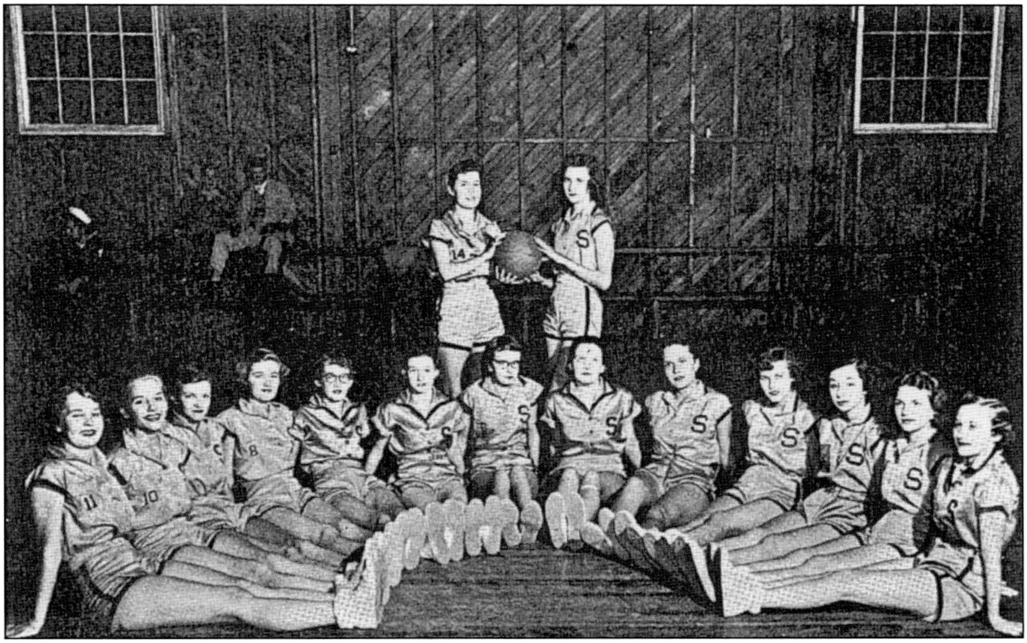

This is the 1955 Stovall High School girls basketball team.

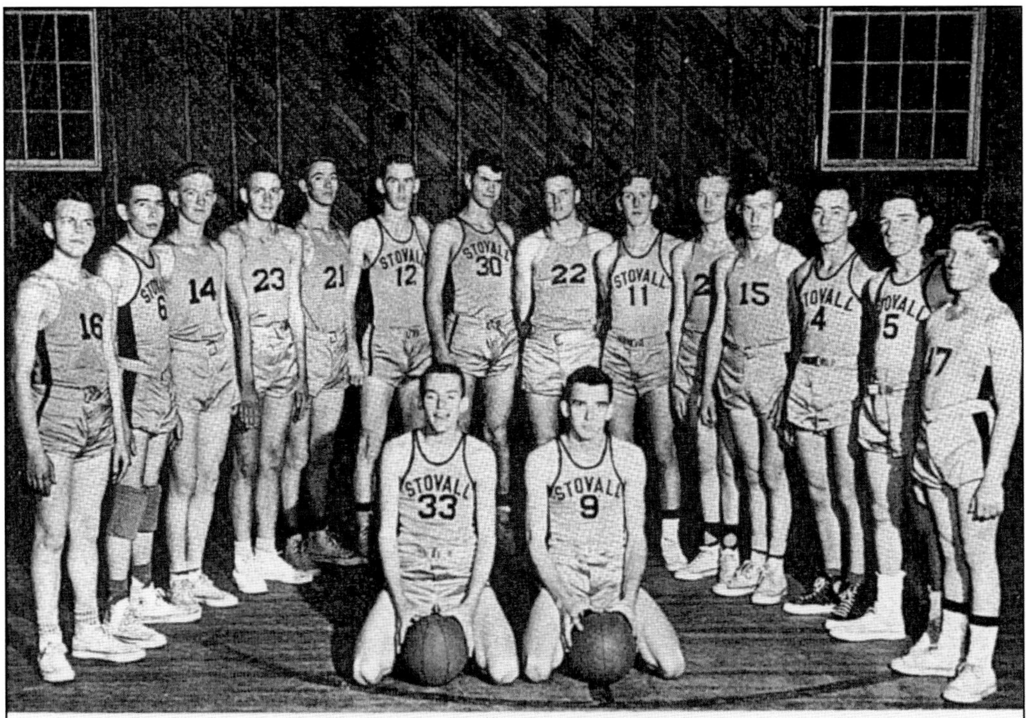

This is the 1955 Stovall High School boys basketball team.

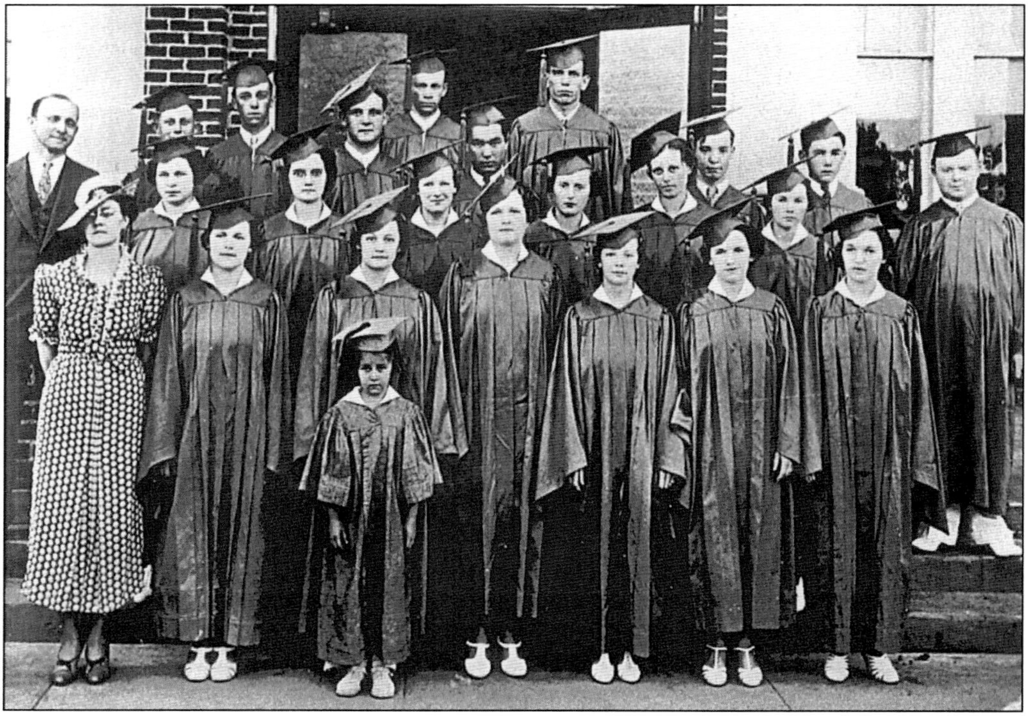

Graduates of Stovall High School in 1936 were, from left to right (front row) Betty Thorpe, Betty Knott, Lillian Hicks, Rebecca Shanks, Kathleen Royster, Adele Blackwell, Madeline Lee, and Blanche Stovall; (second row) Lucille Pittard, Minnie Currin, Elizabeth Campbell, Mary Cottrell, Allene Carey, and Alma Eakes; (third row) E.R.Perry, William Pittard, George Wood, Charles Barker, Frank Eakes,Bernard Munn, Horace Campbell, Charlie Wilson, Gordon Stovall, and Robert Noblin. (Courtesy of Lillian Gill..)

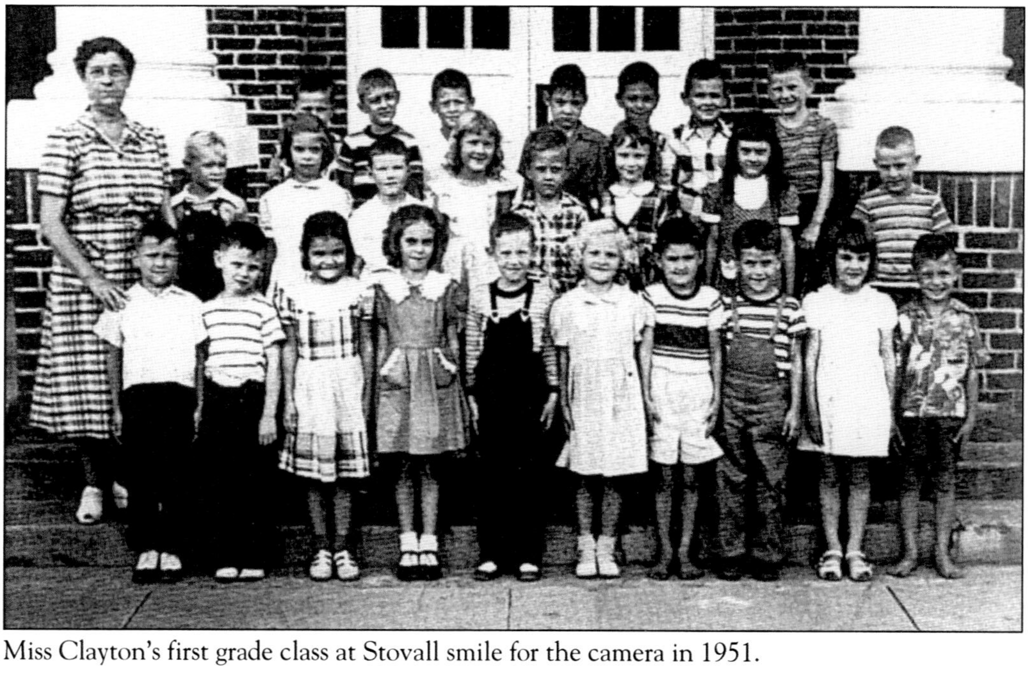

Miss Clayton's first grade class at Stovall smile for the camera in 1951.

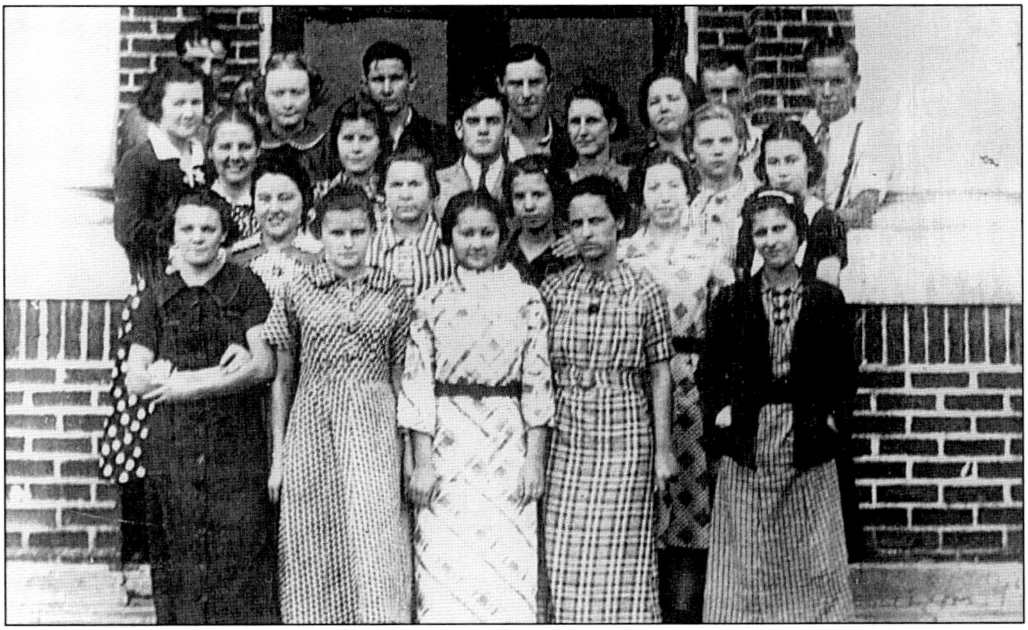

The Stovall High School Class of 1937 is pictured, from left to right (first row) Helen Faucette, Page Knott, Alice Munn, Willie Mae Shotwell, and Ruby Shotwell; (second row) Eula Hockett, Mary Wilson, Hazel Overby, Linville Royster, and Doris Satterwhite; (third row) Nell Harris, Nellie Cottrell, Elvis Cole, Myrtle Critcher, and Jo Daniel; (fourth row) Mary Frances Cutts, Franklin Gill, Juanita O'Brien, Frank Strong, Roy Barker, Alice Raynor, John Hart, and Alexander Green (Courtesy of Lillian Gill.)

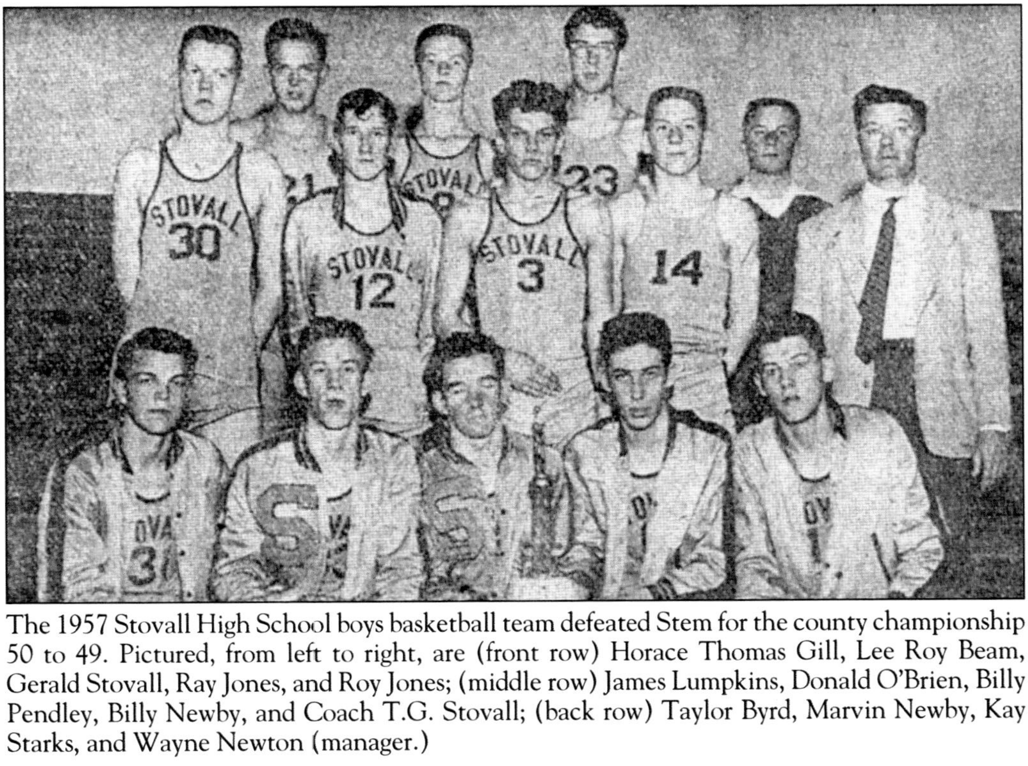

The 1957 Stovall High School boys basketball team defeated Stem for the county championship 50 to 49. Pictured, from left to right, are (front row) Horace Thomas Gill, Lee Roy Beam, Gerald Stovall, Ray Jones, and Roy Jones; (middle row) James Lumpkins, Donald O'Brien, Billy Pendley, Billy Newby, and Coach T.G. Stovall; (back row) Taylor Byrd, Marvin Newby, Kay Starks, and Wayne Newton (manager.)

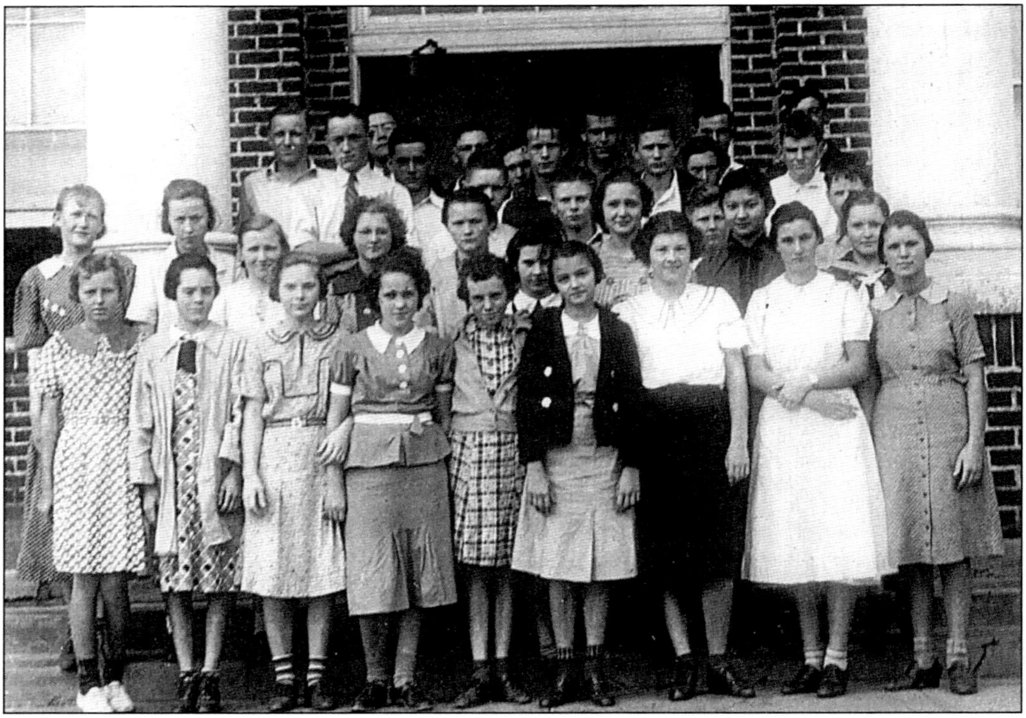

This is the freshmen class of 1936 at Stovall High School. (Courtesy of Emmy Lou Woody Day.)

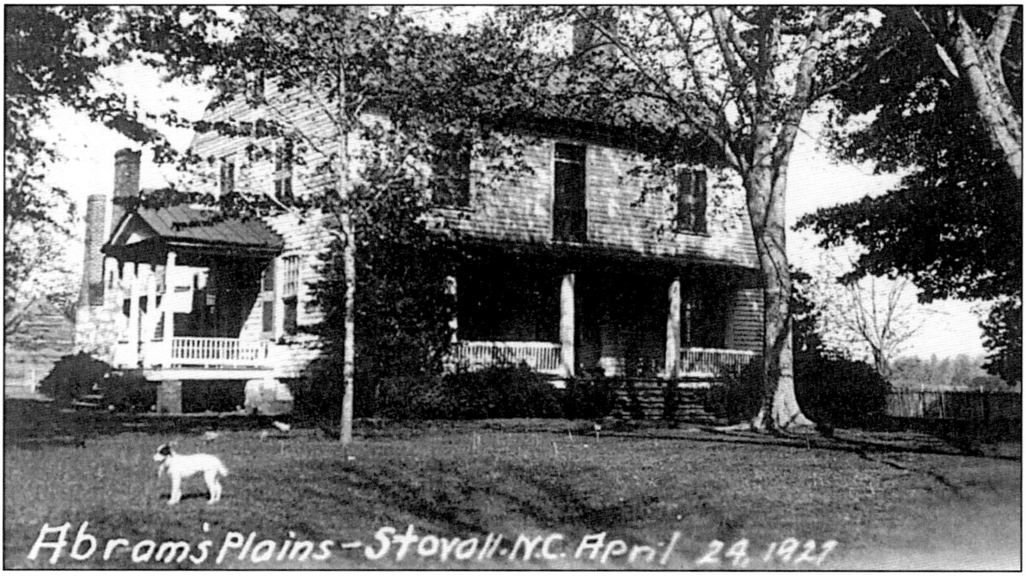

Abram's Plains is located in Stovall; part of this house dates to 1770 and the rest is from the 1830s. This picture was taken in 1927. (Courtesy of Barbara Davis.)

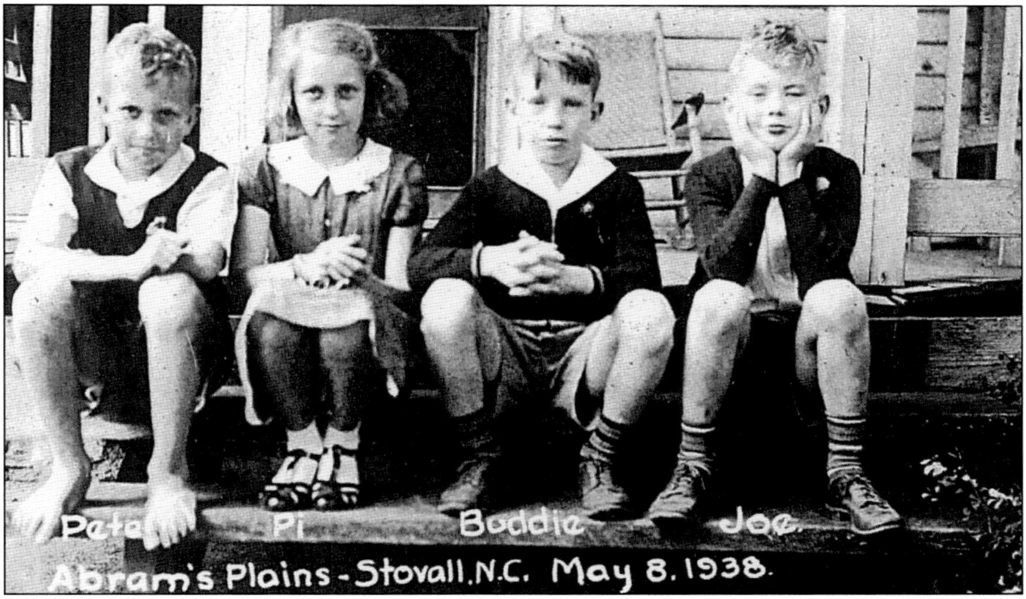

Pete, Pi, Buddie, and Joe take a break from their activities at Abram's Plains in 1938. (Courtesy of Barbara Davis.)

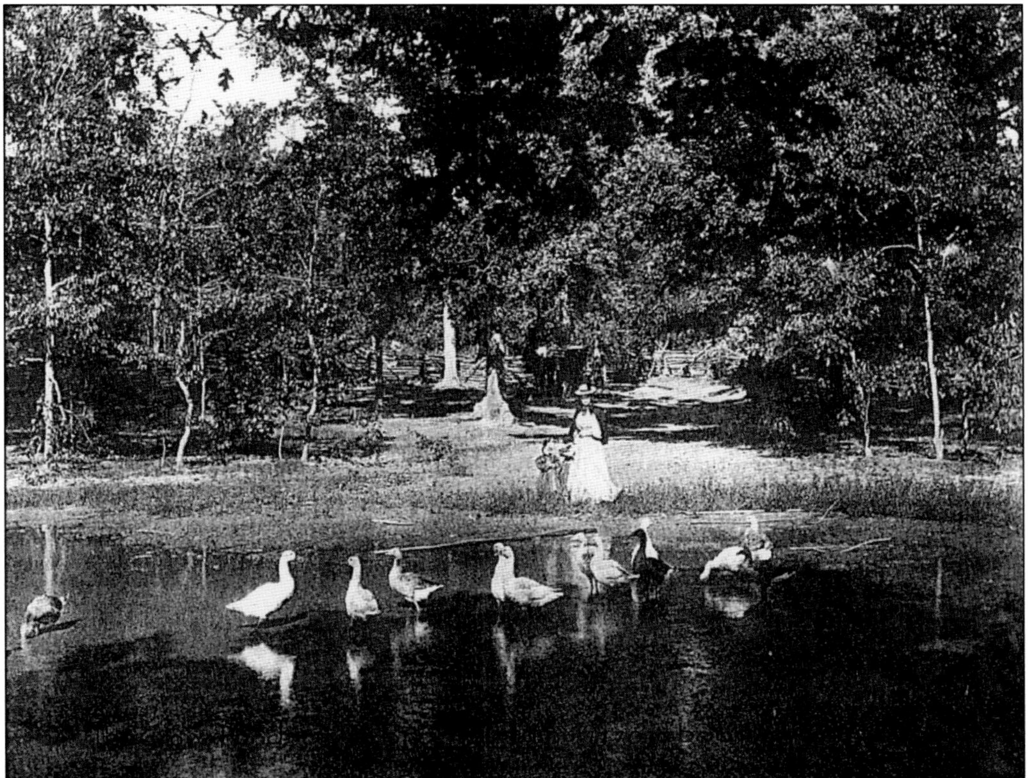

A lady and small child enjoy watching the ducks play at the Grove Pond on the grounds of Abram's Plains in 1896. (Courtesy of Barbara Davis.)

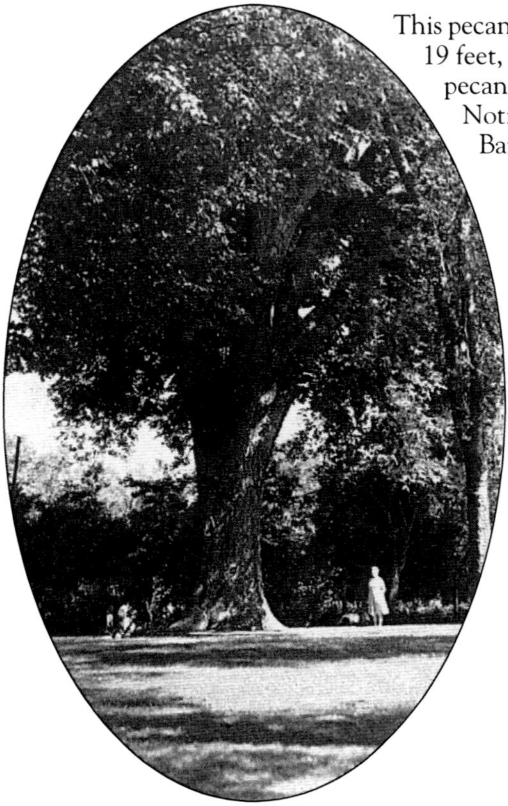

This pecan tree on the grounds of Abram's Plains measured 19 feet, 6 inches in diameter. In 1963, it was the largest pecan tree on the eastern coast of the United States. Notice the lady standing nearby. (Courtesy of Barbara Davis.)

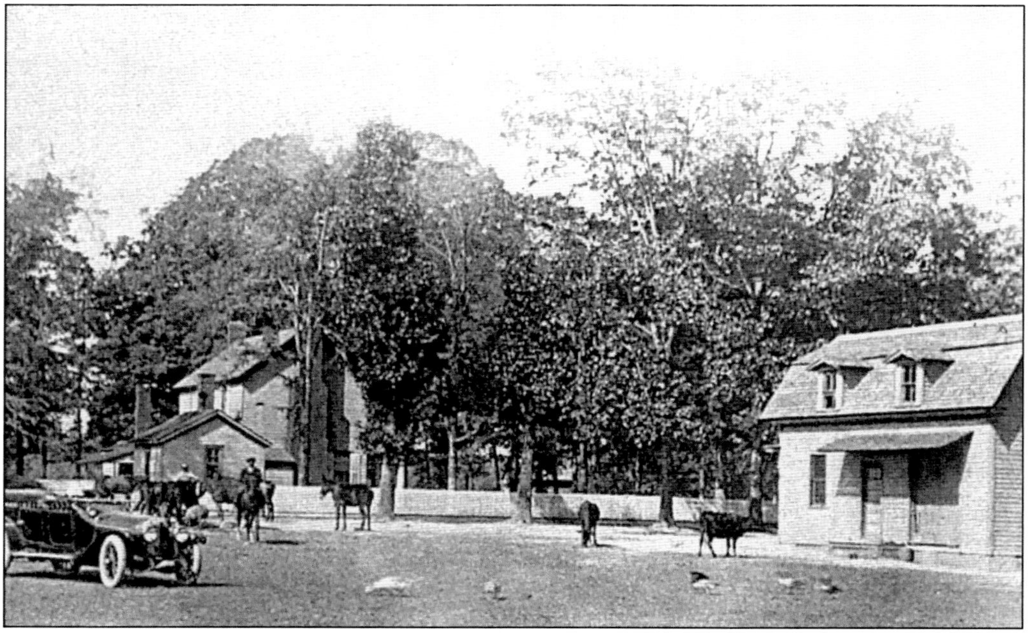

This is a picture from the Gregory Farm in Stovall in the 1920s. Today, this farm consists of 4,000 acres, including a two-mile, paved driveway to the original Gregory house, which dates to the 1830s. The house and grounds were known as the Hill Airy Plantation. Herbert Gregory Jr. currently owns Gregory Farm. (Courtesy of Herbert Gregory Jr.)

William Gregory is shown inside his store on the Gregory Farm in the early 1900s. Gregory and his brother, Francis, introduced flue-cured tobacco to Canada. William always wanted to be a country merchant, so he opened a store on his farm and gave his customers gifts when they visited, as he was a very wealthy man. (Courtesy of Herbert Gregory Jr.)

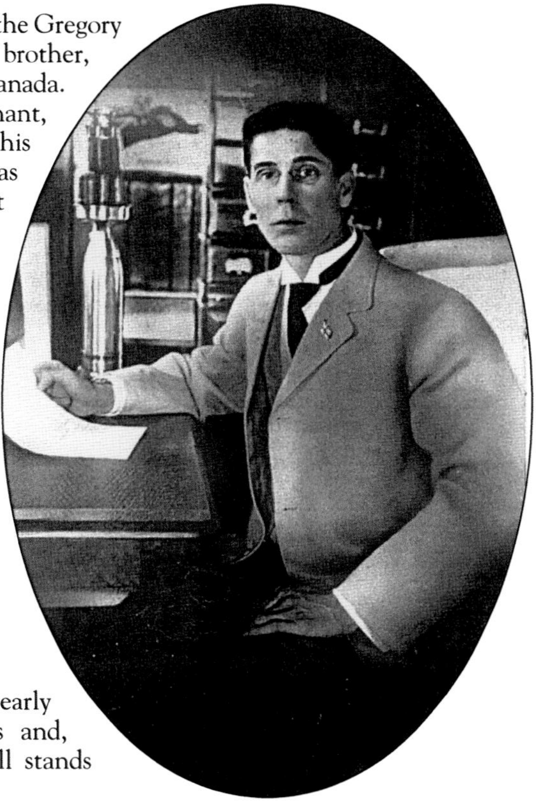

The Gregory Mill in Stovall is seen in the early 1900s. This mill was built in the 1830s and, although it is no longer operational, it still stands today. (Courtesy of Herbert Gregory Jr..)

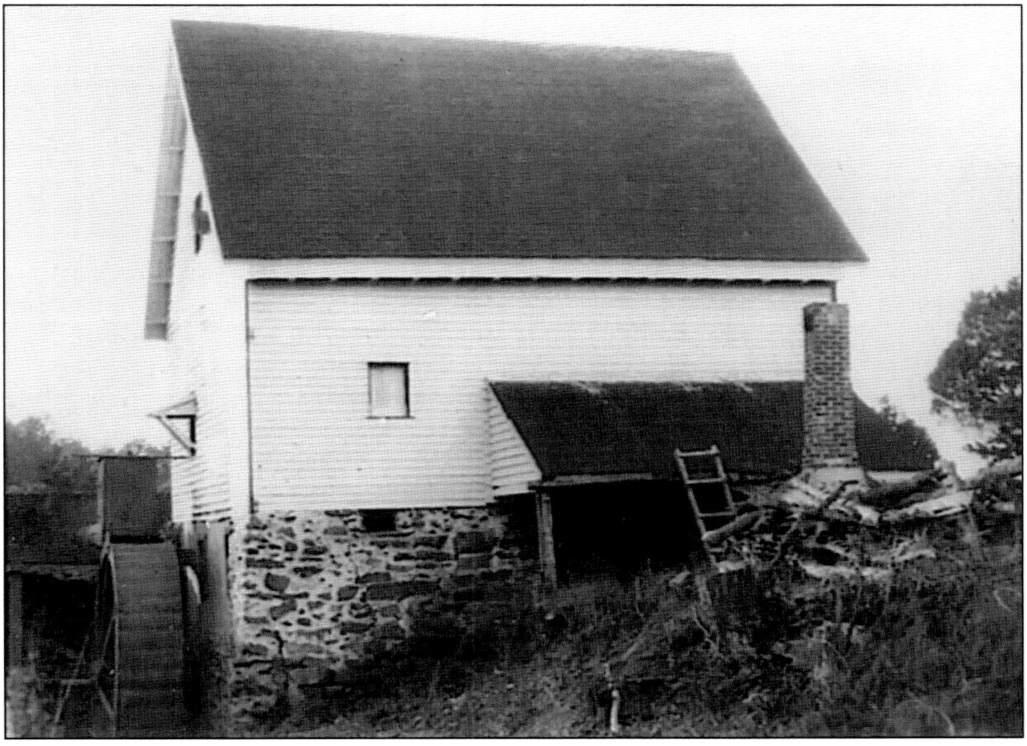

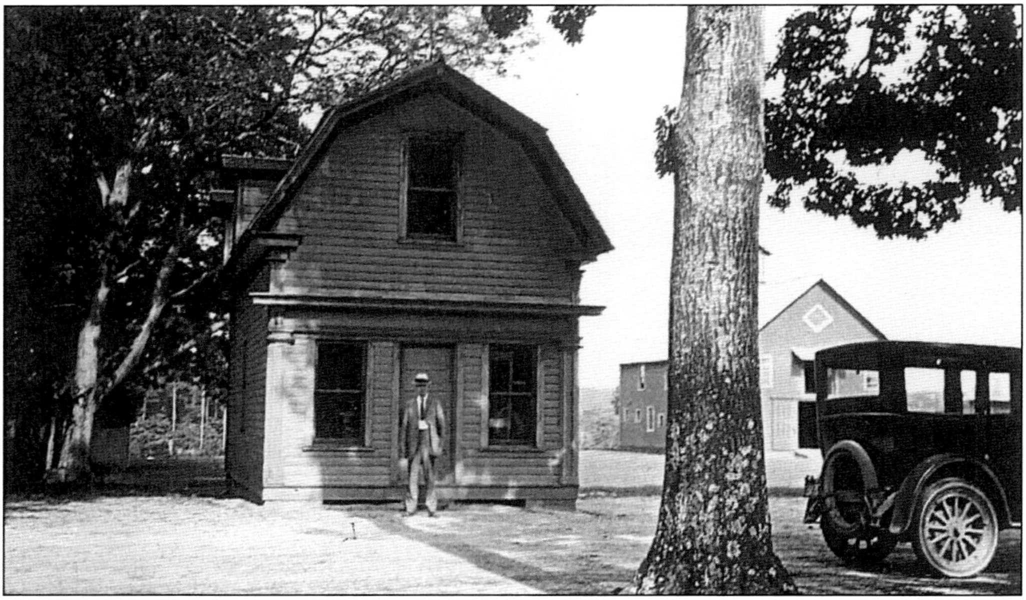

This is the Gregory Store in the 1920s. (Courtesy of Herbert Gregory Jr.)

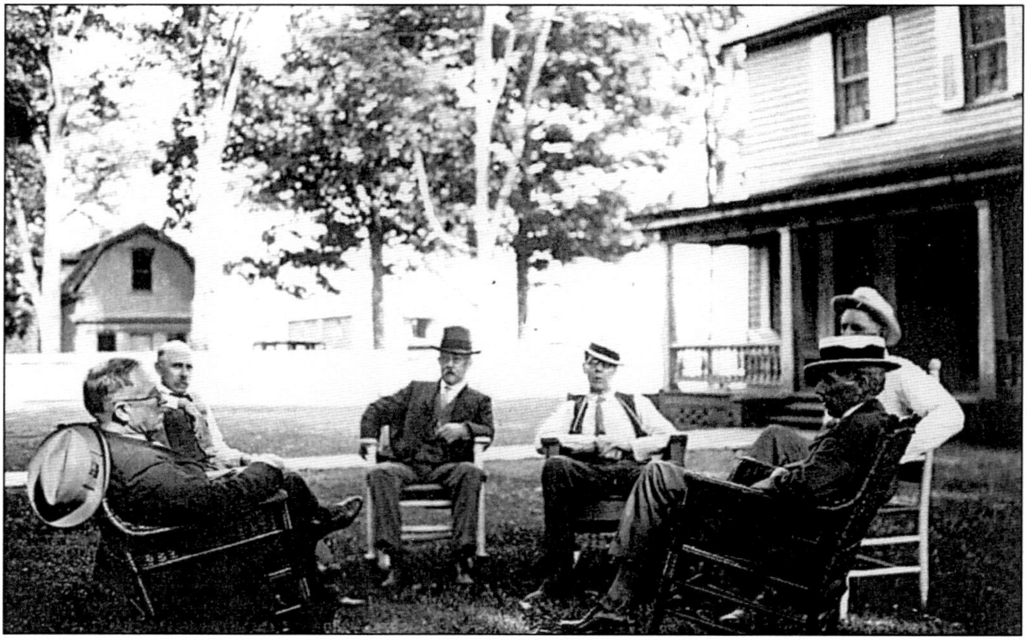

Men at Hill Airy Plantation (Gregory Farm) relax in the shade for some good conversation. (Courtesy of Herbert Gregory Jr.)

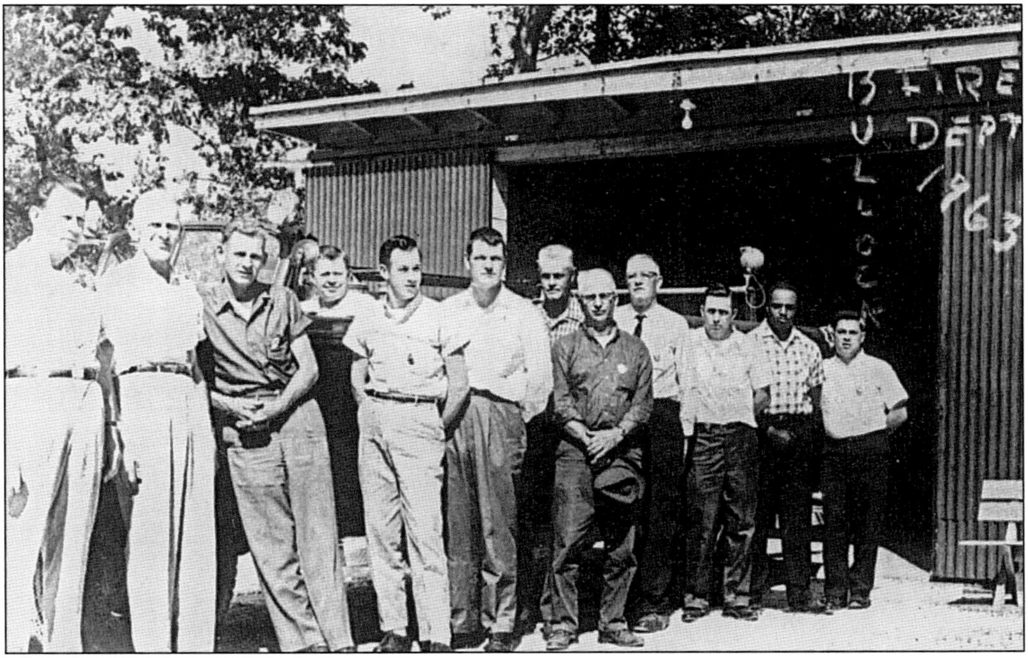

The Bullock Fire Department is pictured in 1963. From left to right are Clifton Capps, fire chief H.P. Pittard, Hammit Cash, Jimmy Capps, assistant chief Bob Hyler (at the wheel), Henry Tilley, Oliver Davis, Irwin Gooch, H.B. Tilley, Sonny Williams, Jesse Marrow, and G.F. Rickenbaker (chaplain). (Courtesy of Lillian Gill.)

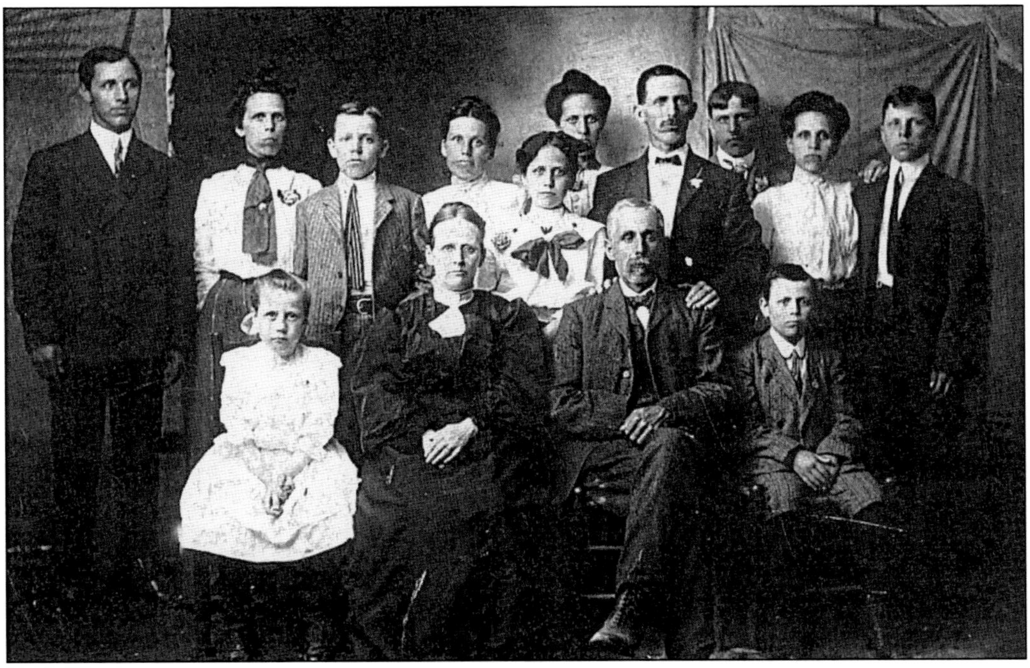

The Hicks family of Bullock gathers for a family photograph in 1902. Pictured, from left to right are (front row) Dorothy Hicks, Virginia Hicks, Benjamin Hicks, and Brodus Hicks; (second row) Buck Hicks, Kitty Hicks, Benny Hicks, Lottie Royster, Grace Shotwell, Mamie Campbell, Jim Hicks, Morgan Hicks, Lora Royster, and Horace Hicks. (Courtesy of Lillian Gill.)

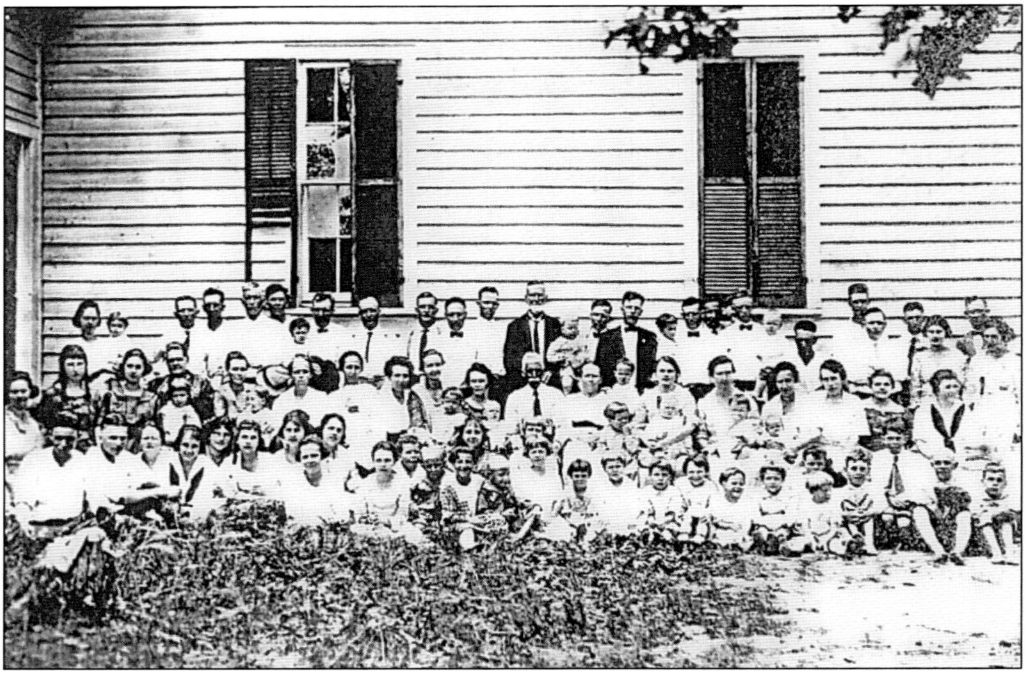

The Hicks family holds a reunion at the Bullock Baptist Church in 1920. (Courtesy of Lillian Gill.)

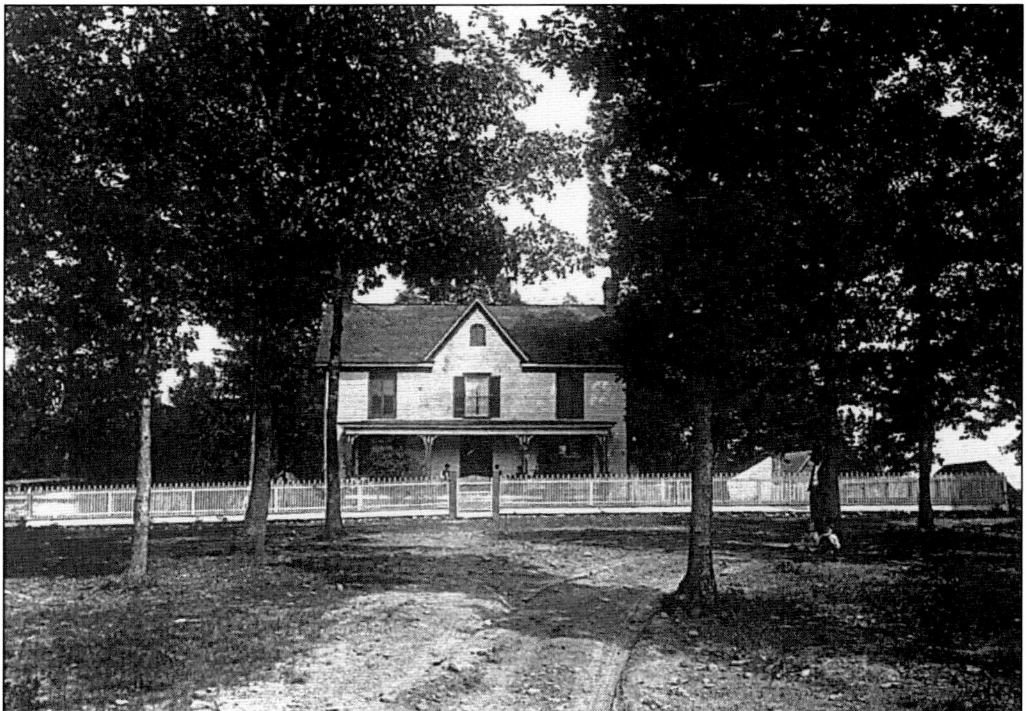

Buckhorn Mineral Water Spring was discovered at the Hicks farm in Bullock, shown here in 1904. This mineral water was bottled and sold throughout the United States and overseas and was known for its positive effect on people's health. (Courtesy of Lillian Hicks.)

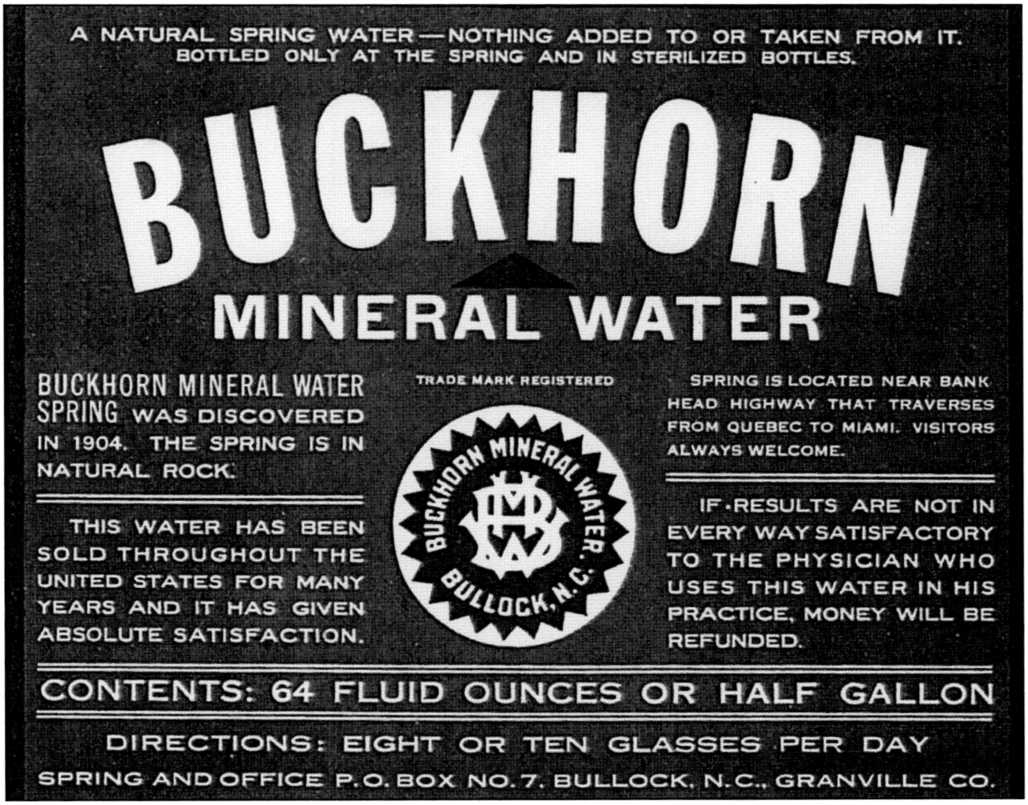

This is one of the labels used on bottles of Buckhorn Mineral Water.

East Douglas, Mass., Sept. 3, 1906.

Buckhorn Lithia Water Company:

Gentlemen—I have everything good to say of your water. My case is one of stomach trouble of long standing, nervous dyspepsia and rheumatism.

I was in the South last winter, and while at Savannah, Ga., I saw in a store several bottles of your spring water standing on the counter. Inquiry led me to try one bottle. It has brought a great change to my whole body. I feel much as I did at the age of twenty-five. I am now sixty-seven. The old machine is good yet and with the aid of Buckhorn Water, I think I am well able to return to business again, which I was compelled to abandon two years ago by reason of stomach trouble, rheumatism and uric acid. These troubles have nearly disappeared, my head is clear and mind natural and active. I cannot say too much in favor of the water, and will do all in my power to enhance the sales.

Very cordially yours,

Dr. C. Houghton.

Dr. Houghton writes quite a glowing report of his thoughts on Buckhorn Mineral Water. He says that he feels as though he was 25 instead of 67 years old and that the "old machine" is good yet. The letter is dated 1906. (Courtesy of Lillian Gill.)

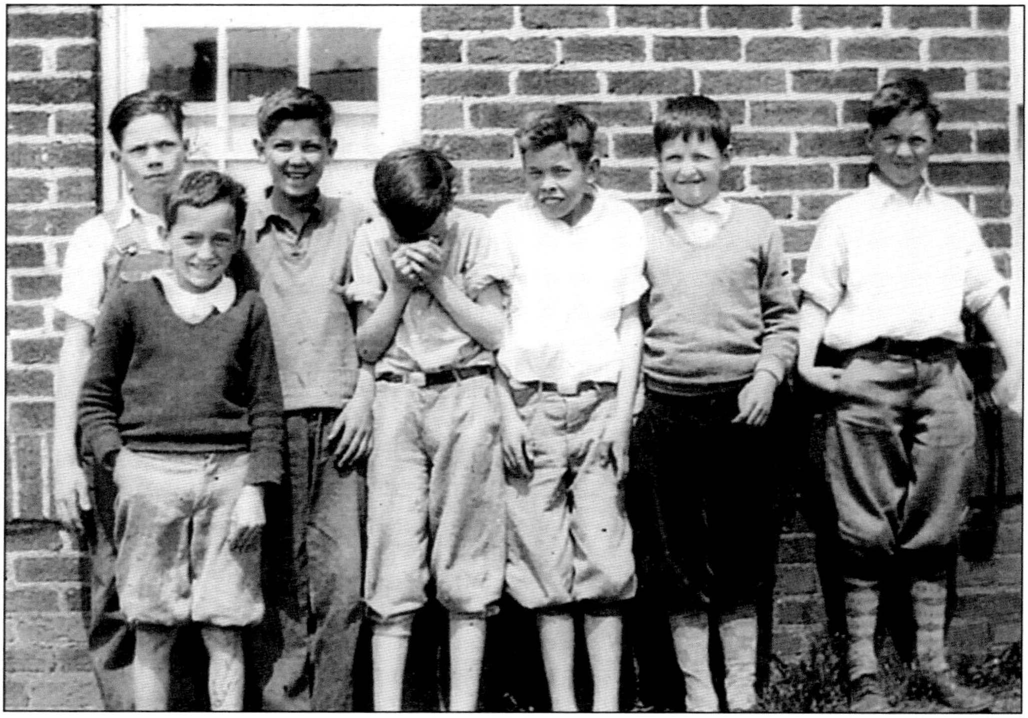

These boys appear to be having a good time at Stovall School in 1934. (Courtesy of Nellie McFarland.)

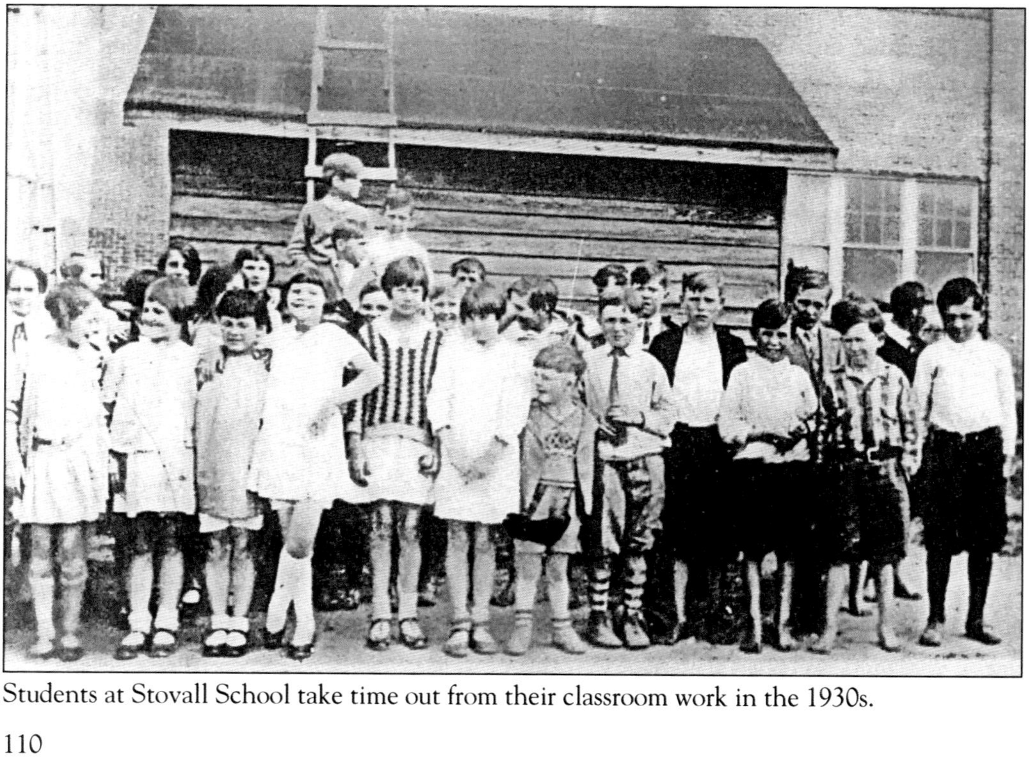

Students at Stovall School take time out from their classroom work in the 1930s.

Five

Communities of Granville

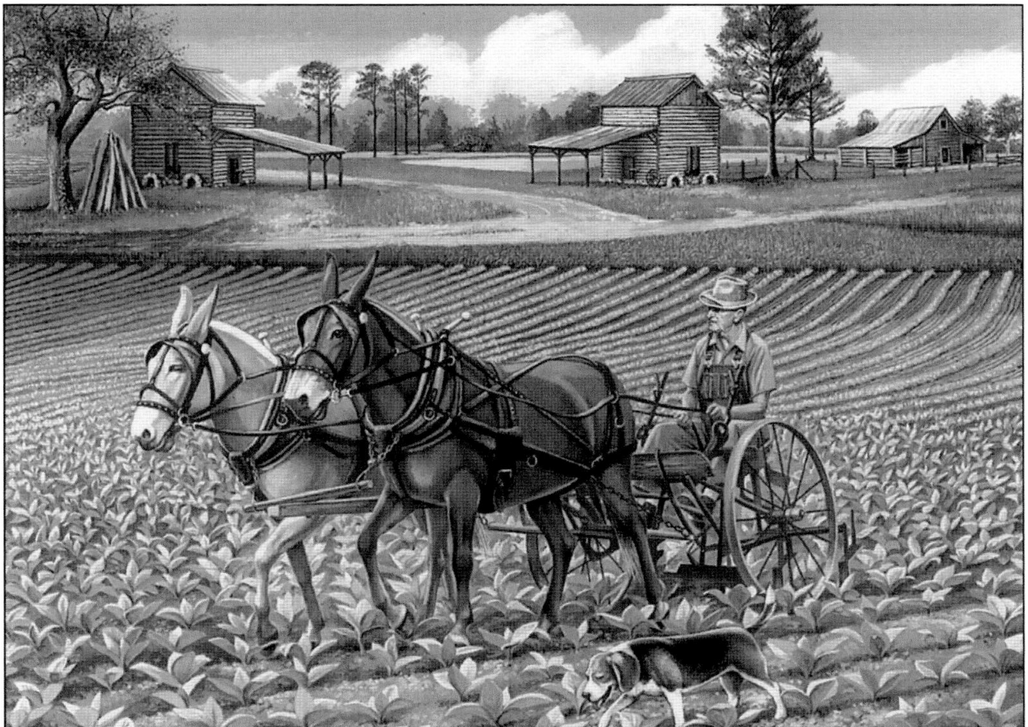

Hugh Ragland is shown plowing tobacco on his farm in Oxford. This portrait was done by Ronald Ragland, Hugh's son. Ronald has completed other country scenes similar to this one, which can be viewed at his website, beagleart.com. (Courtesy of Ronald Ragland.)

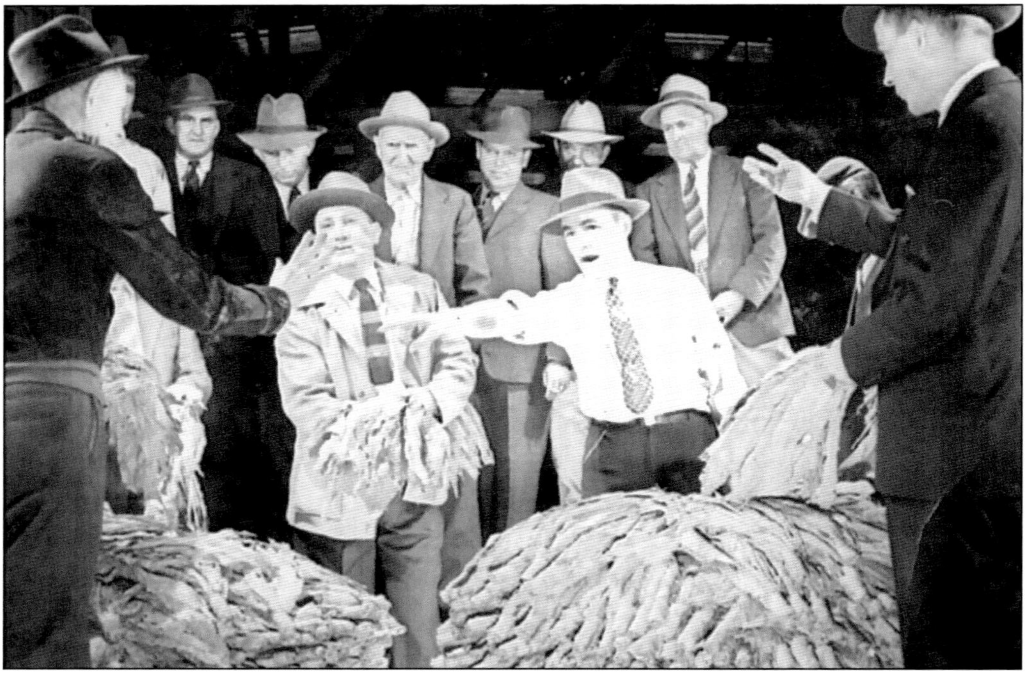

A tobacco auction takes place inside Johnson Warehouse in Oxford in the early 1950s. Among those pictured are Chandler Watkins, Sid Cutts, Jimmy Thomas, Claude Allen, and Leon O'Brian. (Courtesy of Bobby Blackwell.)

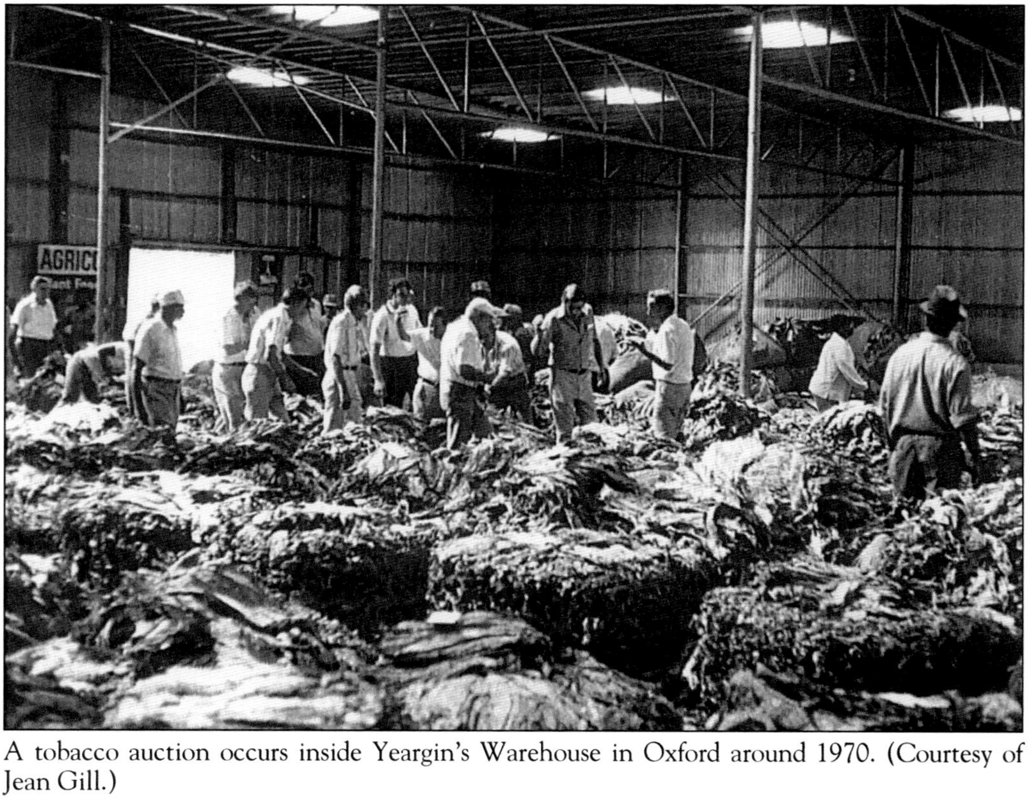

A tobacco auction occurs inside Yeargin's Warehouse in Oxford around 1970. (Courtesy of Jean Gill.)

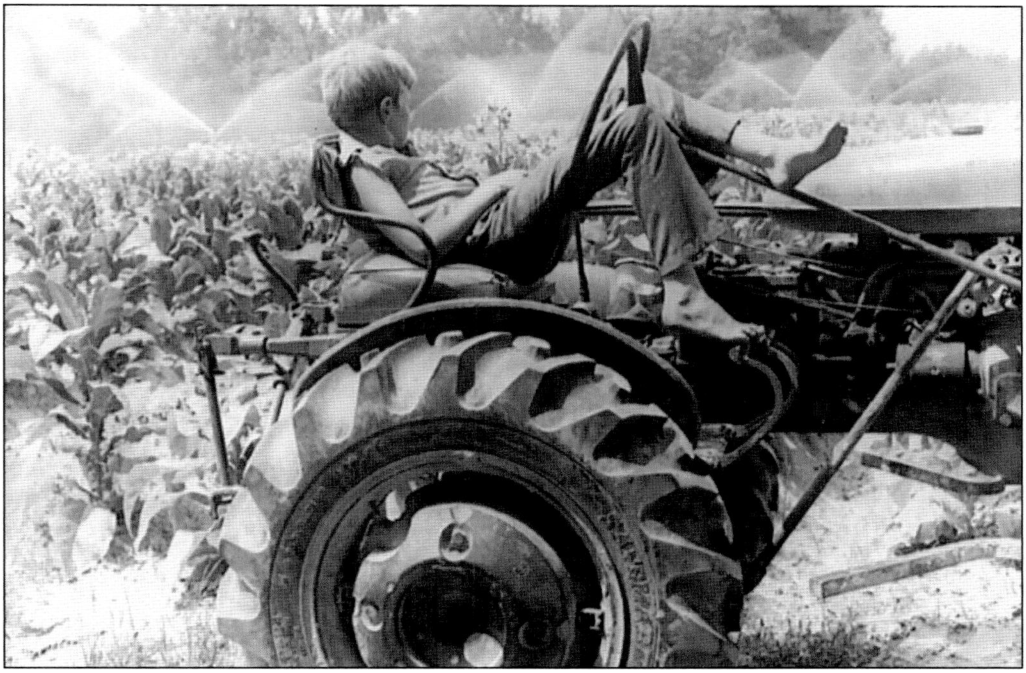

A little boy is watching his father's field of tobacco being irrigated as he relaxes on the tractor. Tobacco farmers are at the mercy of nature: too little rain or too much rain can ruin a crop that required a year's worth of toil to grow. (Courtesy of Harry Coleman.)

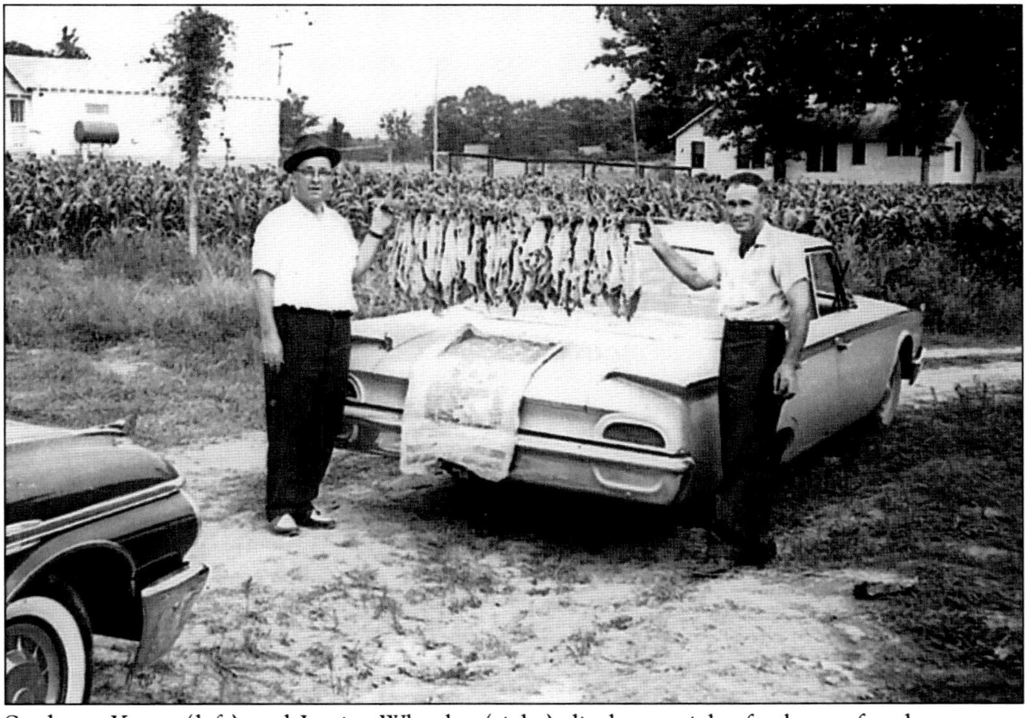

Stedman Knott (left) and Lucius Wheeler (right) display a stick of tobacco for the purpose of advertising fertilizer. This scene is from Providence in 1960. (Courtesy of Lucius and Rowena Wheeler.)

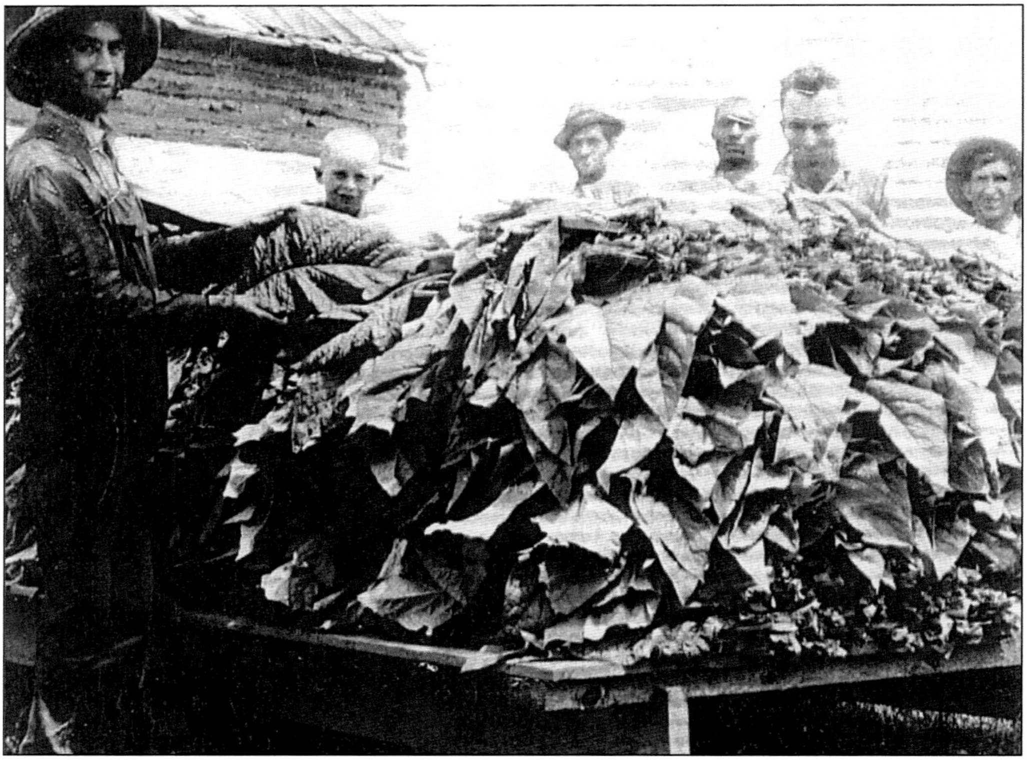

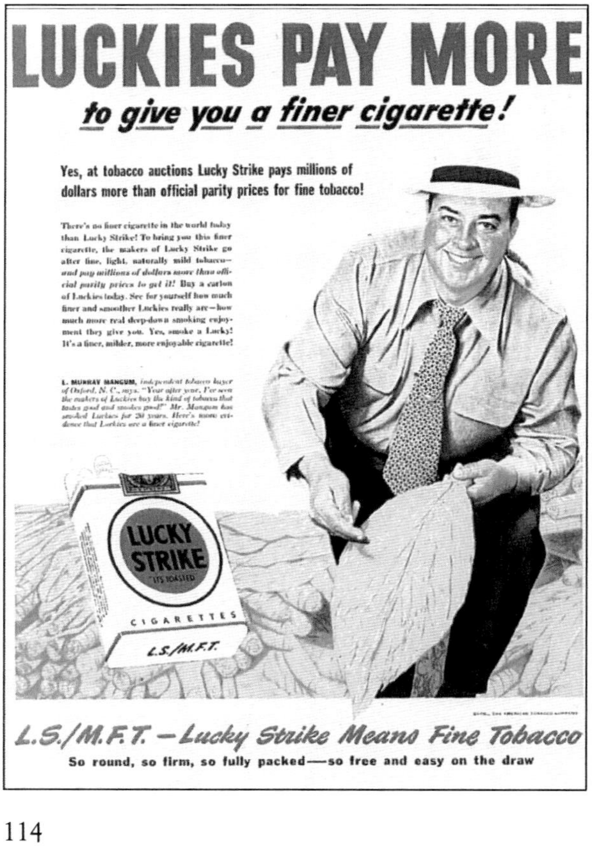

Dewey Averett proudly holds a leaf of his tobacco as he puffs on his cigarette. D.Y. Averett Jr. is the little boy and Gene Averett is on the right.

L. Murray Mangum of Oxford was chosen to make this advertisement for Lucky Strike cigarettes. Mr. Mangum had smoked Luckies for 20 years. The Lucky Strike slogan says "L.S.M.F.T—Lucky Strike Means Fine Tobacco—so round, so firm, so fully packed—so free and easy on the draw." (Courtesy of Josh Mangum.)

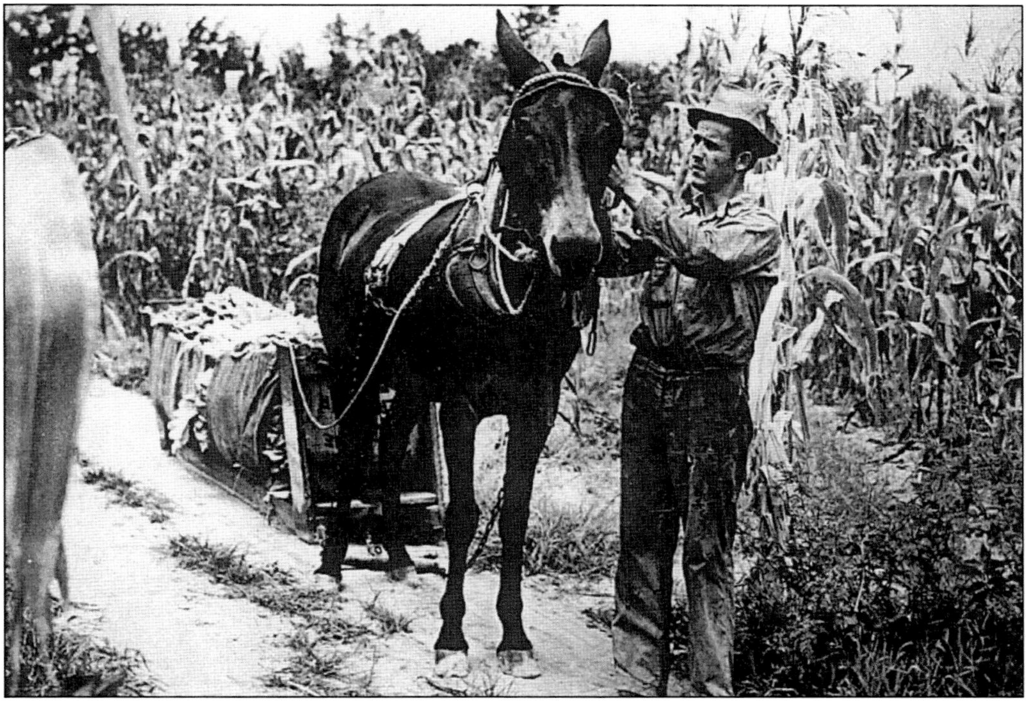

Wilbur Yeargin and his mule prepare to carry their load of tobacco to the barn area. Tall stalks of corn are in the background. (Courtesy of Jean Gill.)

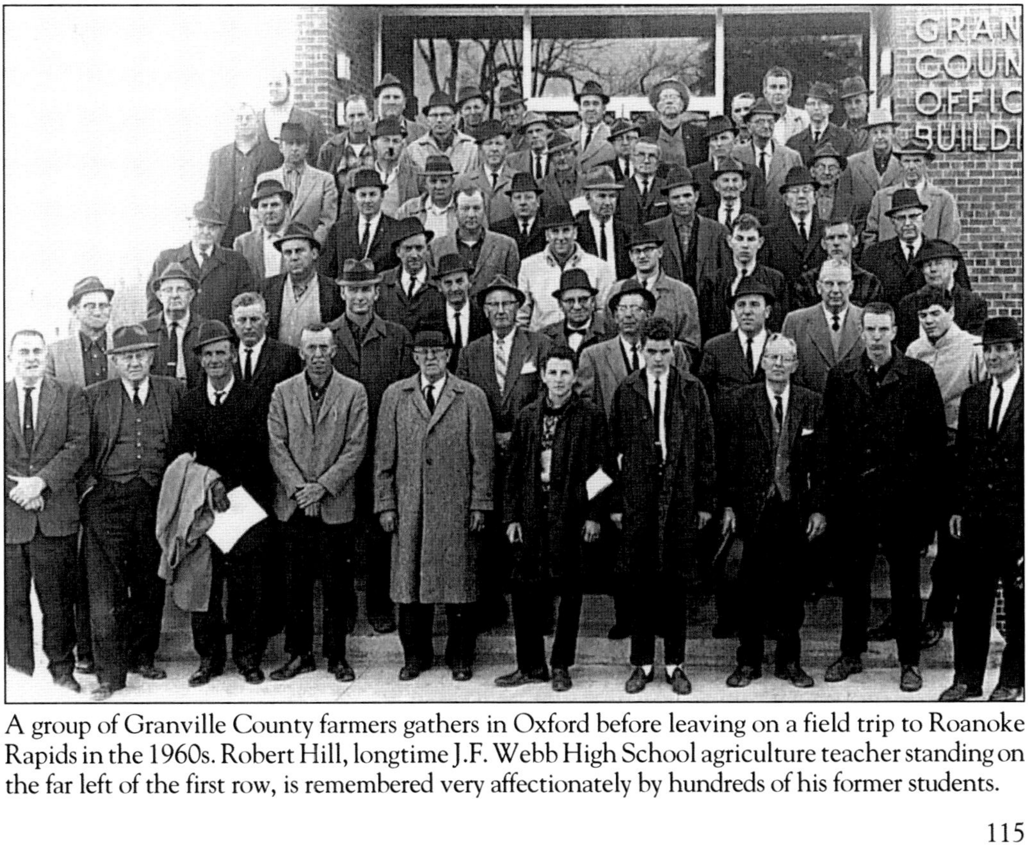

A group of Granville County farmers gathers in Oxford before leaving on a field trip to Roanoke Rapids in the 1960s. Robert Hill, longtime J.F. Webb High School agriculture teacher standing on the far left of the first row, is remembered very affectionately by hundreds of his former students.

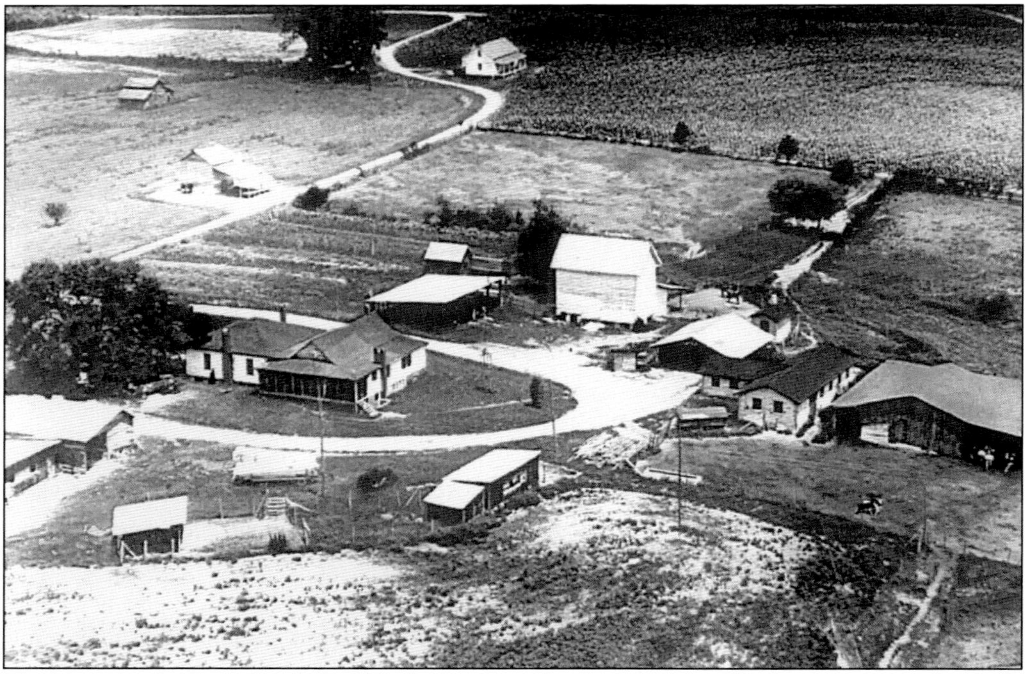

This is an aerial view of the Ralph Green farm in Creedmoor in 1955. C.W. Currin is the present owner of this farm. (Courtesy of Betty Chappell.)

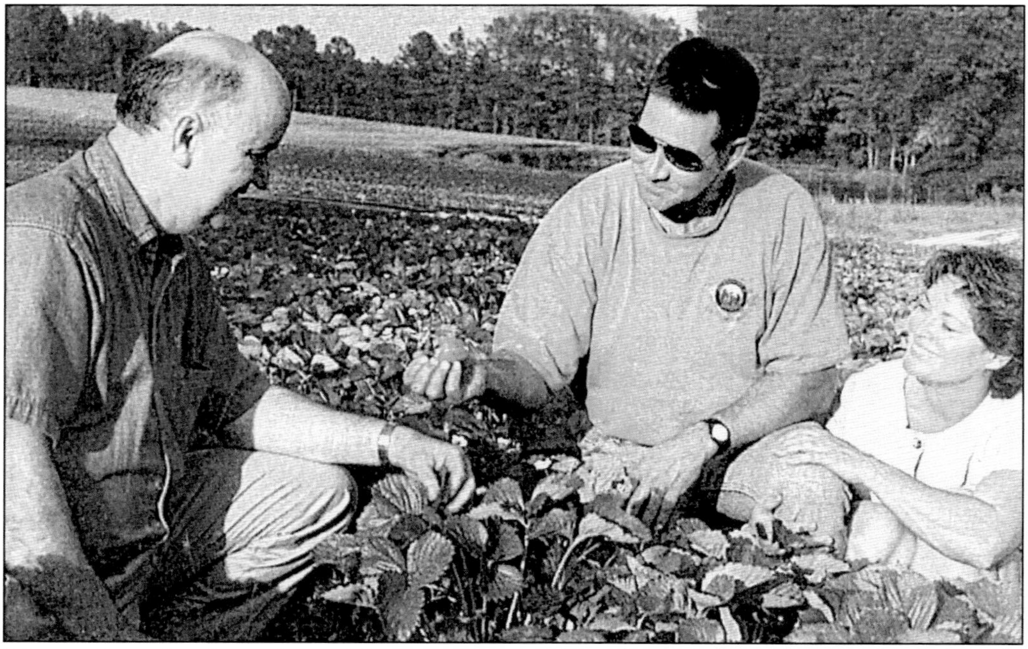

Wayne Goss, Southern States Manager, joins Mark and Rose Lyon at the Lyon Strawberry Farm in Creedmoor. Lyon Farm has been designated as a Century Farm, being owned by six generations of the same family. George Coley, Junnie Coley, Grace Coley Churchill, Alfred Lyon, Mark Lyon, and Coley Lyon are the six generations of Lyon Farm family members, dating to George Coley, born in 1828. Many area residents flock to the Lyon Farm each year for their great tasting strawberries. (Courtesy of Al and Josephine Lyon.)

Libby Clayton, on the left, pauses for a moment in the late 1930s at a corn shucking on the Clayton farm in Stem. (Courtesy of Margaret Moss Cooper.)

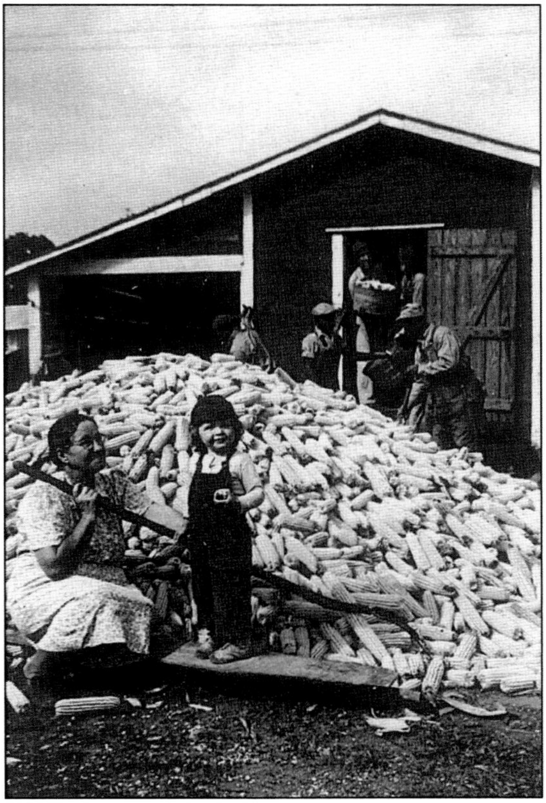

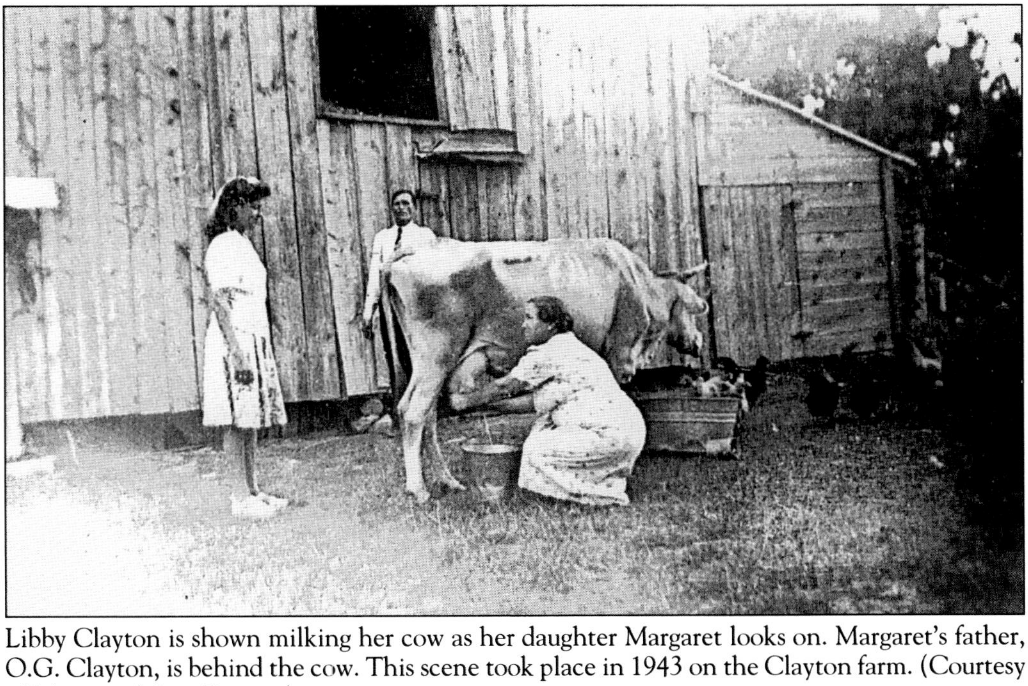

Libby Clayton is shown milking her cow as her daughter Margaret looks on. Margaret's father, O.G. Clayton, is behind the cow. This scene took place in 1943 on the Clayton farm. (Courtesy of Margaret Moss Cooper.)

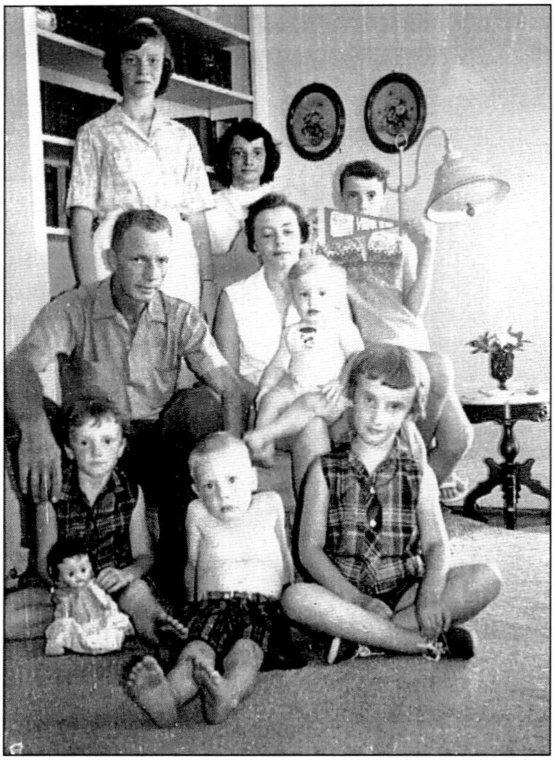

The Bowling family of Providence are all together for this picture taken in 1960. Pictured, from left to right, are (front row) Deborah, Lee, Phyllis; (middle row) O.L. Bowling Jr., Mary, Lewis (the author of this book); (back row) Martha, Dale, and Bonnie.

The Gooch family gathers for this picture taken in 1917. Pictured, from left to right, are (front row) Atlas Greene, Alva Greene, Zelma Gooch, Ollie Critcher, Eric Greene, Beatrice Gooch, Lucy Greene, Lucy Augustus Greene, and Edward Greene; (middle row) Gary Greene, Elmore Gooch, Elvin Critcher, Alise Critcher, Esther Critcher, Earl Greene, Eunice Greene, Lex Greene, and Edward Greene; (back row) Ella Gooch, Hattie Gooch, Ruth Gooch, Catherine Greene, Gussie Greene, Lallye Critcher, Albert Greene, Iola Gooch, and Stephen.

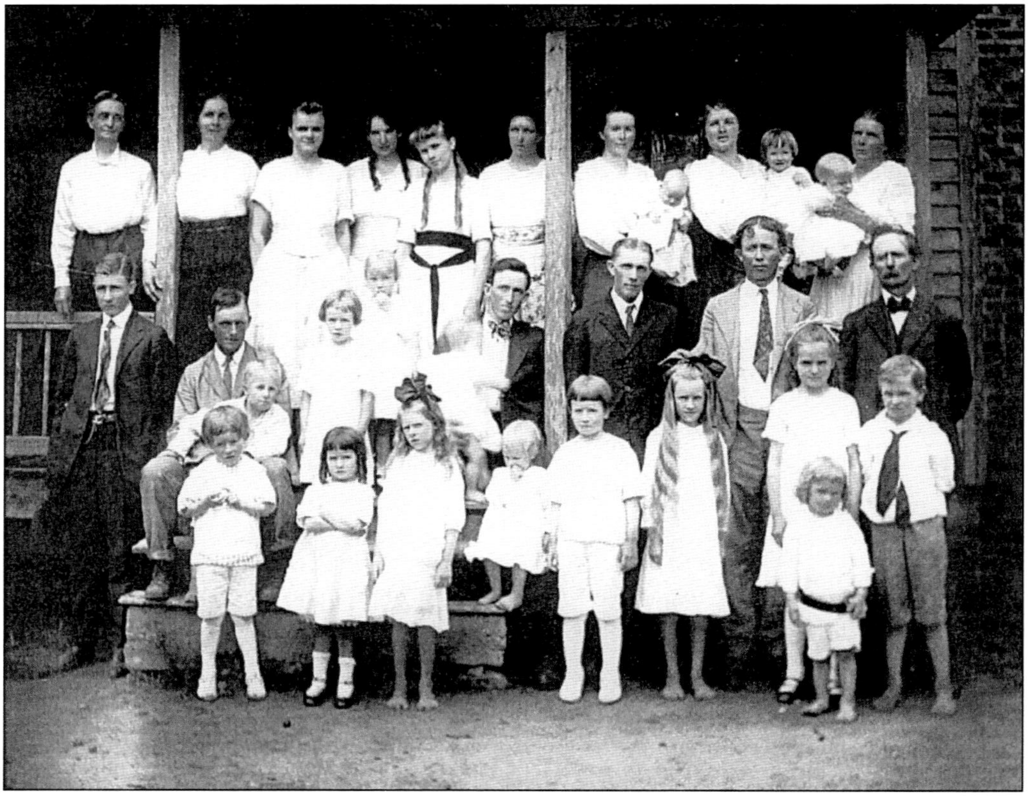

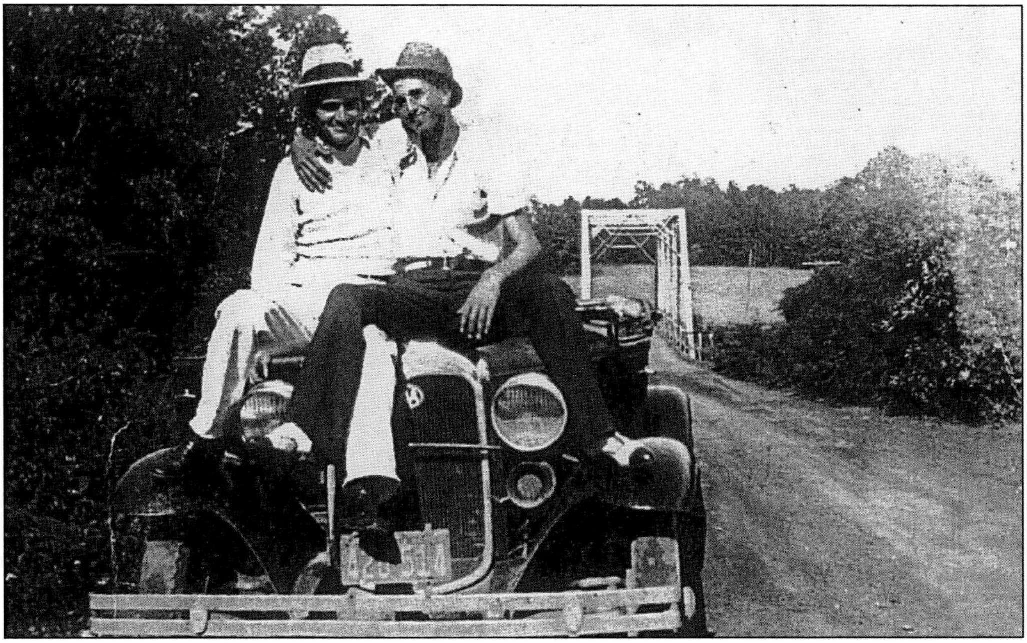

Harry Gold Wheeler (left) and an unidentified friend sit on top of their car in Providence. (Courtesy of Josh Mangum.)

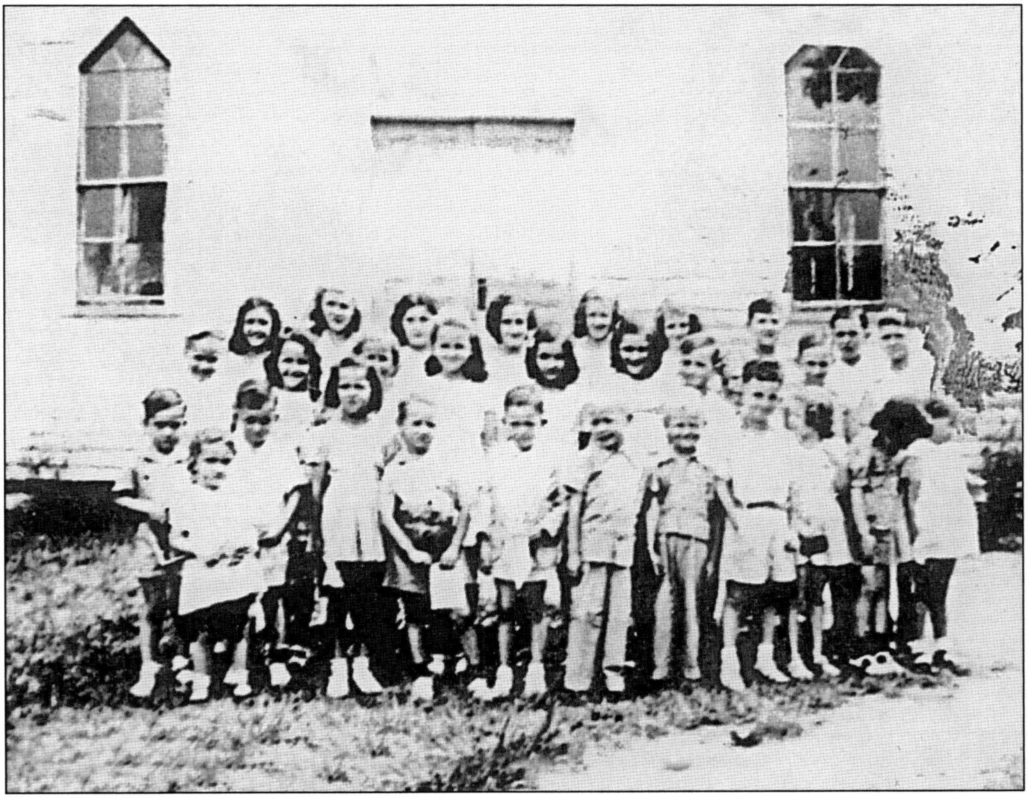

A group of children stands in front of Providence Baptist Church in 1948. (Courtesy of Shirley Currin.)

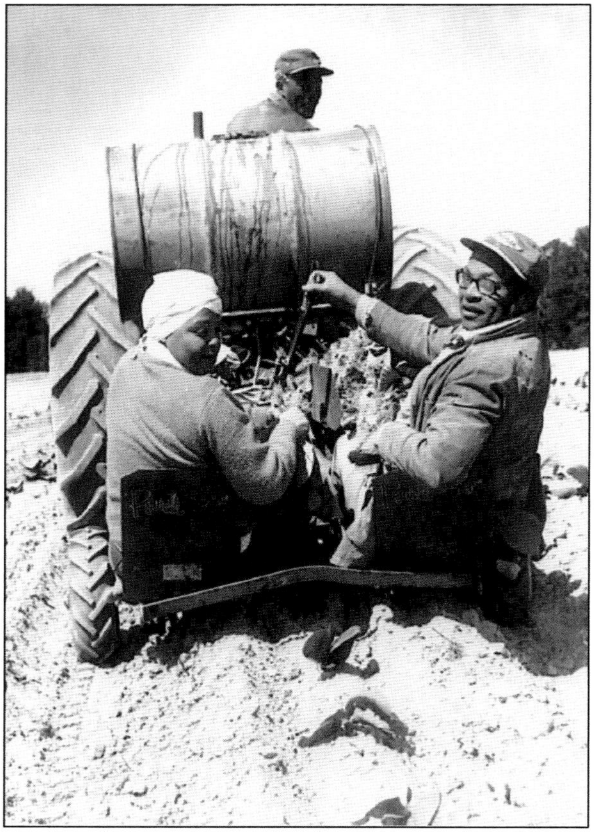

These farmers are planting tobacco. Granville County has a long, rich history of tobacco production that rivals any place in America. Tobacco has played a major role in making Granville County the place it is today; our farming heritage should be valued and never forgotten.

Students line up for a picture at Stem School in the 1920s. Shown, from left to right, are (front row) Vance Adcock, Philip Carden, June Mangum, Evelyn Wortham, Margaret Roberts, Madeline Carrington, Mary Franklin, and John Gooch; (middle row) Welford Roberts, Paul Jenkins, Dela Weaver, Edwin Winters, Philip O'Brien, Charley Green, Roella Bullock, and Bobby Hardee; (back row) unidentified, Catherine Minor, William Royster, Thurston Newton, Marshall Bennel, unidentified, Roy Hopkins, and Battle Suitt. The teacher is Mrs. Janie Clayton. (Courtesy of Nellye Tunstall.)

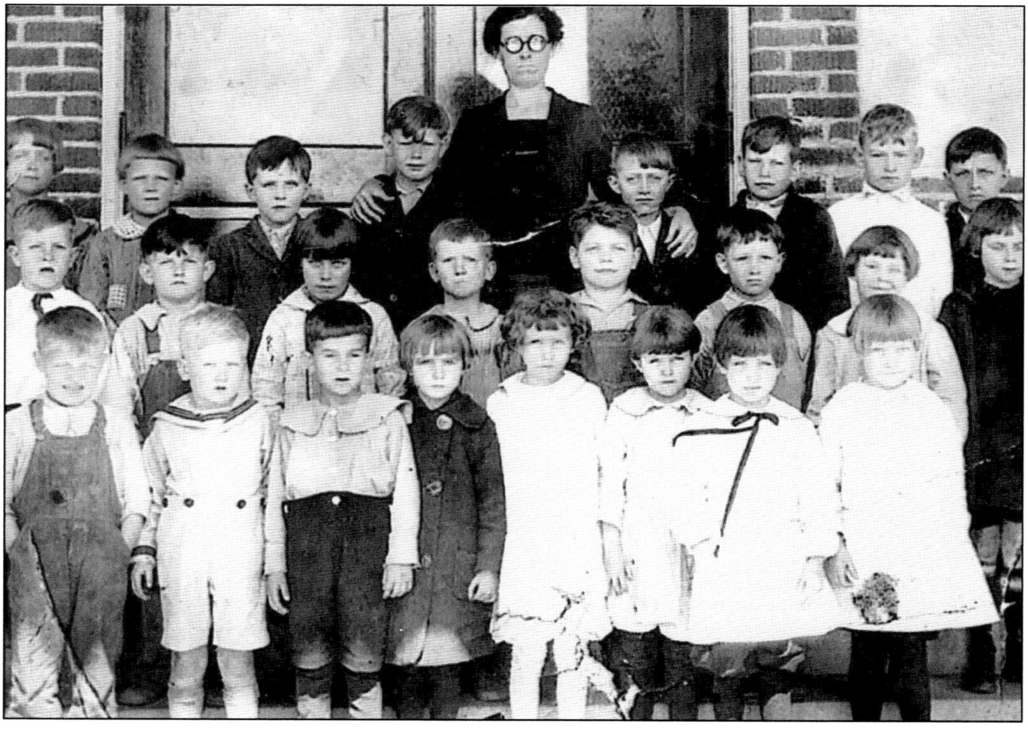

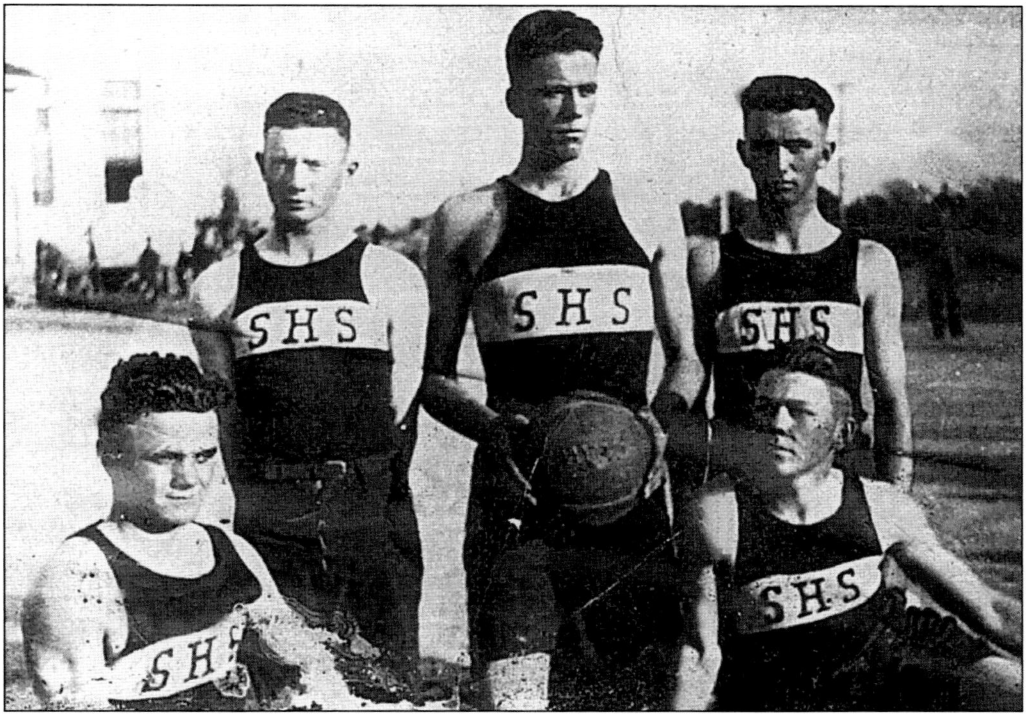

This is the Stem High School boys basketball team of 1922. Pictured are (seated) Bill Jones and an unidentified member; (standing) Roy Gooch, Earl Farabow, and an unidentified member. (Courtesy of Anita Adcock.)

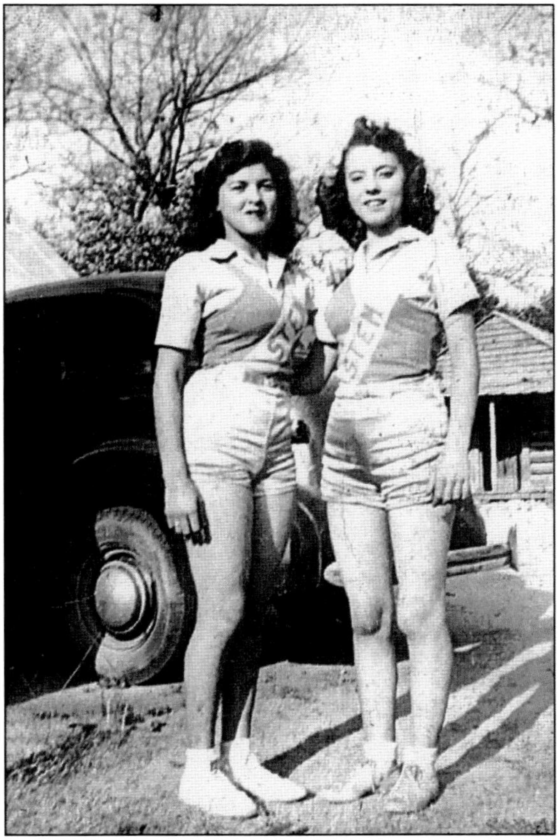

Margaret Moss Cooper (left) and Mary Walker Bowling (right) were members of the Stem High School basketball team in this picture from 1940.

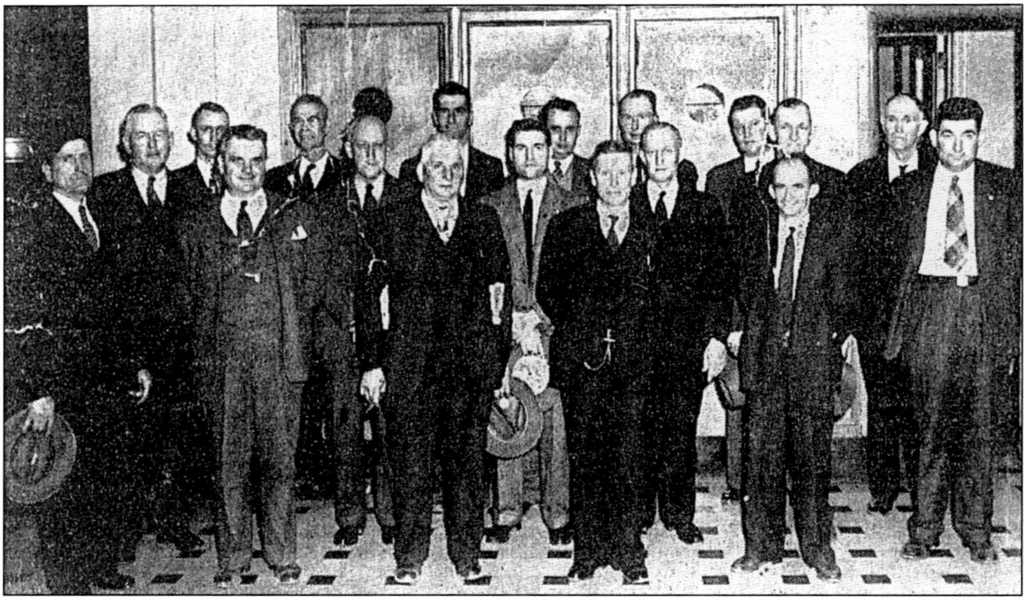

Stem citizens are shown on a visit to Durham concerning the settlement of Camp Butner properties. Pictured from left to right are (front row) O.G. Clayton, William Jones, Ollie Bullock, F.C. Wilkins, J.D. Hales Jr., and J. Mangum; (middle row) L.O. Goss, Frank Pierson, John Clayton, L.W. Hall, and R.T. Walters; (back row) Lewis Gooch, J.L. Williford, T.T.Dean, W.T.Winborne, H.H. Wheeler, Billy Mangum, and A.L. Meadows. (Courtesy of Anita Adcock.)

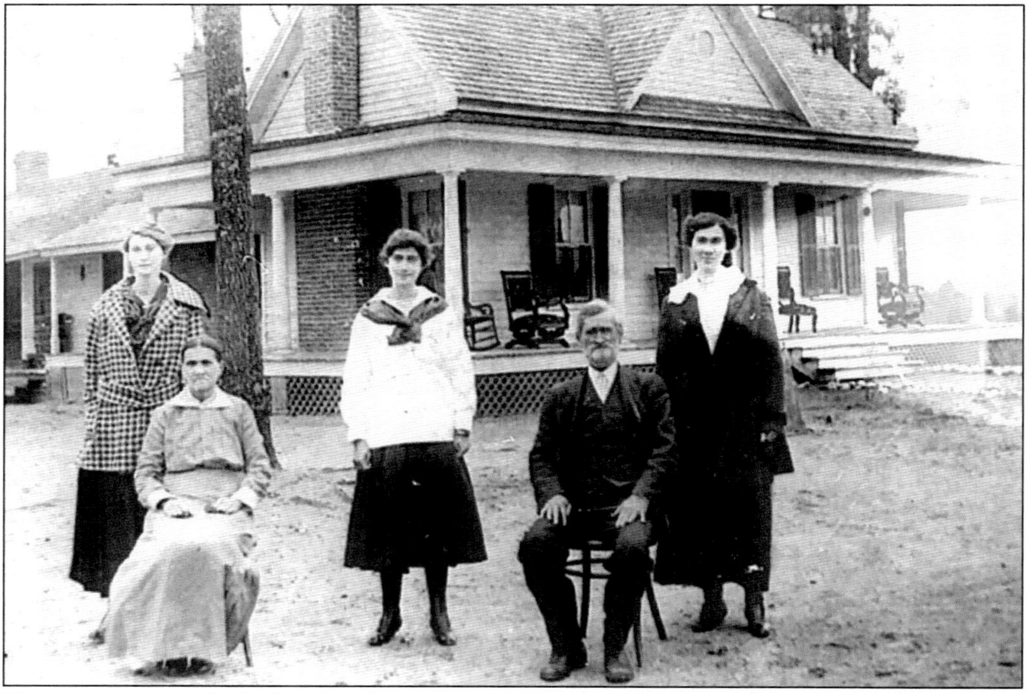

The Burnette family looks into the camera at their home in Providence in the early 1920s. Pictured, from left to right, are (seated) Betty Averette Burnette and Lucius Atlas Burnette; (standing) Minnie Burnette Watkins, Pearl Burnette Wheeler, and Maggie Burnette White. (Courtesy of Lucius and Rowena Wheeler.)

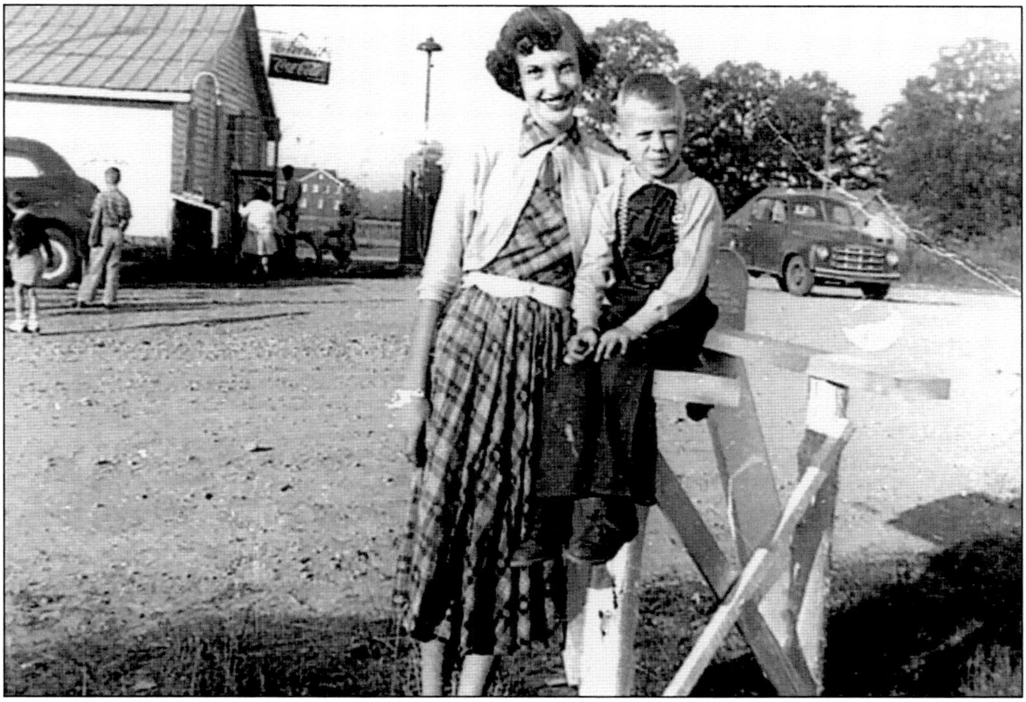

Shirley Wheeler Currin and Eugene Wheeler smile for the camera; the Averette Grocery in Providence is seen in the background in 1953. In 2003, this is the location of Providence Grocery and Grill operated by Lee Bowling. Eugene Wheeler currently runs A&W Grocery and Grill in Stem. (Courtesy of Lucius and Rowena Wheeler.)

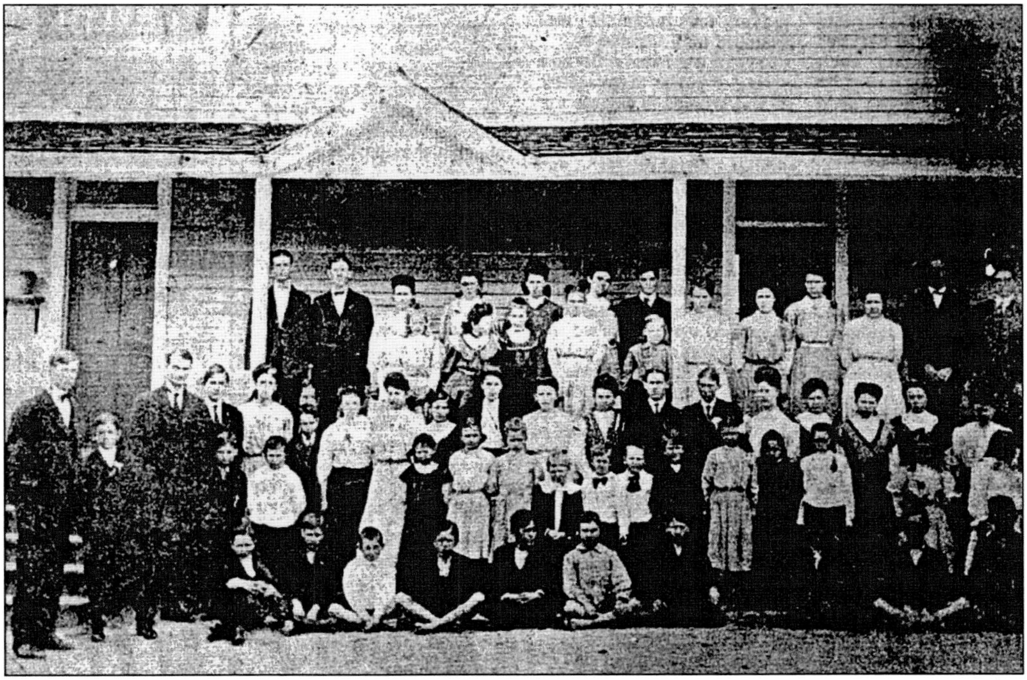

Pictured is the Hester School in 1907. Standing third from the left is D.G. Brummitt, who became attorney general of North Carolina.

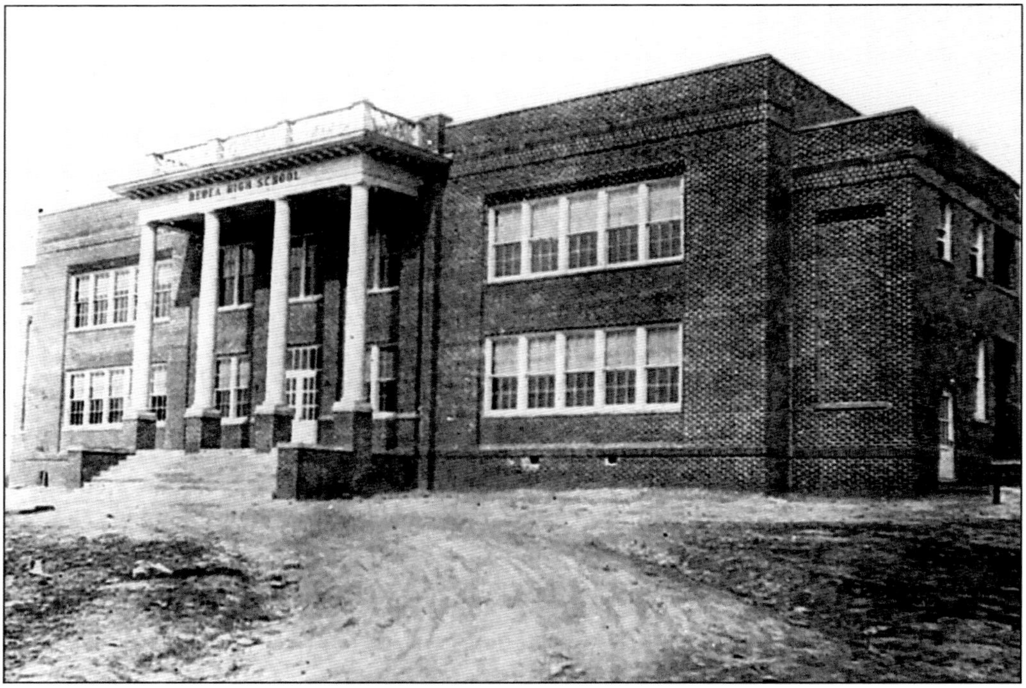

This is Berea High School as it looked in 1927.

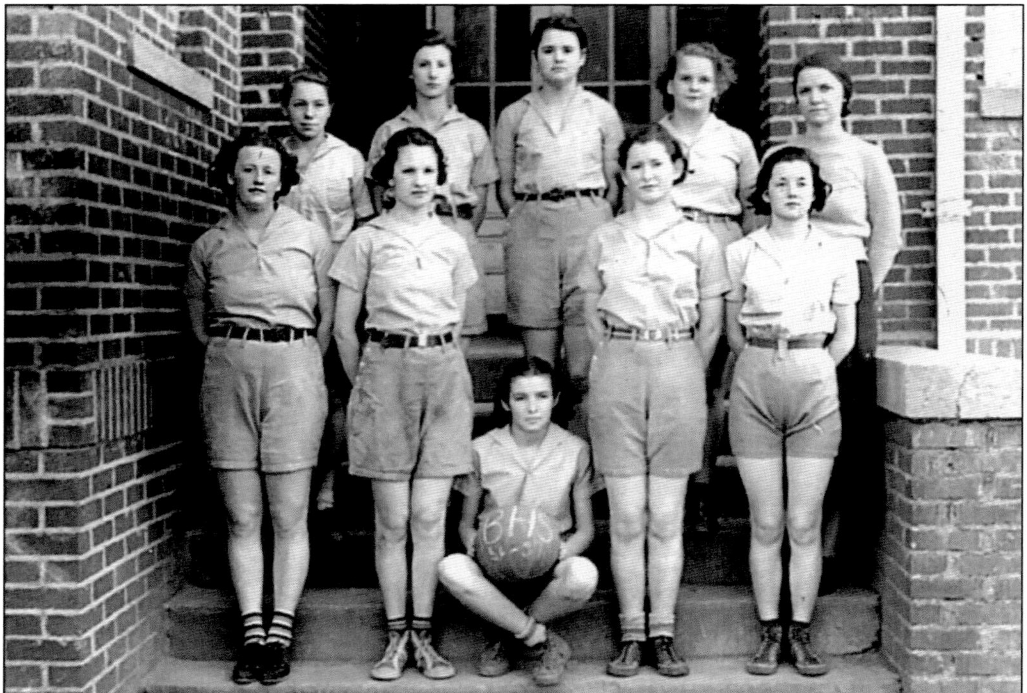

This is the 1936–1937 Berea High School girls basketball team. Pictured, from left to right, are (front row) Ellie O'Brian, Helen Averett, Nettie Riggan Dickerson, Ercelle Jones, and Jane Currin; (back row) Ester Brooks, Mozelle O'Brian, Audrey Dean, Julie May Parrott, and Viola Jones (coach).

Columbus Blalock (seated) and W.D. Mangum (standing) are pictured at Mangum's Store in Berea. The Mt. Zion Baptist Church can be seen in the background. (Courtesy of Josh Mangum.)

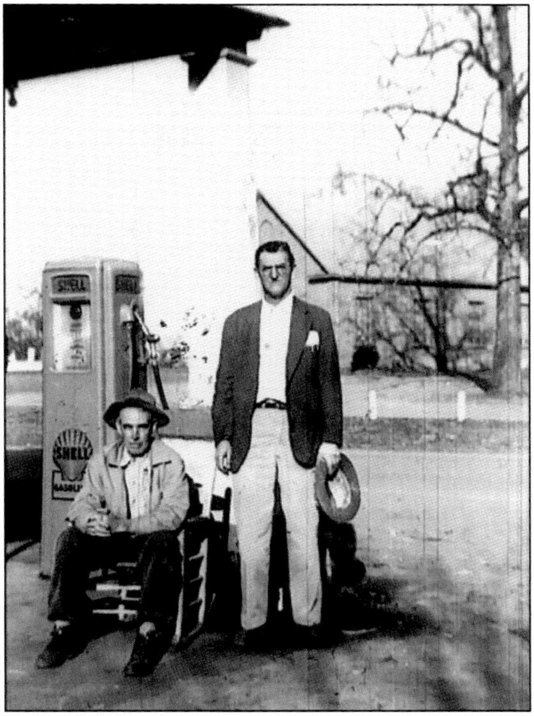

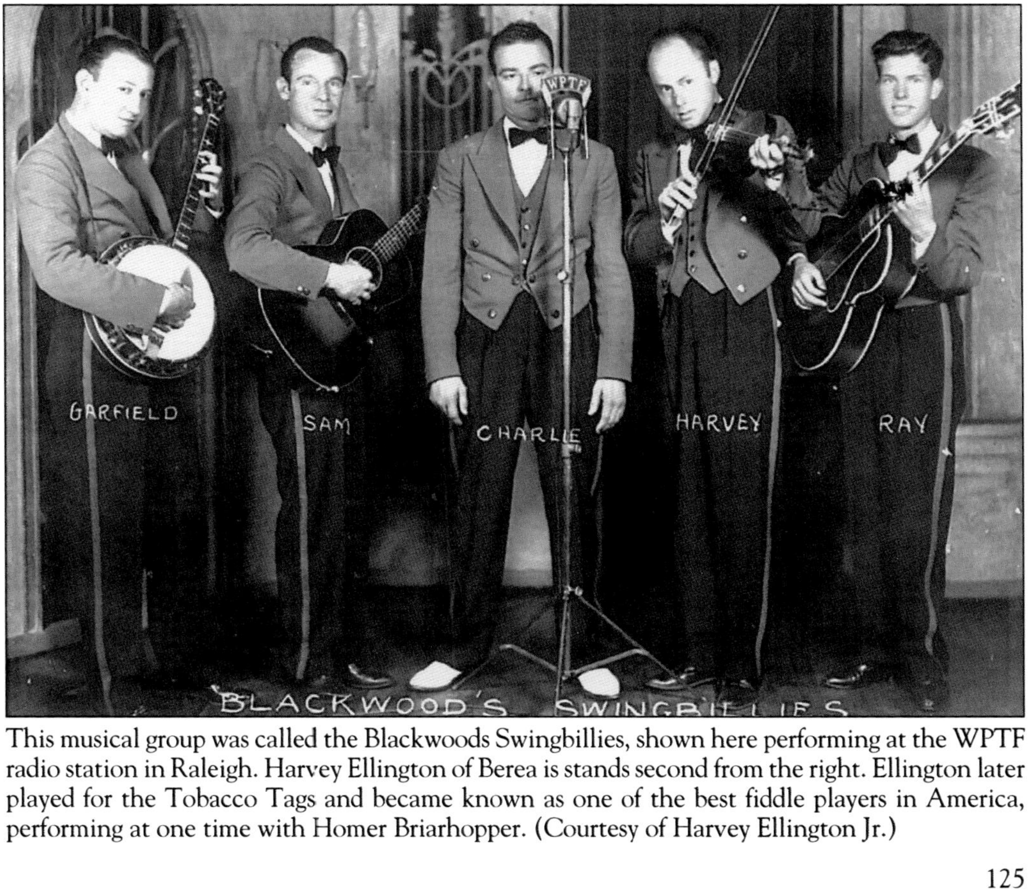

This musical group was called the Blackwoods Swingbillies, shown here performing at the WPTF radio station in Raleigh. Harvey Ellington of Berea is stands second from the right. Ellington later played for the Tobacco Tags and became known as one of the best fiddle players in America, performing at one time with Homer Briarhopper. (Courtesy of Harvey Ellington Jr.)

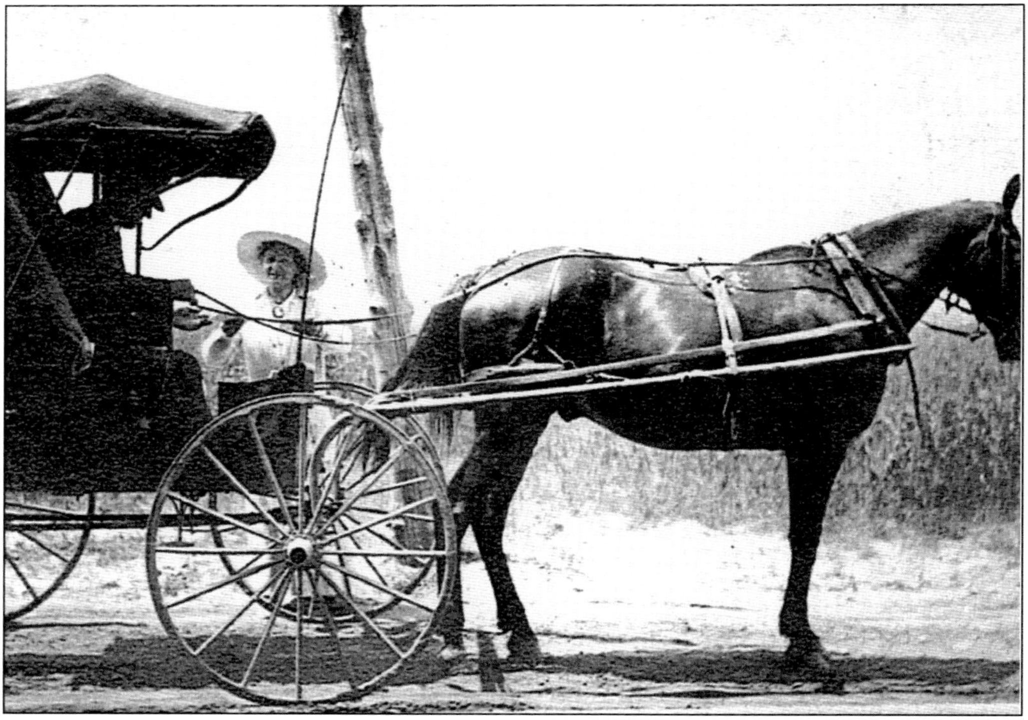

Dorsey Oakley is shown delivering mail to a young lady. Oakley was born in Berea and carried the mail on his horse and buggy for many years. (Courtesy of Nettie Dickerson.)

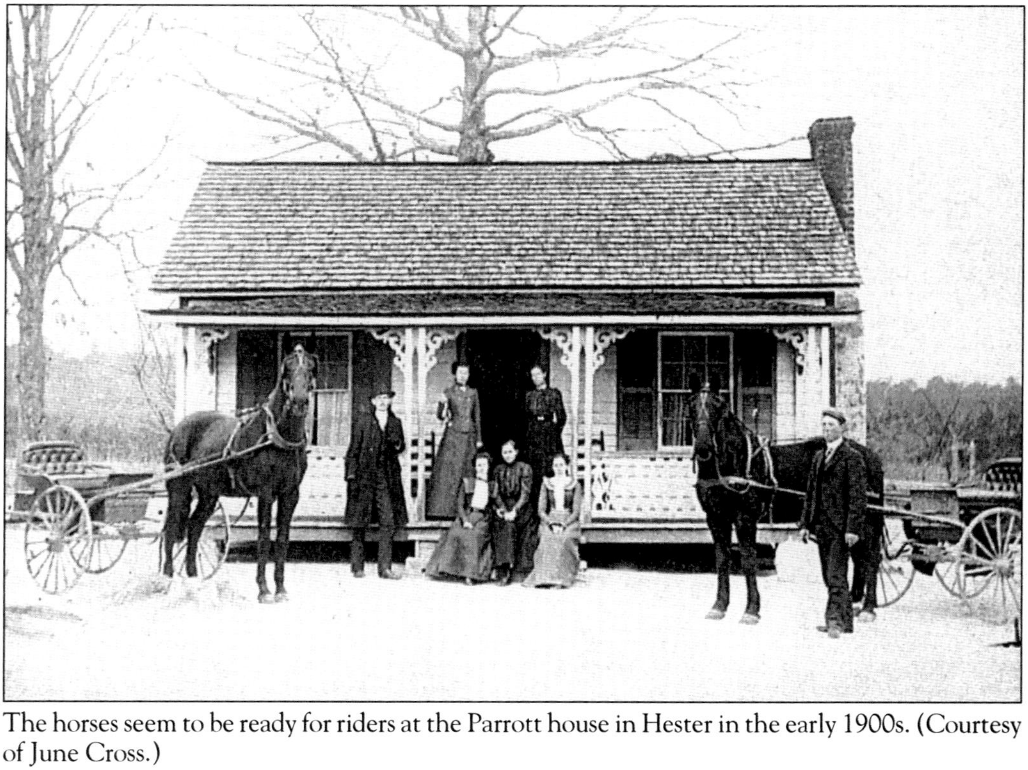

The horses seem to be ready for riders at the Parrott house in Hester in the early 1900s. (Courtesy of June Cross.)

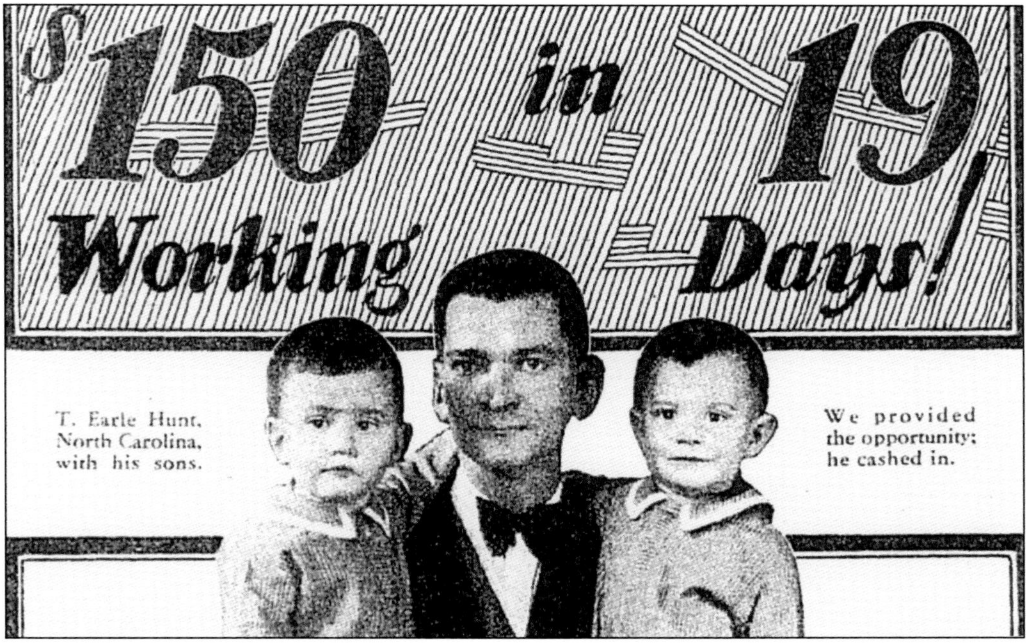

F. Earle Hunt was pictured with sons Bob and Dan in the *Saturday Evening Post* in 1928. F. Earle Hunt was featured in the magazine for selling $150 worth of subscriptions in 19 days. Mr. Hunt later became a columnist for the *Oxford Public Ledger*, writing under the alias of T. Moses Jones. Bob Hunt, one of the sons, served as a longtime teacher and principal in the Granville County school system. (Courtesy of Judy Hunt.)

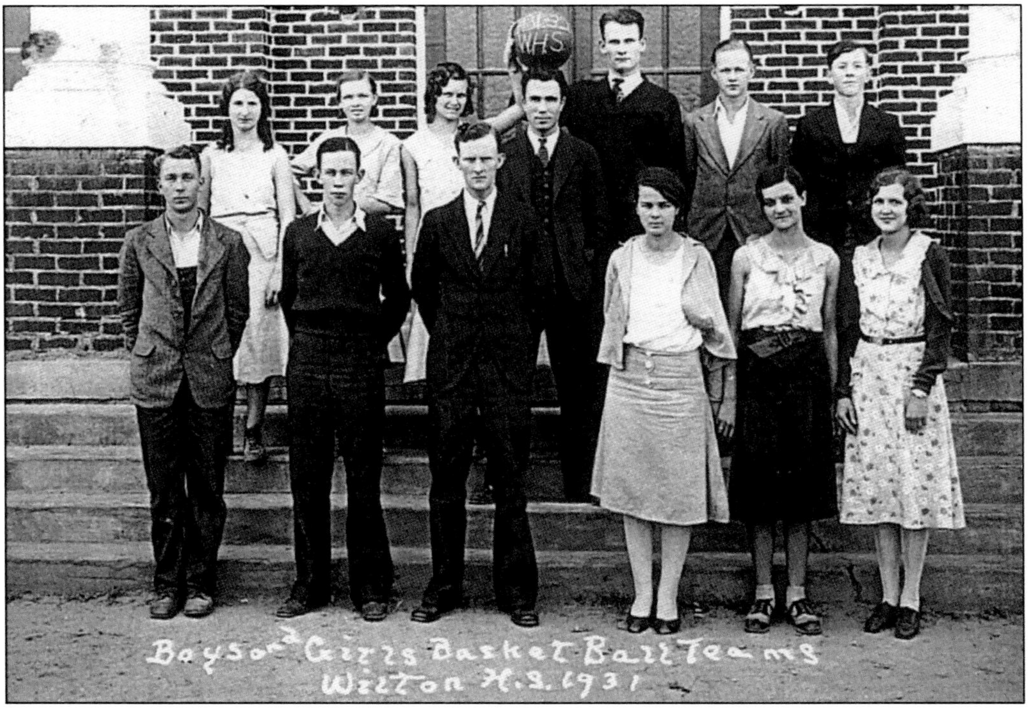

This is the Wilton High School boys and girls basketball team in 1931. (Courtesy of Julia Gooch Vaughn.)

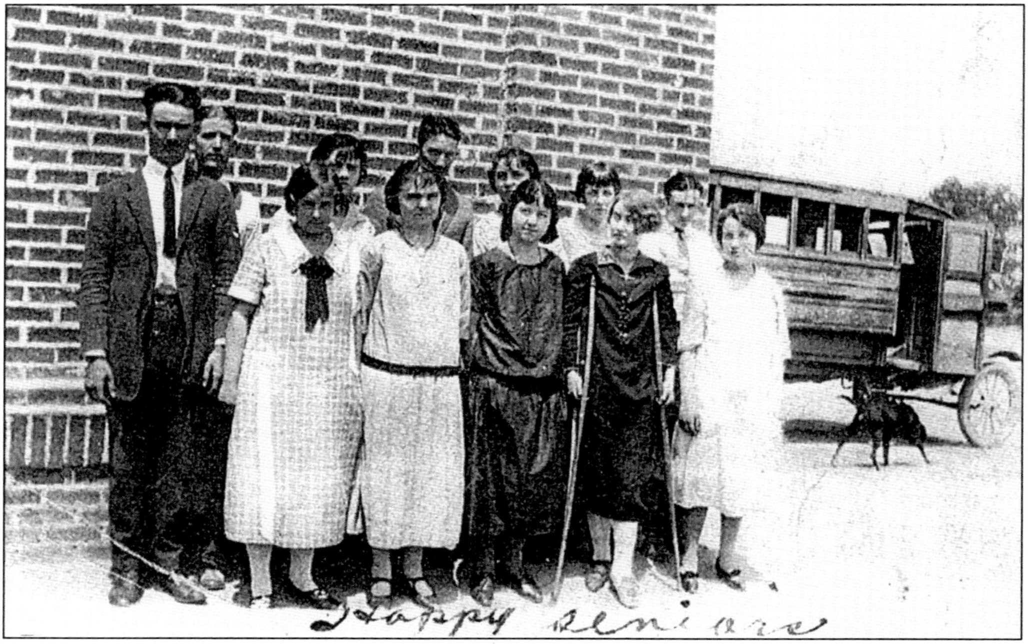

Seniors at Wilton High School pose for a photograph in 1925. Pictured, from left to right, are (front row) Geneva Moss, Louise Bragg, Josephine Mitchell, Ruby Estes, and Estoy Bragg; (back row) Jim Hart, Lee Gresham, Lugene Mitchell, Irvin Smith, Ina Davis, Marie Jenkins, and Robert Davis Smith. (Courtesy of Ramona Byrd.)

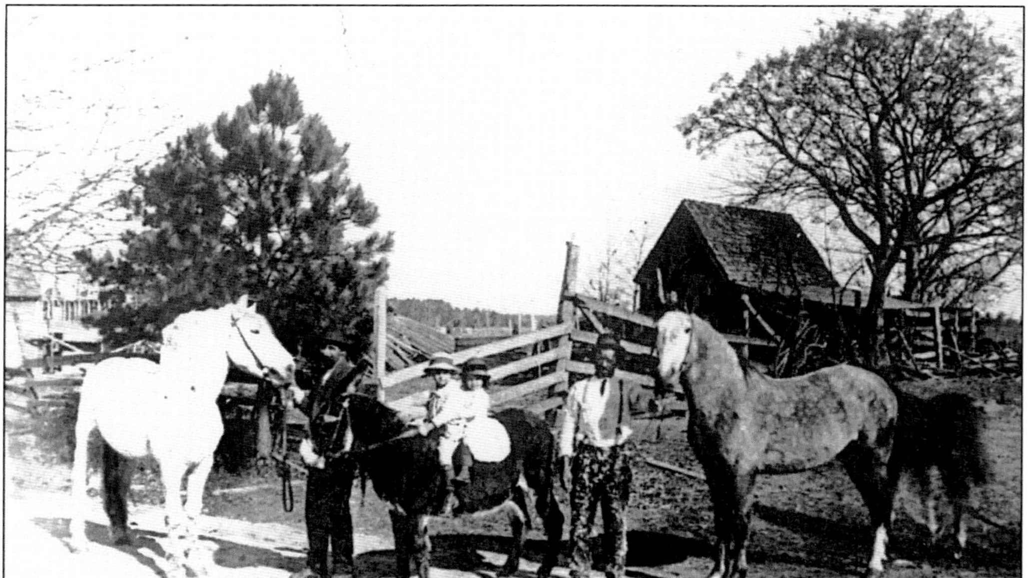

Pictured, from left to right, are Stepper, the white horse; Edgar Gooch; Eddie Gooch Jr. and Julia Gooch Vaughn, both sitting on the "jack;" and Shep Walker. A horse and her colt are to the right of Walker. (Courtesy of Julia Gooch Vaughn.)